T0365148

Good Morning Lord

STARTING EACH MORNING WITH GOD

Alicia Goodwin Jacobs

WestBow
PRESS
A DIVISION OF THOMAS NELSON

WestBow Press books may be ordered through booksellers or by contacting:

WestBow Press
A Division of Thomas Nelson
1663 Liberty Drive
Bloomington, IN 47403
www.westbowpress.com
1-(866) 928-1240

Because of the dynamic nature of the Internet, any web addresses or links contained in this book may have changed since publication and may no longer be valid. The views expressed in this work are solely those of the author and do not necessarily reflect the views of the publisher, and the publisher hereby disclaims any responsibility for them.

Any people depicted in stock imagery provided by Thinkstock are models, and such images are being used for illustrative purposes only.

Certain stock imagery © Thinkstock.

ISBN: 978-1-4497-1158-0 (sc)
ISBN: 978-1-4497-1159-7 (hbk)
ISBN: 978-1-4497-1157-3 (e)

Library of Congress Control Number: 2011921381

Printed in the United States of America

WestBow Press rev. date: 03/23/2011

January

February

May

August

September

October

November

December

Preface

I was born in 1954 and raised in the Midlands of South Carolina. I am the youngest girl with two older sisters and an older and younger brother. I imagine you could consider us a middle class family. We did not live an extravagant life but we always had what we needed. We lived in the country and my father planted an annual garden that fed us for most of the year and we had a few pigs. My parents canned or froze everything they could. I did find it hard to be grateful when Daddy took the pigs to slaughter however that is what fed us. We were raised to do daily chores including working in the garden. Most of my clothes were home made, including accessories. My mother was a genius and could make purses, doll clothes, bathing suits and even winter pants and coats. I will never forget the Barbie curtains she made for my room that I of course shared with my sister. When I started middle school, my mother went to work and my sister and I were expected to have dinner on the table when my parents arrived home from work. Now that I look back, I am very glad that my parents raised me this way because as I became an adult, tasks such as housecleaning and cooking and sewing came easily. I learned early in life to organize my time. I also praise God that I was raised in a Christian home. My mother played the piano, lead the children's choir and taught Sunday School. My father was a deacon and Sunday School teacher. If the doors of the church were open, we were there. My parents had very strict 'old fashioned' religious beliefs. We were rarely allowed to go to parties, never dances, movies were forbidden and any game with dice or cards. Sundays were special days with no work and limited play. Extremely good behavior was expected at church. If we ever acted up, or even spoke out loud for that matter, we were taken outside, received an attitude adjustment and returned to the service. I tell you all this so that you might see where some of my opinions and beliefs come from. As a teenager and young adult I resented my parents for how I was raised. But when I became a parent, I realized why they did some of the things they did and even found myself applying some of the same rules. They did the best they could and I now respect that.

While I was baptized at the age of 11, I did not take my relationship with Jesus Christ seriously until I was well into adulthood. My first step was daily Bible study and talking with God and later started prayer journaling. I have now used a prayer journal for several years and find it to be my lifeline. When I write my prayer, it helps me to focus and speak honestly with God and is especially helpful in difficult and trying times (which are most of the time, right?). You may ask, how are you qualified to write? I am not a Bible scholar. I have a two year Associate Degree from TECH school in Human Services. I have worked in state government since 1974 in public assistance programs. When I started this collection of devotions I was experiencing a crisis in my life. I started putting into words the reflections from my time with God and verbalized how he spoke to me through simple daily activities and encounters with those around me. I find it amazing how God speaks to us in everything we say and do. These devotions come from God speaking to me over the past 15 months. Some reflect my prayer journal entry for the day. I alone am not qualified but the Almighty One who gave me these words is exceptionally qualified. I hope they are helpful to you. Every time I speak with God it is a new opportunity, a new morning, a new day.

This book provides a devotion for each day. There is a Bible reading for each day. Set your alarm 30 minutes early to allocate time to start your day with God. I encourage you to journal your prayers and thoughts. I did not include the scripture text because I want you to read it from your Bible. Use a highlighter and pen to color, date and notate scripture that speaks to you strongly. Your Bible can become a prayer journal in itself. Enjoy your journey over the next 365 days. Daily time with God is what is important. God will see to it that you receive what you need for each day regardless of what I have written.

1

Not a Spirit Of Fear
2 Timothy 1:7

We are often afraid; afraid of heights, afraid of water or afraid of animals. Some things like bugs or spiders simply cause us to look the other way and cringe and some things really cause fear. Since I was a little girl I wanted a horse. I had plastic horses and a couple of glass figures. Financially, we could not afford a horse and we didn't really know anyone who had horses. So I had my TV shows like *My Friend Flicka, The Roy Rogers Show, Bonanza,* and *Gunsmoke.* In the fight scenes, I was always worried more about the horses than the people. When I had my own family, we took our kids horseback riding. I was terrified. I had the slowest horse but was petrified the whole time. I often talked about horseback riding but when it came down to it, I was very afraid. For my fiftieth birthday, my husband found a farm close to our house and purchased five horseback riding lessons for me. I had a wonderful teacher who understood my fear and didn't allow it to ruin what I wanted to do. I don't think she really knew just how afraid I was but she taught me a respect and healthy fear of these huge animals. I prayed every time I went for a lesson. Three years later, I am certainly not a professional rider but do ride regularly on my own horse (another birthday present). I enjoy every ride and still pray before every ride. I am thankful to God for allowing me this joy.

I tell you this to remind you that God does not want us to have a spirit of fear but a spirit of power and love and self-discipline. In 2 Timothy 1:7, Paul was teaching Timothy. Apparently Timothy had a serious lack of confidence. I encourage you to ask God to help you in any area of a lack of confidence, especially if it is something you have dreamed about and really want to do. God wants us to enjoy life, and he is there to take away our fear and give us the confidence we need to find the joy that we may think is unobtainable.

Dear Lord, thank you for your desire for us to have confidence and power and love and self-discipline. Thank you for the joys you bring to us. Help me to trust in you in all things and not allow fears to take away my joy. Remind me that confidence comes from you. Amen.

2

He Surrounds Us
Psalm 125:1-2

I try to start my day with the Lord. My prayer journal entry always starts, Good morning, Lord, thus the name of this collection of devotionals. I don't recall when I came across these verses but I do recall that they touched me so that I copied them and taped them to my computer at work. God promises me that if I trust him, he will surround me like a range of mountains. When we trust him we cannot be shaken. The verse refers to the mountainous area of Jerusalem. As the mountains surround the city, God surrounds his people. The important point to me was that mountains don't move or crumble. I love the mountains. I live in the midlands but love traveling to the mountains. I always feel so close to God and feel his presence there. I see him there not only in the beauty but also in the breathtaking magnitude of how they go on as far as my eyes can see. We take trips to the mountains with friends on motorcycles and ride through the Blue Ridge Parkway which connects the North Carolina Great Smokey Mountains with the Virginia Mountains. Early in the morning as the sun peeks down through the trees it seems like I can see God's face shining down. That's how he wants us to feel. God wants us to feel surrounded by his love that doesn't move and can't be moved and goes without end.

Dear God, thank you for your love that is as immovable as the mountains. Your love surrounds me. While I may move, you tell us you will not move. You promise to surround me both now and forever. Help me to put my trust in you in all that I do. Thank you for the marvelous beauty of our world. Amen.

3

The Bow and Arrow
Psalm 127:3-5

I heard a special analogy on the radio today and these verses came to my mind. It spoke of the fact that we are to raise our children preparing to send them off one day. We raise them prepared to release them. It spoke of our children being the arrow shot from our bow. We slowly prepare for the release, aiming as best we can, and then we let go. And of course it doesn't act like a boomerang. The arrow races toward the target, never to return. We probably all know sad stories of adults who have never left home. They are sad because they are rarely productive adults and have trouble functioning in the adult world.

This passage says children are a gift from God and a sign of his favor. Blessed is the man who has a quiver full of children. Thus we see where the above analogy comes from. Proverbs 22:6 says to train a child in the way he should go. Raising kids is no easy task. It takes lots of prayer and Bible study. God's Word is full of parenting instruction and the wisdom we need to raise our kids. I believe it may be a good idea that even while they are young, our ultimate goal is preparing to release them; guiding them as best we can under God's instruction, aiming at the target he sets for us to hit. We keep our eyes on Jesus and do the best we can.

When I became an adult, I came to understand why my parents did as they did and had only one shot at each child. A parent rarely gets the opportunity to release children, bring them back, and release again. That's why it is so important to stay in line with God's teachings the first time so that we have a good aim as we release. Our awesome God is a loving and forgiving God, which means we have the wondrous opportunity to repent of our sin and mistakes and start a new day tomorrow, no matter how many times we need. Wherever we are today in our parenting, let's pause and ask God for guidance and instruction. There may be something we need to change. It's never too late to change our aim. If the arrow has already been released, let's take time to search our relationship with our adult children or with our parents and seek God's guidance and instruction. In my case, it is too late. My father is deceased and my mother is in the late stages of Alzheimer's. I wish I had spent more time with my parents as an adult letting them know how I felt about them. But I know without a doubt I will see them again in eternity. For that I am thankful.

Dear God in heaven, thank you for the blessing of children. Help us not to take our parenting responsibility for granted. Help me to seriously seek wisdom and daily instruction from your Holy Word. Search my heart today and show me what needs to be changed. Help me to keep my aim on the target set for living a life focused on you and eternal salvation. Thank you for your love for me. Amen.

4

Great is Thy Faithfulness
Lamentations 3:19-24

"Great Is Thy Faithfulness" is one of my favorite hymns. I've learned that this wonderful hymn was written by Thomas O. Chisholm in the early 1900s. Thomas Obadiah Chisholm was born in a log cabin on July 29, 1866, in Franklin, Kentucky. He only had elementary schooling but became the associate editor of his hometown weekly newspaper, The Franklin Favorite. Chisholm accepted Christ at age twenty-seven. Later he was ordained a Methodist minister but had only a year of pastoral work due to failing health. His testimony was that due to his impaired health, his income was hardly enough to meet his needs, although he witnessed the unfailing faithfulness of God for the wonderful displays of his providing care.

This passage in Lamentations tells us that because of God's great love for us, his compassion never fails. Each morning brings renewed faithfulness. He is our everlasting hope with promises of faithfulness and unfailing love. Mr. Chisholm lived a simple, ordinary life. Yet in these words, he appears to be strong and in need of nothing. He claims strength for today and bright hope for tomorrow; blessings, with ten thousand beside. God's faithfulness provided all that he needed, morning by morning. God makes that new promise to each of us every morning. We just need to awake and open our eyes to see it. Find a hymn book and read through this hymn. Sing it out loud! Proclaim, great is thy faithfulness, Lord unto me.

Dear Father, thank you for your unfailing love and your faithfulness that comes with each day. I put my hope and trust in you. Thank you for providing all that I need. Thank you for your great love for me. Amen.

5

Physical Training vs. Godliness
1 Timothy 4:7-10

The Bible is very clear that we are to take care of our body. Exercise and physical training are obviously good for our body and should be a regular routine in our week. However, we are cautioned here that godliness is more important. Our church has a basketball program for children each winter. Volunteers have an opportunity to give a time of devotion for the parents and spectators during halftime. Once I used these verses to challenge folks that while it is very important for the children to learn good sportsmanship and physical activity, it is even more important for them to learn the stories of Jesus and know him as Lord and Savior.

We have time for a morning run and evenings at the gym but did we spend time with God today? We have time to chauffeur our kids from activity to activity but did we have family devotion time today? Are we attending church regularly? Godliness has value for all things, holding promise for both the present life and the life to come. Let's be challenged today to take a look at our lives and identify anything that takes priority over our relationship with Jesus Christ. Let's be sure our activities and relationship with Jesus Christ are in the right order. We need a time of prayer, of Bible reading, and especially discipline of our minds. Then we make time for exercise and physical training. Isaiah 26:3 says God will keep us in perfect peace when our mind is disciplined in him.

Dear God, forgive me when I allow other interests to steal from my relationship with you. My body is very important to you, but I believe the discipline of my mind is more important to you. Nothing has more value than the promises from you for my life here on earth and my life to come, living in your presence. Help me to commit to keeping my relationship with you first and more important than anything. You are my God and I trust you in all things. Forgive me when I fail you. Thank you for your unconditional love and mercy. Amen.

6

The Rainbow
Genesis 9:8-17

Have you noticed how a rainbow seems to excite people? When a rainbow is out, we often see people pointing up, bringing it to others' attention. When driving and I see a rainbow, I keep watching to see it as long as I can. The rainbow is a promise of God's love. Yesterday on the radio I heard a great reference to the rainbow and the daily floods in our life. It was suggested that each time we see a rainbow, we are not only assured of the promise made by God in this passage in Genesis but also an assurance of his daily presence in our life amidst the floods of life. The rainbow assures us that the floods will stop and will not destroy us.

God promised Noah that never again would the waters become a flood to destroy all life. Whenever the rainbow appears in the sky, God sees it and remembers his everlasting promise. Reading this passage reminds me that when I see the rainbow God is seeing it too. At that moment, God is thinking of us and remembers his promise to Noah and to each of us. Life can be hard. When it rains, it pours. How many times do we say that? God's Holy Word also pours out the promises of his everlasting love for each of us and his assurances that he has plans for us; plans to prosper. Yes the showers and rains and storms and floods come but they will not destroy us. Jesus Christ came as the life saving Savior, throwing out the life line to keep us from drowning. The only catch is that we have to reach out and accept it. Look up at the rainbow and receive the promise of God.

Dear God reading this makes me anxious to see the next rainbow. You will see it and think of me and I will see it and think of you. Thank you for your marvelous love for us. Thank you for your promises and for your beautiful rainbow. I look up and accept you as Lord and Savior of my life. My desire is to make you first in my life. Forgive me when I am selfish and fail you. Amen.

7

I Become What I Think
Psalm 42

I often get frustrated with myself for missing opportunities to glorify God and just plain mess up. It is difficult to be patient with ourselves. As I begin this passage, I can imagine a deer running from a foe, panting for water but can't take the time to stop. Do you feel that way sometimes? I certainly do. Yet the psalmist remembers to put his hope in the Lord and praise him even when he feels downcast. On a more positive note, Philippians 1:6 encourages us to be confident, that God has begun work in us and will complete it. God brings salvation. He initiated it, continues it and will complete it.

The Bible overflows with words of confidence and encouragement. We must be patient with ourselves. We mess up, we repent, we shake ourselves off and we move on. I saw a poster on an office wall that read, 'A life without challenges would be like a beach without waves'. It also read, 'People can alter their lives by altering their attitude'.

So when you start to feel downcast, remember that your hope is in God. He is to be praised in all things even when you feel like the panting deer that can't stop for water. Stop and think positive. Take a minute to say a prayer of positive thinking. Be careful of what you think because you may become what you think.

Dear God, thank you for loving me as I am. You are always with me and care for me. I want my thoughts and my actions to glorify you. Thank you for your faithful forgiveness when I let you down. Help me to make time for your Word so that I am prepared to follow your instruction and stand up to downcast thoughts and feelings. You are an awesome God and I praise you. Amen.

8

Said the Robin To the Sparrow
Matthew 6:25-34

A friend showed me a poem she came across:
Said the robin to the sparrow, I should really like to know,
Why these anxious human beings rush about and worry so,
Said the sparrow to the robin, Friend I think that it must be.
They have no heavenly Father such as cares for you and me.

If God cares for the birds and the flowers and grass in the fields, why can't we count on him to care for us? As Christians, none of us should doubt that God knows our every need. His grace sufficiently covers our needs and our situations. Trust is the answer to our anxiety and worry. We are to trust that God is on his throne. I remember as a child hearing a song that said, 'His eyes are on the sparrow, so I know he cares for me'. Psalm 55:22 says to cast our burden on the Lord and he will sustain us and will never let the righteous fall. The dictionary defines cast as to throw with force; to hurl or fling. We cast our burdens on him and leave them there. We cannot cast like a fishing line where we cast it and then reel it back in. We cast it to our Lord, with the intention of letting it go and leave it with him. We trust our Sovereign God to work in our lives according to his perfect will.

Dear God forgive me when I forget to trust you. It takes courage for me to cast my cares on you. Sometimes I think it is easier to hold on to my worries but I know that is a lie and is not true. You are the truth and the way. Help me to resist the desire of Satan for me to worry and doubt you. Thank you for your love for me. Amen.

9

The Empty Nest
Psalm 62:5-8

I never knew that when my children left home it would affect me so. I knew my daughter was preparing to go to college but at the same time my son decided to live with his father in Georgia. She was off to college and he left to start the new school year. I felt devastated. No kids – what would I do? Of course my husband was there, but there is something special about being the Mom. These verses brought me great comfort. God alone gives us rest. While children are a huge part of our life particularly before becoming adults, our rest and hope comes from God. He alone is my rock and I will not be shaken. Everything depends on him. God's presence is often referred to as a mountain or a rock. Why? Because they don't move and they don't break. They are solid. God doesn't move and he doesn't break. He is solid. God's Word tells us to trust in him at all times and pour out our hearts to him. That's just what I did. I cried for a few days but soon realized this was the beginning of a whole new chapter in my life. My kids were still with me just in a different relationship. They are still my 'little boy' and my 'little girl' and my God is still my refuge, my rock and my salvation.

Dear God, I find rest in you alone. My hope comes from you. You alone are my rock and my salvation. I will not be shaken by the changes life brings. Help me find my place in each new chapter of my life. Be my refuge and my strength. Amen.

10

Wholesome Talk
Ephesians 4:29

There is a wonderful book by Florence Littauer, <u>Silver Boxes, The Gift of Encouragement</u>. The book is based on Ephesians 4:29. Our words should be positive, not negative. Our words should be like silver boxes with bows on top.

Words can sting and can cut like a knife. We have all at some time or another had someone to say something to us that hurt. Or we hear someone speak to another harshly and it lingers in our mind. It really takes time for the hurt to go away, even if the person apologizes and we forgive, the sting can remain for awhile. We often are the hardest on those we love. According to this scripture, we should not let any unwholesome talk come out of our mouth but only what is helpful and benefits those who hear. This scripture supports the saying, 'If you can't say anything nice, don't say anything at all'. Be encouraged to not only stop saying unwholesome things but to start saying things that build others up.

Dear Lord, help me to be mindful of what I say to others. Forgive me for the times I have hurt others with my words. Help me to practice saying things that build others up. I want to see and speak to others with unconditional love, as you see and speak to me. Help me to be an encourager and make others feel special. Amen.

11

Keep Watch
Matthew 25:1-13

It has become a rather common thing to see crosses, flowers or other memorials on the side of the road where someone died. These were people going about their day with no idea that they would not reach their destination, sometimes at their own fault or of another. It always makes me wonder if the person was ready to die. This parable in Matthew reminds us to keep watch because we do not know the day or the hour that the Lord will return. Are you ready to meet the Lord? Have you accepted him as your Savior, asked for forgiveness of your sins and established a daily relationship with him? If not, I encourage you to do that today. Do you know where you will go when you die? When the Lord returns, will he know you as his own or will he send you away? Don't let another sun go down without knowing that if you die, you will spend eternity with our Lord Jesus Christ. Don't be like the virgins in this parable that had the door shut in their face because they were not prepared. They were not ready. We should live everyday prepared to meet our Lord.

Dear God in heaven, I accept your gift of eternal life. Help me to live each day knowing that tomorrow may not come. From this day on, I choose to trust you and follow your will for my life. Forgive me of my sins. Thank you for your love for me. Amen.

12

Unexpected Encouragement
Psalm 73:26

My Mom who is 92 years old has Alzheimer's and is in a nursing home. She hasn't known us for a couple years. It is very difficult to see her with that blank stare or smile as if looking at a stranger. We can no longer have conversations with her.

When my father died a couple years ago, my siblings and I had the chore of cleaning out their belongings. One of the items I kept was one of their Bibles. Apparently, Mama and Daddy shared this Bible because there are handwritten notes by both of them. One morning in my quiet time when I was particularly burdened, I came across my Mother's handwriting. It said, Encouragement, Psalm 73:26 with a circle drawn around it.

What a wonderful verse it was for me that day. My Mother was speaking to me through that note, encouraging me with that verse. I wondered with tears rolling down my face, if she had any idea that one day this simple note would give me just what I needed that day when she could not. I know for sure that God did. That's just like him. He knew exactly when she wrote it and the day it would touch me. I felt closer to her for those few moments than I had for years and close to God for giving me that unexpected encouragement.

Dear God, my heart may fail but you are the strength of my heart and my portion forever. Thank you for the unexpected strength and encouragement you bring to me. Thank you for a Mom who knew to study her Bible and make notes of words that gave her what she needed. Remind me to do the same for my children. Amen.

13

Horace the Horse
Jeremiah 29:11-13

There was a song that I sang as a child, "Horace the Horse". I still recall the tune…

> Horace the horse on the merry-go-round
> went up and down, round and round,
> He's been sad since the day he found he was the
> very last horse on the merry-go-round.
> Horace tried and tried and tried but he just never could win.
> Horace cried and cried and cried, 'cause all
> the other horses were ahead of him.
> Then came the day on the merry-go-round, Horace
> turned, looked around, then said Gosh Oh me,
> I'm the very first horse on the merry-go-round,
> 'cause the others are following me.

There are a couple things we can learn from Horace. First, why is it so important to be first? Secondly, why do we consider our worth based on where we've come from or where we seem to be going? I suggest that we focus on seeking God's plan for our life and center our thoughts on what he speaks to us and where he guides us rather than focusing on our own point of view. The scripture says God has plans for us to prosper. If we seek him with all our heart, he will hear us and we will find him. How do we seek him with our heart? – with a heart of confession and repentance. Don't be like Horace, going around in circles not knowing if he was first or last. Seek God's guidance for his point of view for your life.

Dear Lord, help me to trust you in all I do. You are my hope and my future. Help me to have a heart of repentance and seek you daily. I want to accept your gift of a prosperous life. Amen.

14

Encouraging Others
Ephesians 3:16-21

I love writing notes of encouragement. I enjoy finding special note cards to send that fits the person I am writing and the situation. It is a blessing when someone hugs me with a smile thanking me for a simple brief note; such a little thing. I know how encouraging it can be when I get such a note.

We need to be an encourager. Once when driving in to work, I looked at the car beside me and the lady sitting in the passenger seat had tears rolling down her face. She never looked my way. I tried not to stare but it brought tears to my own eyes. She stayed on my mind throughout the day and I prayed for her every time she came to mind. Of course, I never saw her again or not that I know of. So often we greet one another and ask, How are you doing? and get the response, Fine, and move on without a thought. But we all have problems of our own and we all need encouragement. When we are in a discouraging time it is hard to grasp how wide and long and high and deep God's love is for us. Be an encourager by sharing his love with those around you.

Dear Lord, strengthen me with your power and dwell in my heart. Your love is immeasurable. Help me not to be selfish but to be aware of those who need encouragement. Help me to share your love in the encouragement that I give. Thank you for your love. My praise to you; who can do more than I ask or imagine, according to your power that is at work in me. Amen.

15

Holding On To the Reigns
Psalm 94:18-19, 22

Last night I was trying to ride my horse that was being very stubborn. When she is showing her attitude I can't help but stiffen and let fear creep in. Even though she never has, I am afraid she will get frustrated and take off running. I am often reminded that I have the 'brakes' but I still allow the anxiety to move in. I was trying to get her to trot but my trainer noticed that I was holding on to the reigns yet coaxing her to go. I didn't even realize how I was pulling on her and confusing her. I was saying, Go but stop.

When I got home I thought about that. How often do we ask God to work in us and take the reigns of our life yet we hold on and even pull back? The psalmist says here, When my foot is slipping, your love O Lord, supports me. When my anxiety is great, your consolation (comfort) brings joy to my soul. Let's let go of the reigns! Let's allow God to hold us in his hands and allow his strength to move us, not our own.

Dear Lord God, you are my rock and my refuge. I commit to let go of the reigns and allow you to take over my thoughts, my fears and my future. I hand you the reigns of my life and follow your lead. You are the Father of knowledge and wisdom. Amen.

16

Waiting
Isaiah 30:15-21

I am not very patient. I want things fixed quickly. In my job I deal with work plans and business rules daily. I normally have several priorities going at the same time. When I have a project to complete, I develop a plan on paper outlining each step, the person responsible and goals for completion. Unfortunately life doesn't work that way especially if we are allowing God to work in us. This passage tells us we are blessed when we wait for God. In the past couple weeks, God has given me a plan just a few steps at a time. I have felt his prompting to wait after every one or two steps. To stay within his will I cannot develop a plan on my own. I must wait for God's guidance even when it means waiting. I try to be patient, knowing that things will work out best when I follow God's direction.

Last Friday we had a fire drill at work. My office is on the 11th floor. After taking the steps down and waiting outside for the signal to return to the building, I anxiously entered the building hoping to catch one of the first elevators up. I was anxious to return to what I was doing when the alarm started. I made it to an elevator and we stood waiting for the doors to close. Ten minutes later we were still standing there because something had happened when the alarm went off and the maintenance crew was unable to get the elevators off the STOP mode. One by one folks got off, a couple went outside to wait and others located on the lower floors started up the stairs. I cringed knowing there were 11 flights ahead of me. I climbed a couple at a time and stopped to catch my breath. Fortunately, I had picked up my bottle of water as I headed out to the drill. I'm not sure how long it took me but I finally reached the 11th floor, breathless and heart racing, sat down in the first chair I came to and what did I hear? The cling of the opening elevator doors and here come my co-workers who had ridden up. They joked with me saying, You couldn't wait another five minutes? While it had been good exercise for an out of shape person, I was somewhat ashamed for taking off on my own and not showing a little patience.

Why do we have to be in such a hurry? Why do we think we can set out on our own and fix everything quickly? While I recognize that God moves swiftly sometimes, I also think that most often he moves slowly, purposefully. I suggest that he wants to give us time to consider obedience and acknowledge him in every step of the process. Like when we just fix something for someone and don't show them how; they learn nothing and are back in the same situation very soon.

How gracious God is when we cry out to him. As soon as God hears, he answers. In repentance and rest is our salvation and in quietness and trust is our strength. So what's the hurry? Let's remember that our timing may not be God's timing. God knows when and what will best complete his plan for us.

Dear God please give me patience for waiting on your plan. I cannot treat life like a business plan. I must trust you and seek you in all things. Thank you for hearing me when I cry out to you. I praise you as the gracious Lord of All who longs to bless me. Help me to be quiet and listen for your voice. I love you Lord. Amen.

17

Recognizing the Lies
Genesis 3:1-13

I teach the high school girls Sunday School class and we studied the book, Seeing Through the Lies, by Vonda Skelton. This is a great book. I recommend it to girls and ladies. One of my favorite lines in the book is, The Father of lies came up with the Mother of all lies: You can be right up there with God. You can be Number One. Satan's best deceit is lies. John 8:44 says, he is a liar and the father of lies. God is the Father of Truth.

Satan deceived Adam and Eve. He portrayed rebellion as wise and acceptable. And then their excuses started when they got caught. I heard once that excuses are lies disguised as reasons. There are so many things in life to get our attention and deceive us. Being in God's Word on a daily basis and having that regular relationship of prayer is how we learn to see through the lies. Starting tomorrow set your alarm 30 minutes early for a quiet time spent in God's Word and talking to him. Use this time to focus on the truth so that you can recognize the lies. And your worship on Sunday will be more meaningful if you have spent time with God during the week.

Dear God, I commit to studying your Word and spending time with you daily. Help me to make the time so that I will know what is true and not make excuses. I want to be able to recognize the lies that cause me to stumble. Amen.

18

Psalm 8

I once saw 'Psalm 8' on a license tag. After reading through the verses I know that this psalm is written in praise to the Almighty God. O Lord our God, how majestic is your name in all the earth – the first and last verse, as well as a song that we often sing at my church. He is majestic, having supreme authority. I do wonder what was particularly significant that someone would put it on their license tag. It could be to signify their praise or as a witness to those of us who saw it and went home and looked it up. Jesus spoke the very words in verse 2 while preaching in the temple and being questioned by the chief priest and teachers (Matthew 21:16). From the lips of children and infants you have ordained praise. Yet he is mindful of us.

Dear God, I don't praise you enough. How majestic is your name in all the earth, yet your love for us is beyond what we can imagine. I want to praise you in all I do and proclaim you as my Lord, unashamed. Give me the confidence of the driver who proclaims you on their license tag. Amen.

19

Wonderfully Made
Psalm 139:13-16

The story of Rachel and Leah is in Genesis 29 and 30. Jacob was in love with Rachel who had an older sister, Leah. Their father convinced Leah, the less popular, to take part in a scheme to become Jacob's wife. Even though Jacob did later take Rachel as his wife too, the girls fought for years in trying to be the favorite wife of Jacob. They were never satisfied with their own individuality. Apparently their own father didn't believe in them either.

Does God care about me even if I am not popular? Yes. Even if I struggle to live up to someone else's expectations, I can always rest in God's love. Do you find yourself wishing 'I was more…' or 'I wasn't so…' or 'I was like…' or 'I could be….'? Psalm 139 says God wonderfully created us in the womb. He doesn't make mistakes. He knew about each day of our life before we were born. I know that full well, the psalmist says. Don't try to be something you're not. You are loved as you are, for the reason you were created.

Dear Father, thank you that I was wonderfully made. You put me together in the womb and knew me and had a plan for me from the moment I was conceived. I know that full well. Help me to seek your will for my life and grow in the truth that I am special and loved as I am. Amen.

20

Go Tell Jesus
Matthew 14:12(b)

Matthew's rendition of the death of John the Baptist ends with, Then they went and told Jesus. The disciples went to bury John's body then went to tell Jesus. This is one of those verses that I think of often. They went to tell Jesus, probably for several reasons; for sure, just to tell him what had happened. I believe they also went to Jesus for comfort. John's death was important and they went to Jesus because they were sad and upset, and to talk to him about it. Many times I wish I could just crawl into his lap and talk to him. One day I will.

When we are sad or bothered or troubled, we should go tell Jesus. In Matthew 11:28-30, Jesus tells us to come to him and he will give us rest. So why do we so often try to carry our baggage of burdens around and try to fix problems on our own? Let's go tell Jesus. Let's find a quiet place to draw near to him, talk to him and allow him to give us rest and comfort.

Dear Jesus, thank you for being there for me all the time. I come to you and rest in you. You are my peace and my comfort. Help me to share with others the rest we can find in you. Amen.

21

Opportunities To Share
Colossians 4:2-6

This scripture was written by Paul while in prison. He was arrested for preaching the gospel. He asks for prayer from his followers that God would provide opportunity for him and his imprisoned friends to proclaim their message. He says to be watchful. To make the most of every opportunity even in the way we treat strangers. He says this from behind prison bars!!

I believe that we have this opportunity every day whether in a smile or actually speaking God's Word. I catch myself in the elevator in the morning, allowing folks to get off without sharing a smile or a positive word. Or pass someone in the doorway or in the checkout lane without taking advantage of the opportunity. A smile and simple greeting may be just what someone needs and often that will open the door for conversation. Verse 6 says to let your conversation always be full of grace, seasoned with salt, so that we may know how to answer anyone. We need to be in God's Word on a regular basis, hiding it in our heart so we have it when we need it and we are prepared for that conversation. Proverbs 15:4 says, the tongue that brings healing is a tree of life. Let's be encouraged to be wise in the way we treat strangers and those we meet throughout our day. Smiles and positive words can be contagious. As these instructions say, proclaim the story of Christ clearly, as I should. Don't miss out on an opportunity.

Dear Lord, help me to devote myself to prayer, being watchful and thankful. I pray that I will proclaim you clearly as I should. Provide me opportunity to offer a smile to a lonely person and share my story of how you provide for me. Thank you for the freedom that I have to share your Word openly. Amen.

22

A Call To Service
Jeremiah 1:4-8

These verses are the first in the book of Jeremiah where God calls Jeremiah to his service. God reminds Jeremiah that before he was formed in his mother's womb, God knew him and had a plan for him to be a prophet to the nations. Jeremiah claims that he is only a child. I don't know if he meant in age or maturity but God immediately denies his excuse. He assures Jeremiah that he will protect him and be with him everywhere he went. God can use anyone - young, old, educated or simple minded. I see a note my Mother wrote in her Bible at these verses. She wrote, God's command to me for service; turn and move in any direction he shall call.

God's promise of his continuing presence and guidance should calm any reluctance we may feel when called to service. We should hear his call as a command and not a suggestion. My Bible study notes tell me that through God's frequent affirmations of Jeremiah's commissioning as a prophet, he became fearless in the service of his God. Jeremiah is the longest book of the Bible and is full of God's judgment yet also proclaims his promise of hope and prosperity to those who call on him and answer his call.

Dear God, I know that you have a plan for my life. Help me to overcome my reluctance to serve you and trust your continuing presence in my life. Forgive me for my excuses. May I become fearless in my service to you. Amen.

23

Promise Of Restoration
Jeremiah 33:1-11

These verses have been very important to me during difficult times in my life. Mark this in your Bible. Through Jeremiah, God promised restoration. Out of the destruction God promised that the sounds of joy and gladness would be heard once more. He promised to restore them as they were before and more than they could imagine.

God couldn't even look on the destruction and wickedness in the city (verses 6-9). Nevertheless, he says, I will bring health and healing to it. He would forgive their sins of rebellion and cleanse them from their sin. Then others will hear of what he has done for them and will be in awe at the abundance and peace he provides.

What a wonderful story of healing and restoration. We want that same thing for our lives. That same promise holds true for us. He will do that very thing for us, when we call on him, no matter what our situation is. As times become difficult and it seems like we will never get past the troubles, go back to these verses and realize that when we pray, we invite God to respond. He wants us to experience the joy that comes from seeking him. He says, Call to me and I will answer you and tell you great and unsearchable things you do not know. I think he is telling us that he will do incredible things beyond what we imagined or asked for. As we seek him, not only will we get past the troubled time but he will restore us to where we were and better. Invite him to bring this same restoration to your life.

Dear God, how I need you. I cry out to you to restore the rubble around me. Bring health and healing. Let me enjoy abundant peace and security. I give thanks to you. Your love endures forever. Amen.

24

When Life Begins
Psalm 139:15

We often hear that life begins at conception. Well I beg to differ. I believe life begins before conception. Psalm 139:15 says, My frame was not hidden from you when I was made in the secret place; when I was woven together your eyes saw my unformed body. God tells Jeremiah (Jeremiah 1:5), before I formed you in the womb I knew you. Before God formed Jeremiah in the womb, he knew him.

God knew us before we were even conceived. He knew we would be conceived and planned every day of our life. Conception is human. God knows our soul. His relationship with us is not physical. Taking a life before birth is taking a life. The Federal Government Code of Federal Regulations

(CFR) 457.10(3) allows a state to define a child as an individual under the age of 19 including the period from conception to birth.

Abortion is wrong. It is a sin. God forgives sin. Don't think for a minute that if you have had an abortion that it is unforgiveable. God will forgive you. You confess it and you repent and you are forgiven. I know because when I was 17 years old in 1972 I got pregnant by my boyfriend. I was able to get to New York City for an abortion. Not making excuses, but it was something that was arranged and done before I really knew what I was doing. Years later I did realize that I had killed a creation of God. He has forgiven me. A Mother's Day does not go by that I don't remember. I believe that 'baby' went to heaven and when I go to heaven I will know him or her. I am ashamed but I am forgiven. If you need to, find that forgiveness for yourself.

Dear God, thank you for life. Thank you for knowing me before I was conceived. You are the only one who truly knows me. Thank you for forgiveness. I pray that our world will come to know that taking a life before birth is taking a life. Help us to remember how precious life is. Amen.

25

Can You Keep a Secret?
James 1:26

How often does someone ask you not to repeat something they told you? Why is it that when someone tells us that, we often have the uncontrollable urge to repeat it?

Proverbs 17:20 says he whose tongue is deceitful falls into trouble. He who guards his mouth and his tongue, keeps himself from calamity (Proverbs 21:23).

When we repeat things we should not, we are being deceitful. We may not realize it at the time, but we are. I recall being the one who shared something in confidence and learned later that it was repeated, several times and the last person did not hear it right. I wanted to crawl in a hole. The truth was embarrassing enough, while the distorted words repeated, really hurt. I later learned that it was repeated as a prayer request. Right! Hopefully we all learned a valuable lesson and together we found forgiveness but it did cause quite a calamity.

Let's be encouraged to be a person who can keep a secret. It is a wonderful opportunity to set a good example as a Christian – being someone that can keep a secret and can be trusted.

Dear God, I pray that you will be revealed when I am trustworthy and can control my tongue. Let others see you in me when I can be trusted. May I watch my ways and keep my tongue from sin (Psalm 39:1). Amen.

26

Gossip
Proverbs 11:13

Proverbs has many things to say about gossip. A gossip betrays confidence but a trustworthy person keeps a secret (11:13). A gossip separates close friends (16:28). Avoid a person who talks too much (20:19). Without gossip, a quarrel is avoided (26:20). Remember the game we played as a child, whispering something in someone's ear and after several times, the last person says what they heard. I don't believe it ever finishes correctly. That is the point. Playing that game was funny as a child but in truth it is very sad. That is exactly how gossip works. The truth gets twisted and someone gets hurt.

I recently went to visit my staff in an office in another part of the state. The reason for my visit was to discuss the new terms of a contract that supported the staff. I took with me representatives from Personnel and Legal in case questions came up I could not answer. The meeting went well. As I was leaving, one of the staff came up to me and thanked me for my visit; she also told me that the rumor was that I was coming to report that the contract was terminated, terminate the staff and was bringing people to help them apply for unemployment benefits. That made me angry. Who started that gossip and why? I could hardly imagine how they had felt the weeks between the scheduling of the meeting and my visit. I'm sure there was someone(s) who really believed it and was distressed and worried for weeks. Gossip is so unfortunate. Gossip can hurt. Gossip is usually a lie. Let's be encouraged to be a person who stops the cycle of gossip. If someone tells us something, let's not be so quick to repeat it.

Dear God, our words can be so hurtful. Remind me to be mindful of the turmoil and distress gossip can cause. Let me be the one who stops it from going further. Help me to set a good example as someone who can keep a tight rein on my tongue. Amen.

27

I Was Only Joking
Proverbs 26:18-19

In my Bible study, I came across these verses that I do not recall ever reading. Verse 18 reads, Like a madman shooting firebrands or deadly arrows is a man who deceives his neighbor and says, I was only joking. According to my dictionary, a firebrand is a piece of burning wood or someone who stirs up trouble and kindles a revolt. You should be easily able to visualize this situation. Sounds like chaos to me. I do recall that when I was hurt by a word or deed and was told it was a joke, it only increased my hurt or embarrassment.

Not only do we use this excuse when we are deceitful but when we accidently hurt someone maybe in a practical joke. My son always used the excuse, 'It was in an accident' whenever caught at something. He is now 22 years old and we still joke about it.

I'd like to suggest that we strive to own up to our mistakes and guard against deceit. Out integrity is important as a Christian. Titus 2:7 talks about our integrity and the importance of setting a good example, not only in our words but in our lifestyle. Even if we innocently hurt someone, let's confess and apologize instead of using this excuse.

Dear Lord, your Word is so full of unexpected lessons and I thank you for them. Help me to commit my heart to integrity and a lifestyle of honesty and truth. Help me to be mindful of others' feelings and treat those around me as I want to be treated. Thank you for your forgiveness. Amen.

28

Perfect Timing
Galatians 4:1-7

I was going through a time of struggle and confided in a friend that it seemed like God wasn't reacting to my situation. We talked about the fact that his timing is perfect and I needed to put my trust in that truth. The next day, she brought me a devotion entitled *At Just the Right Time* based on this text of scripture. It had helped her and she wanted to share it with me. God's timing is always perfect. He gave her the devotion just at the time when she needed it. He knew that I would share with her my concern and she would share with me just when I needed it. Galatians 4:4 says that God sent His Son at just the right time. So often throughout scripture, God moves unexpectedly. So many times we expect him to come in and save the day, at the time that we think we need it. Our time is rarely in the same time zone as God. He is the God of wisdom and perfection and we need to be patient in waiting for his timing. Let's be encouraged to ask him for the peace and patience that we need to wait for him to move. Let's not get in his way. He will show up to save the day and we will be amazed by his brilliant timing.

Dear God, thank you for your perfect timing. Help me to hold fast to my faith and trust in you. Help me to remember that you do what you say, in your time. Thank you for being my Savior, just when I need you most. Amen.

29

Unforgiveness
1 John 2:9-11

When we allow unforgiveness in our heart and thoughts, it will turn to hate. When we choose not to forgive we are walking in the dark. We stumble. We make bad choices. It shows in our words and actions. We often make those around us uncomfortable. Unforgiveness hinders us from receiving blessings meant for us. Forgiveness is a choice. Forgiving doesn't mean there wasn't hurt. Forgiveness doesn't make a wrong, right. It will give us freedom to receive blessings meant for us.

In Matthew 18:21-35, there is a story of the servant who owed a debt to his king. The king forgave the debt and freed him. However, the servant refused to forgive a fellow servant and took away his freedom. When the king heard what had happened, he sent the servant away to be tortured. Jesus said in verse 35, This is how my Heavenly Father will treat each of you unless you forgive your brother from your heart. We should forgive because we are forgiven. Like the king, God is angered that he forgives us and we do not forgive others. By choosing not to forgive, we lose our freedom and become captive and tortured by the unforgiveness and hatred held in our heart, just like the jailed servant.

Do you need to forgive someone? Do you need to forgive yourself? Do you hold a grudge against God for something? Come out of the dark into the light. There will be an obvious difference in how we see others and how we are seen.

Father, I want to forgive those who have hurt me. Convict me and bring to my mind, those who I need to forgive. Help me to be mindful of how I have hurt others and need to ask for their forgiveness. Thank you for forgiving me. Thank you for being the light that keeps me from stumbling. Amen.

30

Honor Your Parents
Exodus 20:12

This commandment tells us to honor our parents so that we will live long and prosperous. It tells us to honor our parents so that we can enjoy long life. This is the first commandment with a promise according to Ephesians 6:2.

I was raised by very strict parents. I 'missed out' on lots of things the other kids my age got to do. In my teenage and young adult years, I resented my parents and often dwelled on 'their mistakes.' I often had a pity party, even as an adult because I didn't get to go to movies or dances with the other kids. When I became a parent I realized it wasn't as easy as I thought. I later came to realize that my resentment was a sin and I was not honoring my parents as these scriptures instruct. I unfortunately can't say that I reconciled with my parents but thankfully I have with God. I encourage you not to waste time holding resentment in your heart toward your parents. Ephesians 6:1 says, Obey and honor your parents in the Lord, for this is right. I believe it is wrong to resent your parents and how you were raised, compared to your own point of view or compared to your friends' privileges or how you believe in raising your own children. We may need to agree to disagree but let's respect our parents. My Dad often said, You don't have to like what I say but you do have to respect it. I may not have realized it then but this is so true about any authority. A heart of love and respect gives us the freedom to enjoy life.

Dear God, thank you for my parents. Forgive me for how I have dishonored them. Help me to set a good example for my children. Help me to realize that you give us commandments for our own good. You also reward us with prosperity when we obey your commands. I want to honor you as my Heavenly Father. Forgive me for how I have dishonored you. Amen.

31

Finding Refuge
Deuteronomy 4:41-43

I have been blessed with the opportunity to visit Hawaii. One of the most beautiful places we saw was the City of Refuge on the Kona coast of the Big Island. In ancient times, Hawaiians lived under strict laws. The penalty for violating a sacred law was death. Breaking a religious law was believed to bring the wrath of the gods. They would capture an offender and swiftly put him to death unless he could reach a place of refuge. There he could be absolved by a priest in a purification ceremony, then return home with his transgression forgiven. Defeated warriors could also find refuge there during times of battle. I still remember the sense of peace and refuge there, even after hundreds of years have passed. It is a beautiful place and now a national park.

Moses speaks of cities set aside for refuge. A person could flee into one of the cities and save his life. We have a place of refuge. We can flee into the salvation of our Lord and save our life. The Lord is a refuge for the oppressed; a stronghold in times of trouble (Psalm 9:9). We don't need to swim across waters or sneak through the jungle to get to our place of refuge. We simply need to fall on our knees where we are and seek God, allowing him to provide the refuge and strength that we need today.

Dear God, thank you for being our refuge. Bring peace to my life. Help me to live each day in your strength. I will be glad and will rejoice in you. Amen.

32

Comfort For Eternity
John 14:1-4

I heard on the news recently that someone was selling a burial spot next to Marilyn Monroe. The newscaster asked, Do you want to spend eternity next to Marilyn Monroe? The spot was selling for a huge sum of money. I am sure there is someone out there who bought it and saw themselves as spending eternity next to a beautiful woman.

Jesus offers so much more than that! Where will you spend eternity? These scriptures tell us that Jesus is preparing a place for us and is coming back for us. We will spend eternity with him, in the many rooms of his Father's house. The way to spending eternity with Jesus Christ is through a relationship with him. This should bring a sense of excitement and expectation. Our days here on earth are just a whisper compared to the eternity we will spend with Jesus – no matter where our body is buried.

In this passage, Jesus had just told the disciples of his coming death and they were troubled. He gave them these words as comfort. He tells them not to be troubled for there is more to come. He reminds them that he speaks the truth and they can trust in his words. Do not let your heart be troubled. Trust in God. He offers this same comfort to us today. Choose eternal life with Jesus. Prepare now to spend eternity with him.

Dear Jesus, thank you for your truth and your promise. I want to be prepared for when you return for me. Forgive me of my sins and be my Savior. Help me to live life trusting in you. Amen.

33

Finding Success
Proverbs 3:1-12

Proverbs was written by King Solomon and other wise men that were called on to give advice to kings and instruct the young. A proverb expresses a truth or fact. I find several truths in this passage; advice that offers a long successful life.

- To prolong my life and find prosperity, I must remember God's teachings.
- To find favor with God and have a good reputation with others, I must wear love and faithfulness like a necklace and hold it in my heart. I must show love and faithfulness in how I act and in my lifestyle.
- I must trust in God completely and not try to figure out things on my own and he will make my walk straighter. There will be fewer obstacles to overcome if I always pray before making choices and decisions. My goals in life will be easier to reach.

- I will be healthy if I don't rely on my own opinion, stay away from bad influences and have a respectful fear and awe for the Lord.
- If I honor God with a regular portion of my gross pay, I will be blessed with what I need and more.
- God disciplines me because he loves me just like I love and discipline my own child.

Let's be encouraged to be in God's Holy Word everyday so we know his instructions. Following these instructions brings blessings. There is a benefit to each truth.

Dear Father, thank you for offering instructions in reaching the success you have planned for me. Help me to pass these words of wisdom to my children. Let them be a regular part of the choices we make daily. I want to love and honor you in all I do. Amen.

34

Pray Continuously
1 Thessalonians 5:17

In many Christian gift shops you will see the painting, *The Prayer at Valley Forge* by Arnold Friberg. The painting recalls the winter of 1778; the lowest, most hopeless and discouraging time in the revolutionary war. The struggling Americans were defeated by the British army in battle after battle, and were fast losing all hope. It was at such a time that legends say General Washington fell to his knees and humbly asked God for the strength to endure. The prayer is often quoted as, 'I consider it an indispensable duty to close this last solemn act of my official life by commencing the interests of our dearest country to the protection of the Almighty God and those who have the superintendence of them into his holy keeping'.

Throughout the Bible, kings and soldiers seek God in the time of battle. We are at battle everyday. The schemes of Satan are in our thoughts and the peer pressures of this world that we live in are constantly against us. This passage is another marvelous writing of Paul calling us to be joyful, pray continuously and give thanks in all circumstances. This is God's will for us in Jesus Christ. It is often difficult to focus on him in the distractions of life and I am sure even more close to impossible while in battle. However, this is where our strength to endure and resist comes from. Keeping open communication with God throughout the day regardless of our situation is what gets us through the day. Prayer empowers us to resist worry and fear. Prayer is part of our armor. The words of the old Hymn, "Teach Me to Pray" say:

> Living in thee Lord, and thou in me; constant abiding, this is my plea. Grant me thou power, boundless and free; power with men and power with thee.

Dear God, help me to be joyful, pray continuously and give thanks in all circumstances. My strength comes from you. I pray for the leaders of our country, as well as my community. I pray these leaders will fall to their knees and humbly ask you for strength to endure. Amen.

35

Rules For Living
Colossians 3:9-17

I enjoy going through God's word and developing it in words for my everyday life. This passage is Paul giving guidance to the church. Very simple rules to live by.

- Do not lie
- Have compassion
- Be kind
- Be humble
- Be gentle
- Be patient
- Forgive as freely as God forgives
- Over all of these, love.
- Be peaceful and not easy to quarrel
- Be thankful
- Study and live by God's Word
- Teach others
- Sing
- Everything you do should be pleasing to God.

Dear God, help me to follow these rules and teach them to my family. I want to do all things in your name. Sometimes these simple rules are hard to follow and I ask you to guide me and help me to follow them. Amen.

36

Rules For a Christian Household
Colossians 3:18-25

Here are more rules. Be careful not to take the word rule negatively. We try to explain to our children that rules are made for our protection. We all need boundaries. This is true for the rules that God sets for us, but additionally God sets rules so that we can be blessed. He always offers a blessing for our obedience. Here are a few for Christian households.

1. Wives, submit to your husbands, as is fitting to the Lord. My Bible study notes explain this last phrase as an act of submission to the Lord. To submit means to yield or submit to the authority of another. Wives are to honor and respect our husbands as head of our household (and I remind myself as I write this). I believe God mandates the husband as the head of the Christian household. Caution. There is no *if* here. I'll not delve into this any deeper. If this brings concern to your mind, take it to God.
2. Husbands, love your wives and do not be harsh with them. We are to treat each other with love and respect. I think one of the most important things to remember here (again I remind myself) is that we each have an opinion. Neither has to be right or wrong. Sometimes we must agree to disagree.
3. Children, in everything obey your parents. Children must be taught and expected to obey their parents.
4. Fathers, do not embitter or discourage your children. There are several levels of verbal abuse and each can grow bitterness and hopelessness.
5. As an employee, we must perform our duties as if we were working for the Lord himself. It is God we serve and an eternal inheritance that we strive for.
6. God will repay wrong and he will be just.

So what do you think? Can we deal with these? We can with God's help. Not one of these comes easily but with God all things are possible, even obedience. Let's take time to pray about this asking God to guide us as we strive to live within his will for us.

Dear God thank you for the rules you give us to live by. Thank you for your blessings that come from obedience. I need your help in living by this guidance. Show me how to live a life that pleases you. Help me to teach my children in the right way. With your help I can do this. Amen.

37

God's Promises
Psalm 3

God never promised skies always blue, flower
strewn pathways all our lives through.
God hath not promised sun without rain, joy
without sorrow, peace without pain.
But God has promised strength for the day,
rest for the labor and light for the way;
Grace for the trials, help from above, unfailing
kindness and undying love.
(Unknown author)

Psalm 3 was written by the psalmist with confidence when threatened by many foes. Verse 8 says From the Lord comes deliverance. We have confidence that this promise never fails. God is our shield. We can cry out to him and he will answer. Sometimes, we need to be still so that we can hear him. He speaks softly to quiet the loud storm around us. We can all look back and give testimony to this. Be encouraged to think on these promises when troubles come. His promises are more than we need. Start your day thanking God for the blue skies as well as the peace without pain.

Dear God, you are a shield around me. You never promised blue skies every day but you do promise unfailing love for each day. Help me to never doubt your promises. Thank you for your deliverance. Amen.

38

James Cash Penney
Matthew 7:12

As a child, J. C. Penney was taught by his parents to live by the Golden Rule - to do unto others as you would have them do unto you. While critics predicted failure, he revolutionized the world of retail. The son of a poor farmer, he watched every dime he made however built his business through serving the community with fair dealing and honest value. He often spoke to his sales associates, If you treat your neighbors and customers good, that's what will keep them coming back. The original Golden Rule Store opened in 1902 and was incorporated as J C Penney eleven years later. By the time he died at age 95, the company had 1660 stores and now yields annual revenue of $18 billion. J C Penney grew a nationwide company using Matthew 7:12 as its basis.

While this is one of the first verses we learned as a child, it may be the most difficult to live by. The JC Penney story sounds simple and easy, however I am sure it was difficult to live by in the competitive business world. Yet it appears that he stuck with it and lived successfully. Striving to live a life of devotion to God and a commitment to be in his Holy Word everyday for a dose of strength and support, we too can choose to live by these words.

Dear God help me to treat others as I want to be treated in everything I do. Forgive me for my selfish ways. Help me to live by this rule and teach it to others around me. Thank you for your forgiveness and your unfailing love for me. Amen.

39

On Eagles Wings
Isaiah 40:28-31

As I write today I feel burdened with family issues. Sometimes we feel like taking off to live on a deserted island where we can forget the difficulties in life. As I cry out to my God, he brings relief and comfort, for I know that he knows my situation and he is in control. No matter who I think of to go to for advice, I know God is the master of wisdom and he is the one that can lift me. As this scripture passage begins, Don't you know, the Lord is the everlasting God? He does not grow weary as I do. He understands what was, what is and what will be. My comfort and strength for the day comes from him. This hope renews my strength to soar like an eagle.

Have you seen an eagle soar? It looks like it is hanging in the sky, moving with the wind with very little effort. And I understand that no matter how high it goes, it can see the littlest creatures on the ground. It has no fear of falling, suspended by the will of God and no worry for provision. This is the comfort God provides for us no matter how weary or tired we may be. We can trust God to carry us, just like that eagle, while we wait on him and his infinite wisdom to handle whatever we bring to him. That hope and trust is what gets us through each day. We can walk and not faint.

Dear God hold me and provide me strength for this day. My hope and trust is in you. While I feel faint, I know that you can support me, to soar like the eagle, effortless and fearless. Hold me in the palm of your hand. Amen.

40

Love
1 John 3:16-24

Love talked about is easily ignored. Love demonstrated is irresistible. Jesus set the perfect demonstration of love. He had no sin in him, yet gave his life as the ultimate sacrifice for our sin. Active love is evidence of salvation. Romans 5:8 tells us that God demonstrated his love for us in that while we were still sinners, he gave his Son for us. God says, If you say you love me and other people, don't just tell me or tell them. Show me. Show them. Be a person of action. Do something about the people around you who need something. Then experience all the blessings I have for you. Verse 23 tells us God's commands are to believe and to love others. Love as he loves us. This is a command not a suggestion. I have a bookmark that says God does not love us because we are valuable; we are valuable because God loves us.

Not everyone is easy to love. Some don't seem to deserve anyone's love while others reject it. Nothing in the scriptures tells us that it is okay to love some people and not love others. God's gift of love is available to everyone. Our love should be available to everyone. Active love can tear down walls and mend bridges. We receive unexpected and unintended blessings from showing love to others. There is a young Hispanic girl that works for a friend of mine. She barely makes ends meet as a single parent. She got pregnant. While I didn't think this was a very good choice on her part, I wanted to do something for her. I purchased a gift card for her and had a friend write in Spanish in a note card, Jesus loves you and so do I. I felt such a rush from head to toe when I gave it to her. Tears came to both our eyes. When we see each other now, there is a special smile and greeting between us. God is love, all the time.

Dear God, help me to love others deliberately. Let unselfish love be my goal. Help me to love in obedience to your command. Thank you for your unfailing love for me. Amen.

41

Teachings For a Long Life
Deuteronomy 6

This passage of scripture includes direction from Moses as given to him from God. It was the commands and laws the Israelites were to observe in the Promised Land. As usual, our gracious God provides benefits in following him. These are the commands and their benefits that I find here. I encourage you to read this passage and find the promises that God speaks to you.

1. Honor and respect the Lord as long as I live by keeping his commands so that I may enjoy a long life.
2. Life will go well and full of blessings when I am obedient.
3. I must love the Lord my God, as my one and only god, with all my heart and soul and strength.
4. Talk to my child about obeying God, everyday, in everything we do.

5. I must not forget him when things are going good. I must remember that he provided the good things and the good times.
6. I must not anger God by putting anything or anyone before him.
7. I must not test God.
8. I must serve God only.

In verses 20–25, the scripture talks about explaining to our children why we are to follow these commands. You nor I may have come from slavery, saw miracles or inherited a promised land....but then have we? I think we often find our selves in situations just like the Israelites. Sometimes I find myself feeling just like those in the Old Testament, wandering, wondering what tomorrow will bring. I have seen miracles. And I have been delivered from bondage. The benefits are great when we live a life of respect and devotion to the Lord our God, and teach this belief to our children.

Dear God thank you for making it clear how to receive blessings in our life. It is not a mystery or a risk. Your Holy Word provides instructions on how you want us to live and how you will bless us for following your instruction. Thank you for your Holy Word and for your gracious provision. Forgive me for the times I have failed. I want to live a long life committed to you. Amen.

42

Saying I Love You
John 21:15-17

I grew up feeling loved with plenty of hugs and kisses, however we did not make it a practice to say I love you, very often. When I met my husband, he was surprised at that. I remember going to see my Dad in the hospital after he had minor surgery. When I left the room, my husband asked me in the hall why didn't I tell him I loved him. I just wasn't comfortable saying it. I often told my husband I loved him and I told my children I loved them every time I dropped them off at school but told very few others. I have worked at it and do better now, but missed opportunities to share my love with friends and family.

In this passage of scripture, Jesus was allowing Peter to claim his love for him after denying him three times (John 18:15-27). This reminds me of the need to say these words as well as hear them. Jesus knew Peter's heart, but he questioned him three times to hear him say the words. The word love is in the Bible many, many times. We are often told that we are to love God and he loves us. We are to love others as ourselves. God is love was probably the first Bible verse many of us learned. The word love should be a common word for us but should not be used carelessly. We should be comfortable speaking our love for each other.

I remember someone in a movie that told his wife, Ditto, after she told him she loved him. She longed to hear him say the words but he didn't. Let's be encouraged to give serious thought to saying, I love you to those that we love whether family or friend. Let's tell our Father in Heaven how we love him too.

Dear Father, I love you. Thank you for your love for me. Help me to love those around me and not be afraid to tell them so. I pray others will see your love in me. Amen.

43

Gesundheit
Ezekiel 34:25-31

What is a sneeze? According to the dictionary, it is a compulsive expulsion of air from the lungs through the nose and mouth caused by an irritation in the sinus passage. I read that sneezing can be triggered by sudden exposure to bright light, a particularly full stomach or a virus. I was surprised at that, wondering what this had to do with the sinus passage. I always thought a sneeze came from pepper or dust. We normally say, God Bless You or Gesundheit when someone sneezes. Why? Some believe when you sneeze you expel demons. Some have the idea that you ask God to bless you so that the sneeze doesn't develop into something worse. And some believe that the heart actually skips a beat during the sneeze and the wish is that the heart starts again. I'd like to suggest that we ask for God's blessing for our self and others, at the start of each day as well as when we sneeze.

Ezekiel is a prophet of God. He spoke words given to him by God. God promises blessings in these verses. He promises peace, showers of blessing, food and safety. Then God says, Then, you will know who is God. Verse 31 says, You my sheep, the sheep of my pasture, are people, and I am your God. Earlier in this chapter, God says, I will search for my sheep and look after them. He seeks us out to take care of us. He wants to be our shepherd. But as silly sheep do, we often run off into danger. He is the faithful shepherd that will search for us and bring us back into the safety of his promises.

Take a few extra minutes to read this entire chapter. Mark this in your Bible as a promise for you and your family. Gesundheit.

Dear God, thank you for being my Shepherd. Thank you for your promise of blessings and safety and peace. I want to stay close to you and not run off like a silly sheep. You are my God. Bless me and those around me. Amen.

44

The Love Chapter
1 Corinthians 13

This passage of scripture is often called The Love Chapter and is read sometimes at weddings. This passage is from Paul to instruct and inspire the church. It describes true love. Without love we are nothing. Even a massive faith is nothing without love. Love is patient and kind. There is no pride or envy in love. Love is not self centered or easily angered and forgets past mistakes. Love rejoices in the truth and does not delight in evil ways or thoughts. Love always protects, trusts, hopes and perseveres. Love never fails. Love is mature. Of faith, hope and love, the greatest of the three is love.

God is love and commands us to love each other. If our words and our deeds are not in love, we only make noise. We usually focus on our family and dear friends when we think of loving others. We show our love at special celebrations and certain times of the year such as Valentines Day or Christmas. Sometimes the love of material things or achieving our personal goals gets in the way of showing our love. We must share our love with everyone, in obedience to God everyday, in everything we do. 1 John 4:8 says that if we do not love, we do not know God. It's very easy to tie conditions and expectations to our love. God loves us unconditionally. He forgives as many times as we ask. We must have a selfless concern for others, regardless if the person seems lovable. We love in obedience to God as he made the ultimate sacrifice of love by offering the life of his Son in payment of our sin.

A friend told me that dog is God spelled backwards because only a dog can love unconditionally as God does. That comes to mind as I write this. It is funny, but seriously, my dog often loves me better than I love others. Show someone today, the unconditional love of God.

Dear Father, thank you for your love. Help me to grow the love of this chapter thirteen in my heart. Help me to memorize this description of love and carry it with me. Forgive me when I love only when there is something in it for me. Give me an opportunity to show your unconditional love to someone today. Amen.

45

The Excellent Wife
Proverbs 31:10-31

Many men look for, and many women want to be, the perfect wife. Let's start by agreeing that no one is perfect except Jesus Christ. However, this Proverbs passage describes a wife of noble character, the excellent wife.

As a wife, she is worth more than jewels, trustworthy and kind.
As a homemaker, she works joyfully, is thrifty,
disciplined, energetic and diligent.
She has compassion for the poor and those in need.
She is devoted to her family and does what
it takes to keep them clothed.
She sets an example with her kindness and
words, and has no worry for the future.
She manages her home with organization rather
than idleness and her family praises her.
And last but certainly not least, her beauty comes
from within, for she fears the Lord.

Our noble character or excellence comes from our humility and fear of the Lord. I'd like to suggest that we females follow this guidance not only as a wife but as we live busy lives as a single Mom, sister, aunt, daughter, friend, etc. Please don't let me take away the importance of these words to wives but as I read through it I see character in lives other than wives. I see character of Godly women. We need to teach these ideals to all girls. Women and girls live so many lies of what it takes to be perfect. Let's be encouraged to put God in the center of our lives no matter our position. And especially as we strive to be the wife of noble character in a marriage God has ordained, for as long as we live.

Dear God, create in me a heart that desires the Godly woman you intended me to be. Help me to recognize that my beauty comes from within. You created me to be joyful and trustworthy. Help me to keep you in the center of my life and be an excellent example to others around me. Amen.

46

It Is Well
Isaiah 61:1-3

Horatio Spafford was a successful Chicago lawyer. He was devoted to the Presbyterian Church and the father of four daughters. In 1873 he planned a vacation for he and his family to Europe but was detained by business and had to send them ahead of him on the S.S. Ville du Harve. Halfway across the Atlantic, the ship was struck by another ship and sank. Mrs. Spafford was miraculously spared but all four daughters were lost at sea. Horatio took a ship to reunite with his wife. As his ship passed the site of the earlier ship wreck, he claims to have felt an over powering comfort from God and the words, When sorrow like sea billows roll, it is well with my soul, came to his mind. He later wrote the words to the song we know today as, "It Is Well With My Soul".

Hebrews 13:5 tells us to be content with what we have, because God has said that he will never leave us or forsake us. When I think of the grief that Horatio was feeling that day as he passed over waters where his four daughters died and he felt comforted by God, I am overwhelmed with the magnitude of God's promise of peace. He wrote the words …whatever my lot, thou hast taught me to say, it is well with my soul. Horatio wrote words of praise to God for forgiveness and the price paid on the cross for him, looking forward to the day when the Lord will descend and return for us.

Some days are easier than others. Some days are really hard. No matter what our day brings, God promises to be with us and to never forsake us. He sees every tear and every smile. We can find contentment and thanksgiving in his promise, whatever our lot.

Dear God, thank you for the peace you can bring even in times of devastation. Help me to be content with what I have, knowing that I can trust in you. Thank you for the price you paid for my sin on the cross. Thank you for preparing a place for me in eternity with you, where there will no longer be pain and suffering. Amen.

47

Living Our Dreams
Proverbs 16:3-4

Did you watch the TV show, *I love Lucy*? I loved watching her and still do when I can. It is rare to see such simple, clean humor these days. Lucille Ball was never accepted in drama nor acting school because she was repeatedly told that she had no talent. She actually started her career as a model and show girl. These positions gave her exposure and she finally caught the attention of Hollywood. *I Love Lucy* ran successfully for six years, winning numerous awards including five Emmys. While Desi Arnaz had a magnificent voice and musical talent, he often was known to complain that Lucy was the star and carried the show. While I believe they complimented each other and would never have been as popular alone, she really could make me laugh, sitting on the edge of my chair wondering what she and Ethel would do next. And it was the opinion of many that she had no talent. While I cannot judge her heart, when I've read stories of her life, I never came across any indication of a relationship with God. For her sake, I hope here was one. She did live her dream.

Proverbs 16:3 tells us to set our goals, committed to God, and we will succeed. Psalms 20:4 assures us that God will give us the desires of our heart and make our plans succeed. When I was a little girl, when asked what I wanted to be when I grew up, my Mom tells me that I would answer, a rabbit. Well, as a small child that was as good of an answer as any. We can't just wish what we want to be, like a child. We must seek God's plans for our life and follow him. In other words, ask God what he wants you to be when you grow up. You may be an adult and haven't grown up yet because you have not yet asked him what he wants you to be. It is not too late. It may not be that his plan is for us to be a successful actor like Lucy, but when we follow his will, we will be as successful and I imagine happier.

Dear God, thank you for creating me with a plan for my life. Give me a desire to live within your plan for me. I pray that I will not live by selfish dreams but according to your desire for me. What do you want me to be? Open my ears and my heart that I will hear and know. Amen.

48

The Sabbath
Exodus 20:8-11

My parents impressed on me as a child, that Sunday was a special day. It was special in that it was 'The Lord's Day' and we did very little other than go to church on Sunday. I remember going to the lake to my aunt and uncle's house to visit. While others went out on the boat and swam, we were not allowed to. It was strictly a day of rest and quiet. I will not argue whether they were right or wrong, it's just how they were. While I have been known to take a boat ride on Sunday, it did instill in me that the day is special. There are some things that I try not to do on Sunday. The farm where I board my horse gives Sunday as a day of rest for the school horses used in lessons during the week. I believe this is the intent of this first day of the week.

The fourth of the Ten Commandments tells us to remember the Sabbath Day by keeping it holy. We are to observe this day after six days of work, as God did when he created the heavens and earth. At the time this command was given, it was also to allow the servants to participate in a day of rest just as God delivered the Israelites from slavery. In Mark 2:27-28, Jesus told the Pharisees that the Sabbath was made for man - intended for physical, mental and spiritual rest. Isaiah 58:13-14 provides instruction on how to find joy in the Lord. When we keep from doing as we please on his day and call the day a delight and honorable, we will find joy in the Lord and experience blessings. Take a minute to read these verses.

I am not prepared to give a list of Dos and Don'ts for the Sabbath, however I do suggest that we seriously consider how we spend this day. Let's ask God to show us how to spend our Sunday and convict us for anything we do that takes away from its intended holiness. We may be surprised.

Dear God, I want to keep your day holy. I ask you to clearly speak what you would have me do on this day of the week and convict me when I do not keep it holy. Help me to instill in my children the importance of this day. Thank you for your instructions that will bring us blessings. Amen.

49

Salt

Matthew 5:13-16

Salt flavor is one of the basic tastes, an important preservative and popular food seasoning. In the Sermon on the Mount in which Jesus gave several standards for living, he said, You are the salt of the earth. I think this simple statement can have several perspectives. People of God are to stand out from the rest of the world and impact others in a positive way. We are to preserve his teachings. If our flavor is lost, we are good for nothing. The dictionary defines flavor as a distinctive yet intangible quality felt to be characteristic of a given thing. If we lose our flavor for God, we are of no use to his mission. Our influence is to be positive and make things better, as salt adds to food. If we are negative or neutral, we add nothing, as salt with no saltiness. We are called to be like salt and be of unlimited value in taste and preserving.

Colossians 4:5-6 tells us that our conversations should always be seasoned with salt - wisdom and knowledge. Take a look at Mark 9:49-50. This suggests that we can expect to suffer but will be preserved and purified. We are cautioned about losing our flavor. Salt cannot regain its saltiness if lost. Next time you pick up the salt shaker, or see it on the table, ask yourself how much flavor you have added to someone's life lately.

Dear God, I want to be the salt of the earth. I want to have a positive influence and add flavor to those around me. Remind me that when I am idle or negative or even neutral, I lose my flavor for you and have nothing to add. Help me to trust in you in all I do. Amen.

50

Hoodie-Hoo Day

Psalm 47

February 20 is Northern Hemisphere Hoodie-Hoo Day. This is the day folks express their desire for winter to end. At Noon they go outside, wave their arms and hands, and shout Hoodie-Hoo!, Hoodie-Hoo! Hopefully, this song and dance will bring on Spring. While I'm sure it has nothing to do with the change of seasons, it would certainly bring a smile to the faces of those who have seen mostly cloudy and cold weather for many days. I am certain that this would lift everyone's spirit and outlook.

Have you noticed how contagious laughter can be? When you hear someone laughing and it goes on and on, what do you do? I know that I break out into a laugh as well. Especially when you hear a baby or a child laughing, you can't help but laugh yourself. Sometimes we don't laugh enough. There are times that I don't realize how solemn I am until someone appears with a smile or laughter. I have a good friend who hugs everyone. When you see her coming, she will give you a hug. She is always so lively and happy. It is contagious when she is around. It seems like she never has any down moments, but I am sure she does. She will quickly tell you that she is happy because Jesus is in her heart.

Psalm 47:1 tells us to clap our hands and shout to God with joy and thanksgiving. We serve an awesome God and joy should come easily regardless of our circumstances. I am experiencing a difficult time in my life right now and God gave me this verse this afternoon and I learned for the first time of Hoodie-Hoo Day. I turn on the radio so that Christian tunes fill my head. God knows just what we need and when we need it. God is the King and reigns over the nations. When we focus on our Lord, peace comes. When we take our eyes off of him, confusion and frustration sets in. Are you feeling down today? Read Psalm 47 out loud and Hoodie-Hoo! to you.

Dear God I thank you for laughter. I thank you for the joy you can bring. Help me to keep my eyes on you regardless of my circumstances today. You know everything about me and I know you care for me. I know you have plans for me; plans to prosper. Thank you for your love for me. Amen.

51

I Must Not Tell a Lie
Zechariah 8:16-17

We all know the story of George Washington cutting down his father's prized cherry tree and admitting to it saying, I cannot tell a lie. It is one of the things we remember about him most. What an admirable way to be remembered. How different our world would be if we all lived by this motto, every hour of the day. In this passage of Zechariah, God instructs the people to speak the truth to each other. He offered instructions to them on how they were to live under his protection and blessing. God hates lies and deceit. I hate all this, he said.

Proverbs 12:22 says that the Lord detests lying lips and delights in truth. We often hesitate at speaking the truth. We often later wish we had told the truth. Why? Sometimes we think it is in the best interest of another. Sometimes it is to prevent conflict. Whatever the reason, we usually look back and see that telling the truth the first time would have been the best move. We forget the peace that telling the truth can bring to our heart. Satan is the father of lies. God is the father of truth. God is delighted when we speak the truth and will bless the outcome. When in such a situation, we can ask God for guidance and he will take control and provide direction. He will not advise us to lie. He will bless our obedience.

Dear God forgive me for being untruthful at times. Give me courage to speak the truth. Help me to remember that you delight in the truth and you will bless my obedience. I want those around me to know I am honest and truthful. Help me to be the example of your words of truth. Amen.

52

Prayer Of Jehoshaphat
2 Chronicles 20

This chapter of scripture is an action packed story of King Jehoshaphat at battle. I find his prayer in verses 5-13 to be a model prayer for us. This king was told that a vast army was on its way. Alarmed, he resolved to ask the Lord for help and called his people to pray. In his prayer he:

- Started by stating who God is
- Remembered what God had done for them
- Recalled God's promises
- Stated the problem
- Released the problem to God
- Rejoiced
- Rested in confidence

2 Chronicles 17:3-4 tells us that the Lord was with King Jehoshaphat because in his early years he sought God and followed his commands. He

knew what to do when difficult times came. We know what to do when difficult times come. Mark this chapter in your Bible as a place to go when faced with battle. Use King Jehoshaphat's prayer when there is a battle at hand.

Dear God, I praise you for you are the King of Kings. You have blessed me in more ways than I can count. You make promises of fighting battles for me. I lay my fears and concerns at your feet. You care for me and take my fears from me. I praise you for the peace and confidence you bring. I rest now in knowing that you are the solid rock of my life. Amen.

53

God's Response To King Jehoshaphat
2 Chronicles 20

Yesterday we looked at the prayer of King Jehoshaphat. Today we will look at God's response to his prayer. God's response begins in verse 15. God advises him (and us), Do not be afraid or discouraged...for the battle is not yours but God's. God tells him exactly how to defeat the oncoming army. He tells Jehoshaphat to have faith and to rejoice. The faith of Jehoshaphat released God's power. This is like a dramatic movie scene. I can see him falling to his knees in relief, his heart racing.

God gives these same assurances to us. The battles are not ours, they are his. God wants us to acknowledge him and hand our battles over to him so that his power is released and his will is accomplished. What a wonderful story to encourage us. This is our only real hope. When we react in obedience, we receive his blessings.

The story ends telling us that the fear of God came upon all the kingdoms of the country when they heard how the Lord fought against the enemies of Israel. And the kingdom of King Jehoshaphat was at peace. Not only did Jehoshaphat save his people, but was a witness to those around him, even far away. Let's be encouraged to follow his lead.

Dear God, my battles are yours. Help me to trust you as I should and be obedient to allow you to fight my battles for me. Give me the faith and strength I need to be obedient. Bring peace to my life and those around me. Amen.

54

Our Work Ethic
Colossians 3:23-24

In my job I am responsible for many individuals across the state. The number of disciplinary actions that I am required to take is alarming to me. Individuals are often consistently late or absent or neglect to have a harmonious relationship with their coworkers. These are adults that often act like children. When disciplined, they often want to blame others or act disrespectful to those handing down the discipline. I often discuss with my peers that there is a vast difference in the work ethic of these individuals.

Colossians 3:23 and 24 instructs us that we should work at whatever we do with all our heart, as working for the Lord, not for men, since we know our inheritance will come from the Lord as a reward. It is the Lord Christ we serve. Do I perform my duties based on what I think I should be paid or following this instruction? Is my work ethic different when the boss is around compared to when he or she isn't around? Does my performance at work reflect that I am working for the Lord and not my boss? And what about my voluntary duties at church or school or for my community; does my performance of my responsibilities that I volunteer to do, reflect the same or is it different because I don't get paid for it? In this passage in Colossians, Paul is speaking to the slaves, not paid workers or volunteers like us. This is humbling to me. If slaves were to do their jobs this way, what does that say to us? What a difference we would make in this world if we followed these instructions in everything we did and taught our children and youth this type of work ethic. Our reward in eternity far exceeds any amount of pay we receive here from man.

Lord, forgive me for the times that my performance and my behavior does not reflect that what I do, I do for you. Help me to have the work ethic that glorifies you with a heart of service. Let me be an example to others. Let those around me see a difference in me and know that it is you in me. Help me to have a sincere heart and reverence for you in all I do. Amen.

55

A Beautiful Prayer
Colossians 1:9-14

In this passage of scripture, Paul writes to the church in Colosse. He wrote this either while in prison or under house arrest for preaching the Gospel. He writes, grace and peace to you from God our Father. Verses 3-6 speak of faith and love that spring from the hope that is stored up for us in heaven. Paul wrote these words while behind bars. I believe Paul was an ordinary man used by God. The power and greatness that we see in him came from his faith in God. Our sin and lack of faith puts us behind bars, and separates us from this hope, making us feel small and inadequate. God offers each of us a share in the inheritance of salvation from sin and eternal life. We can find that same power and greatness that we see in Paul in our faith in God.

I have this marked in my Bible as *My prayer.* These are lovely words of prayer. There are words asking for blessing, words of encouragement, strength, joy, promise and forgiveness. I once had a Sunday School teacher and dear friend who often encouraged us to pray the scriptures. Pray these words out loud. Pray for someone you know in need. Pray the words as thanksgiving for your salvation.

Dear God, I pray for you to fill me with the knowledge of your will. I want to live a life worthy of you and pleasing to you. Give me strength and joy and thanksgiving. Rescue me from the darkness and bring me into the kingdom of your Son, in whom I have forgiveness of my sin. Amen.

56

Good Advice
Proverbs 19:20

Advice from a Horse

Take life's hurdles in stride.
Loosen the reigns.
Be free spirited.
Keep the burrs from under your saddle.
Carry your friends when they need it.

Keep stable.
Spur yourself on to greatness.
Author Unknown

Proverbs 19:20 advises us to listen to advice and accept instruction and in the end you will be wise. Proverbs has a couple other things to say about advice. Verse 12:15 says a wise man listens to advice. Verse 20:18 advises us to make plans by seeking advice. Who do you seek advice from? Actually, the horse who wrote the above gives some pretty good advice. I caution the high school girls in my Sunday School class to seek advice from someone who is wise and not from a friend who will tell them what they want to hear.

God's Word is full of advice and guidance. He always has an answer for us, if only we would seek it from him. We must be in God's Holy Word daily and spend time with him in order to hear it. Thoughts and words from Satan will make us edgy and anxious, misleading us because he is the father of lies. God speaks to us with a sweet spirit giving us confidence and peace knowing it comes from the Father of truth. Seek advice from a smart horse, or better yet, from our heavenly Father.

Dear God, thank you for the advice you give me. Thank you for the truth and knowing what is best for me. Place people in my life that will offer good advice and guidance based on your truth. Make me aware of lies and untruths that come to mind and help me to ignore them. Amen.

57

Treasures In Heaven
Matthew 6:19-21

In traffic today, the car in front of me had a bumper sticker that said, Don't let the car fool you, my treasure is in heaven. As the traffic moved I ended up beside it. It was a pretty bad car with several dents and in bad need of a paint job. The lady driving turned to me and smiled broadly. I smiled back. That moment made me feel warm inside. Verse 21 of this passage says where our treasure is, there our heart will be also. I believe this lady's heart was in the right place. While her car was pretty beat up, she felt rich with treasures in heaven.

Our treasures should not be earthly. Money and material things cannot be our treasure. Moths, rust, thieves and rust can destroy earthly treasures. Having money and riches is not wrong. Centering our status in life, our hope and our trust in these material things is where we can go wrong. Whether driving a car with dents and in need of a paint job or a shiny car just off the new car lot, our heart should be centered on our relationship with our Heavenly Father and spending eternity with him. We were not created to obtain and store treasures here on earth but to store treasures in heaven through our acts of kindness, faithfulness and contentment in what we have while temporarily here. Don't let life here on earth fool you, store up for yourself, treasures in heaven.

Dear Father, my heart is with you and not in the earthly things of this earth. My treasure is my devotion to you and looking forward to eternity with you. Help me to be content with what I have and to long for a better relationship with you rather than material things. Amen.

58

People Need the Lord
Philippians 4:19

Recently I went to a birthday party for a friend. An acquaintance mentioned that the school his girls attend handed out Bibles in the cafeteria that day. He was angry about it, cursing, saying they had no business passing out Bibles to the kids. I felt like saying, Honey, you don't know what you're saying. Father, forgive him. Have you ever had such a moment? I don't know this man very well but I do know he and his wife are military. He had just returned from Germany and she is currently in Afghanistan. And I know he needs the Lord. Of course, not everyone we run into knows the Lord but it really stands out sometimes. He is missing so much. I didn't find an opportunity to say anything at that moment, but I immediately said a prayer for him and still pray for him and his family. I pray God will send someone into his life that will lead him to salvation. I never heard him say whether or not a Bible made it into his home. I pray that it did and he will read it. We need the Lord. Life is hard. God is the constant hope to help us through each day.

There is a beautiful song by Steve Green, "People Need the Lord". The lyrics say,

Everyday they pass me by, I can see it in their eyes.
Empty people filled with care, headed who knows where?
On they go through private pain, living fear to fear.
Laughter hides their silent cries that only Jesus hears.
People need the Lord. At the end of broken
dreams, he's the open door.
When will we realize? People need the Lord.

What can we do? When the opportunity arises, we can tell others what Jesus means to us. And we can pray. We can pray for those we know and those we do not know who cross our path. We can keep our relationship with God strong and active, so that he is evident in our daily life for others to see.

Dear Father, you meet all my needs according to your glorious riches. Thank you for salvation in you. We need you. I pray for those who don't know you. Give me the courage to share my story. Forgive me for the opportunities I have missed, please send them my way again. Amen.

59

Finding the Right Path
Acts 2:25-28

When my daughter first started driving, and got a part time job, we bought her a car. Before we allowed her to drive it to school, I took her to school and let her drive my car. We took the same path every morning for a couple weeks, driving a side road parallel to the expressway and to the school. I finally felt comfortable and allowed her to drive her car. I really didn't plan to follow her (honest) but it worked out that we left at the same time, me following behind her. As we went along, she turned right onto the expressway and took a different route to the school. I was fuming but went on and took my route to work, fuming all day long. Later, when we were finally home my first question for her, was why did she take the different path to school. She explained that she didn't realize that was the way she had to go. Well, that was over 10 years ago and we survived her early driving years.

God outlined a path for us even before we were conceived. He has made known to us the paths of life in his Holy Word. God is not a bully.

We can take the path of our choosing or we can follow the path he outlines for us. Even when we get off the path, God is always there to pick us up, dust us off, and get us back on the path. We must be in his Holy Word regularly and open to his guidance in order to know the path he chooses for us. And that path may not be the expressway but the side road. Let's not be too anxious to take a different route.

Dear God, my heart is glad, my tongue rejoices and I live in hope. You are always beside me. I will not be shaken. You make known to me the paths of life. Give me faith and courage to follow you and not be too anxious to take the expressway. Amen.

60

Doing As I Do
Romans 7:15 - 8:2

This passage of scripture is written by Paul regarding our struggle with sin. Reading through it is almost like a rhyme or tongue twister. The word 'do' is there 21 times. As I read these verses, I feel his anxiousness and frustration. Just how I feel when Satan whispers in my ear, lies and suggestions of sin. I also find relief that my struggle with sin is normal. The sin living in me leads me to do what I want to do. I try not to sin but I keep on doing it. My mind and my body want to sin and make me prisoner to it. Who can help me? God – through Jesus Christ our Lord. As a believer, when we make the wrong choices, the Holy Spirit speaks to our consciousness and convicts us, reminding us of the truth. This is not an excuse, just the fact of the sin we live in because of that first sin in the Garden of Eden. We need to recognize this so that we are prepared to resist. The passage closes with Paul's cry of relief and triumph. Victory through Jesus Christ. Those who do not know Christ do not have this relief. That's why it is so important that we spread the truth of Christ. The struggle is there whether we know Jesus Christ or not, but the strength to resist and forgiveness comes only through him. Be reminded of 1 Corinthians 10:13 that tells us God is faithful not to let us be tempted beyond what we can bear. He will provide a way out so we can stand up to the temptation. Phew! I feel better. We all have that same struggle. The angel on one shoulder and the devil on the other. When we know Jesus Christ as Lord and Savior, we can find relief from the struggle and confidence that we can resist temptation.

Dear God, thank you for the relief you bring. Help me to be mindful of the struggle with sin that will come everyday. Help me to find the time to be in your Holy Word so that I am prepared to resist sin. Open my eyes to the way out that you will provide me. Thank you for the forgiveness that you give freely. May my life be an example to others of the peace that I know in you. Amen.

61

Thankfulness
Psalm 100

This is a psalm of thankfulness. Read it out loud. It is a call to a grateful praise and why. There are several action verbs for us. Shout – Worship – Come – Know – Enter – Give - Praise

We are called to praise God and be thankful. There is nothing here about the time of day, the day of the week or the situation we are in. It just tells us what we are to do. We are called to worship God with grateful praise. Why? Because he made us and we belong to him. God made us to worship him. We are the sheep in his pasture. God is good and his love and faithfulness is with us forever.

Dear God, I praise you with a grateful praise. I come to you with a joyful heart, no matter what today brings. I belong to you and I need you. Thank you for your never ending love and faithfulness. I want to praise you and worship you, every day, in all that I do. Amen.

62

By Faith
Hebrews 11

I encourage you to read this entire chapter. It encourages me each time I read it and restores hope in my heart no matter how I feel at the time. Faith is being sure of what we hope for and certain of what we do not see. Each person listed in this chapter is a great example of the faithful. Most importantly they never saw completion of what they were promised yet they still followed what they believed God spoke to them. Their goal was reached because they found eternal life after their time here. We often pray for those we love and for fulfillment of goals we want to reach. Sometimes we see the answer from God and sometimes we do not. That doesn't mean he isn't working. Maybe he has another plan. Maybe it isn't for us to see. Maybe he has other timing in mind. But as the verses say, we can still be certain of what we can not or do not see. This is our faith in him.

I will be the first to say this isn't easy, in fact, this is hard. And I know it was hard for those heroes of faith listed in this passage. We tend to trust what we can see. And we want a response in our own timing. It doesn't work that way with God. We only need to tell him the desires of our heart and lay our burdens at his feet and let him do the rest. Many times I have looked back and wondered why didn't I settle for the peace God offered me and let him take care of the matter rather than painfully struggling through the ordeal like I was alone? We can't ask for his guidance and then start working on our own. We must have total faith and trust in him and allow him to guide us and work through our issues of life. Our reward is the peace he brings during the storm and spending eternity with him in the place he has prepared for us.

Dear Father, thank you for the awesome stories of the faithful ones who set an example for me. They came from all walks of life and various acts of faith. I know that you want the same for me. I lay my burdens at your feet and wait to hear from you. Give me courage to find the faith that I need to trust without seeing. Show me when to step forward in faith and when to be still and quiet as you work in me. Amen.

63

Cheering Us On
Hebrews 12:1-3

Have you been in a relay race, a game or competition and others were cheering you on? It makes us feel better even if we lose to know that others are encouraging us as we go through the game or race. Sometimes we have the opportunity to cheer them when it is their turn. We often lead hectic days just so we can get to our child's game or band concert or recital. We know it is important to be there, to cheer them on and support them. And it is important for them to see us there. They often ask, Did you see me? Hebrews 11 reminds us of the many people of the past who are commended for their faith. Ordinary people (just like us) who were sure of what they hoped for and certain of what they did not see. They have completed their life on this earth and now live the promise of eternal life due to their faith. Romans 12:1 tells us they are now surrounding us as witnesses. I believe they are cheering us on as we run with perseverance the race of life that God has marked for us. They have lived the difficulties of life. They have lived the test of faith. They know what we are going through and are encouraging us to keep going and keep our faith in our Heavenly Father. These verses encourage us to fix our eyes on Jesus, who lived on earth when these others did, was crucified for our sin and now sits at the right hand of God. This truth keeps us going when we grow tired and weary. I always find it encouraging when someone has experienced the same situation that I have and can support me in knowing just how I feel, offering guidance in a time of difficulty from their experience. This scripture offers us that same kind of support from the ancients who lived long ago. We have the responsibility to pass on this encouragement that we receive to others; especially the truth that Jesus Christ died so that we can live in eternity with him. When life gets hard, turn to this passage or look up to the heavens for that cloud of cheering witnesses who are there cheering us on. Fix your eyes on Jesus.

Dear Lord, thank you for the encouragement you send my way. Thank you for Jesus who gives the gift of eternal life. I pray my faith will be as strong as the ancients listed in this scripture. Help me to be sure of what I hope for and certain of what I do not see. Amen.

64

Forgiveness
Psalm 32

This Psalm is about the joy of forgiveness. When we carry sin in our heart, we are uncomfortable. Verses 3 and 4 speak to the discomfort we feel before we acknowledge our sin and confess. Then we receive the blessing of forgiveness. I remember a time when someone said something to me that I did not like, actually it embarrassed me and hurt my feelings. The next day, I practiced over and over in my mind what I intended to say to get even. The time finally came. My heart raced and when the opportunity came, I said my peace. She and everyone else standing there were shocked.

I turned away, my face burning, ashamed and feeling worse than ever. I went home and asked for God's forgiveness. The next day, I found myself apologizing to her but the friendship was destroyed not because of what she said to me, but because of what I said to her.

I am blessed because I know that my Savior has forgiven me and does not count it against me. I confess and he forgives. My heart was broken over the situation, but he surrounded me with deliverance just like these words say. I remember the hurt that I felt from my sinful reaction. God allowed that pain so that I would learn from it. And I remember the comfort and peace of his forgiveness. Verse 9 says not to be like the horse or mule that must be controlled by a bit. Sometimes I feel like God needs to put a bridle and bit on me to control me. But that is not how he works. We are allowed to make our own choice and must work through the consequences even though he will forgive us anytime we repent and change. The Lord's unfailing love surrounds me when I trust in him. Rejoice in the Lord!

Dear Father, you are my hiding place. You protect me and surround me with the songs of deliverance. I want to be open to your instruction and counsel. I need the presence of your unfailing love. Forgive me of my sin and remember them no more. I trust in you in all things. Amen.

65

Song Of Praise
2 Samuel 22:31-33

David sang to the Lord the words of this song when he delivered him from the hand of all his enemies and from the hand of Saul (verse 1). God's interactions and blessings in David's life showed him to be the living God. David experienced the Lord's favor and his forgiveness. I have prayed verses 31 – 33 for my son. These words of praise remind me that God's way is perfect. We often pray for our desire for our children. I often catch myself telling God what I want for my son. I have to stop myself to ask God for his way because I know it is perfect, and much better than anything I have in mind. Verse 7 in this chapter reminds me that God hears when I cry out to him. He hears my voice from his temple. The entire chapter speaks words of praise and reminds us over and over that God is our rock.

Life can be like a roller coaster with ups and downs, full of laughter, thrills and fear. Sometimes I feel alone and tired of trying. Yet when I read a passage such as this, it brings peace and comfort to me. The battles are not mine to fight. The battles are mine to give to him and let him handle in his perfect way. He is a shield for all who take refuge in him. We must sing words of praise in the good times and the bad. Praise to a God who arms us with strength and makes our way perfect. The Lord lives! Praise be to my Rock and Savior.

Dear God, you are my refuge and strength in times of trouble. I praise you for the good times and the bad. My hope and trust is in you. I am comforted to know that my words fall on your ear. You hear me from your heavenly temple. I praise you with all my heart. Amen.

66

Jesus' Mission
Luke 19:1-10

This is the story of Zacchaeus. It is also The Story of Jesus' Mission. It wasn't so bad that Zacchaeus was a tax collector. He was a cheating tax collector. He collected taxes and took extra for himself. I believe that Jesus chose this street to walk through so that he would engage with this man. I believe that this incident took place not long before Jesus' trial and death. It was an opportunity for him to show the people his mission – to show them why he came. He came to earth to find the lost and save them. He came to bring salvation and eternal life. Zacchaeus was the perfect example and his life was never the same after he met Jesus and found forgiveness.

Our lives are never the same after we come to know Jesus. Our lives are never the same when we stray or rebel and return to him. Life is different after forgiveness. We stumble and fall over and over, but Jesus' mission is to seek and save the lost and the sinners – you and me. No matter what our sin is, he is here to forgive and to change us. Zacchaeus returned all that he had stolen. We don't know how he lived his life after this but Jesus said that salvation had come to his house. I believe his life was different because he found Jesus. I believe those that knew him saw the difference in him and may have trusted in Jesus through his testimony. You and I have that same opportunity every day. Each morning brings a new opportunity to live for him. Jesus' mission was to seek and save the lost. Our mission is to spread his word to our community. We must get past our comfort zone and seek those who need them. We are to seek the lost and show them the way to salvation and eternal life.

Dear Jesus, thank you for coming to our world to seek us and save us. Thank you for forgiving me of my sins. I want my life to be a testimony of your mission for others to see. Help me to remember the change that you brought to Zacchaeus and that you want to do the same for our world. Amen.

67

Robbing God
Malachi 3:8-12

I was taught at an early age to give God a regular offering. As I grew older, I was taught and chose to follow, giving God a tenth of my gross wages. These verses I find very serious. It says to me that not giving to God is robbing him. I give because I believe it is in obedience but also because I know God will provide for me and add to the amount that I give. I do not miss it. I do not go without nor pay bills late because I give. If my finances are not right, it has nothing to do with my giving. I do believe our finances are affected if we do not give our tithe to him. Tithing is an act of obedience.

A friend of mine told me a story about her son. He had promised a friend a loan of $500. When he gave it to him, he told him not to worry about paying it back to consider it a gift. The very next day he lost his job. He spent the next couple weeks in limbo not knowing what his future would bring. He admitted that he could have used the $500 that he gave away. However, another job did come through for him and he received an extra $5000 in severance pay and moving costs. You can believe what you want. I believe God blessed him many times over for his willingness to give. I know this wasn't an offering to God but I believe this is what God is talking about. Leviticus 27:30 says a tithe of everything belongs to the Lord; it is holy to the Lord. When we are obedient, God blesses us. When we are disobedient, we rob him.

The amount of your tithe is something you work out with God. I believe in a tenth of the gross of what I receive. If you are not attending a church regularly and not giving a regular tithe, I encourage you to pray right now for guidance and direction. I believe you will see a change for the better in your relationship with God and in your finances.

Dear God, thank you for how you provide for me. Thank you for the opportunity to give back a portion of what you provide. Help me to seek your direction when I am not sure and be obedient when you speak. Amen.

68

Recovery
1 Samuel 30:19

1 Samuel 30:1-20 is a wonderful story of recovering a loss. The Amalekites raided Ziklag, taking the people captive, including David's two wives, stealing their animals and property. When David and his men discovered this, they were so hurt it says they wept until they had no strength left to weep. David asked the Lord what to do. God told him to pursue the Amalekites and he would be successful. Skipping some of the details that you can read, they recovered everything. No life was lost and all property was recovered.

Have you ever been so hurt or experienced such a difficult loss that you cried until you were simply exhausted? When this happens, we can cry out to our Heavenly Father and ask him what to do. Now I am not here to say that this recovery such as David's will be the result each time. I am here to say that God will pick you up, wipe your tears and restore you. Sometimes we are restored back to where we were, sometimes to a better place and sometimes to a totally different place. But we are restored and our hurt is healed. We can look back and see God in his glory as he fulfilled his purpose for us, and look forward with hope in our heart. David rejects his men's idea that their victory came from their own strength and skill. God allowed the victory therefore no man could claim any greater right to the recovered property than any others.

The final verses in the chapter tell how David equally shared the plunder that was recovered to all who fought the battle, those who were too exhausted to fight and other friends. He shared his restoration with others and God's glory was revealed to them. Let's be encouraged to let this story set an example for us as we face difficulties and losses.

Dear Father, thank you for how you restore my losses and bring me to a place of recovery. I give you all the glory and celebrate your goodness. Remind me to share with others the stories of your faithfulness to me and the blessings you provide me. Amen.

69

The Potter
Jeremiah 18:1-10

Some of us understand things better when we see a picture rather than hear a description. Apparently, God wanted Jeremiah to see what he had to tell him when he sent him to the potter's house. Jeremiah saw the potter molding the pot from the clay. Because his hands were covered with clay, the shape would not take form so he changed his plan and shaped another type of pot. Jeremiah understood that God had intentions for the people but because of their behavior, he could and would change his plans for them, sometimes for the better, sometimes for the worse. As the potter could control the shape of the clay, so the Lord has authority over his people. He can allow blessing or he can allow disaster.

I believe God works in our lives this way. When we are obedient and walk close to him, he will bless us and pour out his mercy. However, when we rebel and let go of him, we make bad decisions and wrong choices which may alter his response to us. Keep in mind, the bad decisions and wrong choices are ours to make and ultimately cause hardship to come upon us. We mustn't see it as God cracking the whip on us because of our disobedience. We should see it as consequences of our choosing. We can miss his blessings because of our choice or we can prevent disaster because of our choice. Life brings good times and bad. God is always there to comfort us in the hard times and sing with us in the good times. He never steps away from us. We step away from him. Isaiah 64:8 tells us we are the clay and the Lord our Father, is the potter. We are the work of his hand. Maybe we should all take a trip to the potter.

Dear God, I am the work of your hand. Thank you for allowing me to make my own choices. Help me to remember that my choices are better when I walk close to you. Even when disasters come, you are there to bring comfort and peace. Thank you for your Holy Word that brings me these words of encouragement. Amen.

70

Though Your Sins Be As Scarlet
Isaiah 1:18-20

After reading these verses one morning, I could not get the old hymn, "Though Your Sins Be As Scarlet" off my mind. I just kept singing it over and over in my mind.

Though your sins be as scarlet, they shall be as white as snow.
Though your sins be as scarlet, they shall be as white as snow
Tho' they be red like crimson, they shall be as wool.
Though your sins be as scarlet, though your sins be as scarlet,
They shall be as white as snow. They shall be as white as snow.

Isaiah, which means The Lord saves, is speaking the word of God in this passage. God says he will change our sins from scarlet to white as wool if we are willing and obedient. This passage is referred to as a message of rebuke and promise. According to the dictionary, scarlet means vivid red and it means sinful, unchaste, whorish. What an excellent word to explain sin. Forgiveness is changing our scarlet sinfulness to white as wool or snow. When we think of white, we think clean, fresh, brand new. I am from the midlands of South Carolina and see very little snow. But I do recall seeing the white and perfect first fallen snow. After a while it melts and becomes mushy and dirty. That first perfect white snow is the symbol of forgiveness. And the wool that is sheared from sheep is perfect as well. God is willing to forgive. We must repent and change our heart to remove the scarlet stain of sin. As the song says, God will forgive our transgressions and remember them no more.

Dear God forgive me of my sin. Thank you for your forgiveness. Remind me daily of how my sin is dark and ugly without forgiveness. You promise that we will eat from the best of the land if we are willing and obedient. Help me to seek your way to stay within your perfect will. Amen.

71

John 3:16

John 3:16 is one of the most widely quoted verses from the Bible. It has been called the 'Gospel in a nutshell' because it is considered a summary of some of the most central doctrines of traditional Christianity. The verse occurs from a conversation in Jerusalem between Jesus and Nicodemus, a member of the ruling council. Jesus' miracles have convinced Nicodemus that Jesus was sent from God. In reply, Jesus declares, I tell you the truth, no one can see the kingdom of God unless he is born again, (verses 5-6). John 3:16 summarizes Jesus' lesson to Nicodemus; that belief in him is the only path to eternal life. Take a few minutes to read verses 1-21.

The phrase John 3:16 is very short and can be written in out-of-the-way locations. We see it everywhere, often on bumper stickers. Apparently it is often written in places that we may not see as a tribute to the meaning of its message. *Google* tells me that in the U.S., the In-N-Out fast food chain prints it on the inside of the bottom rim of their paper cups. The restaurant chain has developed a loyal customer base and has been rated as one of the top fast food restaurants in customer satisfaction surveys.

God loved us so much that he was willing to give his Son as the ultimate sacrifice to give us eternal life. What great promise these few words bring us. Simple enough for a young child to recite yet big enough to save the world. The words roll off our tongue without recognizing the magnitude of them. The salvation Jesus Christ offers results in eternal life. Life, unending, lived in his presence. Our belief must grow into a relationship with him to receive the full blessing of this promise while here on earth. Let's be encouraged to keep this verse in our heart and use it to share our testimony to a world hungry for hope.

Dear God, thank you for your love for me and the sacrifice you made for me so that I can have eternal life. My hope is in you. Give me courage to share my hope with the lost world that we live in. Amen.

72

A Roadmap To Heaven

1 John 5:11-12

Unfortunately, some people see getting to heaven as a life long difficult road, that they are not worthy to travel; therefore they never accept the offer and take the first step. Some believe that one must be perfect to even start the journey. Some are afraid of what they have to give up, to take the road. I am not saying it is an easy road but it is not a lonely road. The hills are easier if we allow our strength to come from God and not on our own. It is also easier if we drop that backpack of burden that we insist on carrying instead of allowing Jesus to carry it for us. And each morning brings new opportunity for growth in him.

These two verses give the simple plan regarding the road to heaven. If we have the Son of God, we have eternal life. The dictionary defines the word have as, to be in possession of; to hold in the mind; to accept; to use or exhibit in action. Does this describe your relationship with God? I hope so. If not, stop right now and ask Jesus Christ to show you the way.

I had a friend to tell me once when I was trying to witness to her, 'I'm just not ready to walk that way'. I could not get her to see that there is no preparation, just taking the first step toward Jesus and he leads the way from there on. To this day I don't really know her heart. I pray that the seed I planted will grow within her. Jesus says in John 14:23-24 that the Father loves anyone who loves him and obeys his teaching. He will make our home with him. Love and obedience are linked.

I love you Lord. I lift my voice to worship you. Take joy my King in what you hear. I long to see the eternal home that you have prepared for me. Forgive me of my sin and help me to walk obediently. May my actions reveal to those around me, my love for you. Amen.

73

Changing Color
1 Peter 2:1-3

A foal's (baby horse) color can change as it grows. In the autumn of its first year, after losing its foal coat, its adult color usually emerges. Gray horses become lighter as they age until their hair coat is nearly completely white. Some horses get darker with age. Color can be defined in terms of the observer. Color can define not only the appearance but the opinion, character or position. Color defines the outward appearance which can be deceptive or misleading.

When we accept Jesus, our color should change. These verses tell us to rid ourselves of malice, deceit, hypocrisy, envy and slander of all kind. Like a newborn we grow in our salvation. Like a newborn, we should crave spiritual milk. Our color, our outward appearance, should change as we advance in a life lived for Jesus. Others should see us differently, not perfect, differently. My Bible study notes say the unrestrained hunger of a healthy baby provides an example of the kind of eager desire for spiritual food that ought to mark the believer. This spiritual food is vital nourishment for the growth of our relationship with Jesus Christ. Just like a baby grows in what it can do intellectually and a foal changes color, we should be growing and changing. Later in verse 12 of this passage, Peter encourages his listeners to live such good lives among the pagans that they see their good works.

My horse, Strawberry, is a red roan. A horse with intermixed white and colored hairs of any color is called a roan. While I love her, I don't want my color to be intermixed. I want to be clearly defined as a child of God, striving to live obediently in anticipation of eternal life in his presence. I want my outward appearance to be of strong character and of honesty. I have good days and I have bad. I am strong some days. I am weak some days. I sin. I am forgiven. But Jesus lives in my heart and I praise him for his full color of everlasting love for me.

Dear Father, thank you for the lessons we can learn from the wonderful world of nature that you created. Thank you for your unfailing faithfulness and your unconditional love for me. May my color be of faithfulness to your teachings and honest to those around me. May my color show the hope and confidence that I have because of you. Amen.

74

The Prayer Of Jabez
1 Chronicles 4:10

The first time I heard of this verse, was a conversation that I overheard a man talking about how the verse had changed his life. His perspective of blessing was a matter of giving rather than getting. I became curious and read through it. I have marked in my Bible many times that I prayed this prayer for myself and others.

There is very little history of Jabez in the Bible. Jabez is only found in a few verses in chapter 4 of 1 Chronicles. His story is easily missed, because it falls in the middle of lineage. Yet in these two verses, is a powerful message for us.

Oh that Thou would bless me indeed, and
enlarge my boarders, and that your hand

might be with me, and you would keep me from
evil, and that it might not cause me pain.

Jabez asked five things of God. Jabez asked God to bless him indeed
or greatly. It may be hard to ask God to bless us a lot. Verse nine tells us
that Jabez was honorable which suggests that he was not asking for God's
blessing for selfish reasons. He wanted to do God's will, and honor God.
Jabez asked God to expand his influence. I think he was asking God to
expand his ability to proclaim his testimony. Jabez asked God to keep his
hand on him. He knew that when God placed his hand upon him, he was
truly blessed. He wanted God's protection. Jabez asked God to keep him
from evil. He asked God to protect him from evil and also to keep him
from thinking or doing evil. Jabez asked to be free from pain. The name
Jabez means born in pain. Jabez asked God to keep him from experiencing
pain and from causing pain.

I encourage praying scripture. I believe it gives God joy to hear his
words come back to him in praise. Pray this prayer regularly. Anticipate
blessings from God. Listen for God's voice. Look for opportunity to
expand your influence. Expect to expand your comfort zone. Seek God's
protection through obedience. Remember and testify the Jabez moments
you experience.

Dear God bless me indeed. Give me opportunity to testify your love
and faithfulness. Keep your hand upon me. Protect me from evil and pain.
I pray I will not stray from you in sin and will not cause others pain. Thank
you for your grace and mercy. Amen.

75

Living In Harmony
Romans 12:16-21

I love watching westerns on TV, especially *Gunsmoke*. Those who
know me well, know how I dote on James Arness, Marshall Matt Dillon.
The show took place in frontier Dodge City with problems of Indian
raids, robberies, rustling, and family feuds. The task of dealing with these
issues within the law fell on Marshall Dillon. I enjoy all of the characters
especially Festus who had a special knack with words. Marshall Dillon
often solved crimes through observation and reasoning, rather than the

use of his gun in his quest to keep peace in Dodge. I still keep up with 86 year old James Arness through his website. Over the years he has given his time and personal donations to non-profit organizations. One closest to his heart is the United Cerebral Palsy organization. US Marshall Matt Dillon (fictional of course) tried to live in harmony.

Paul's teachings in Romans 12, tells us to live in harmony with one another. In these few verses is quite a list of instructions for living in harmony. Do not be proud. Be willing to associate with anyone regardless of their position. Do not be conceited. Do not repay evil with evil. Do what is right for everyone to see, living at peace with everyone. Revenge belongs to the Lord. Be kind and good to the enemy. Overcome evil with good. Only God can equip us to follow these instructions. Without him in our heart, it is impossible. There is much discord around us at work, in our community and within our families. Our obedience could bring those around us to repentance and salvation. We should also recognize that living in harmony brings a peace within us that is denied when we choose to fight and live in discord. Responding to anger and hurt with anger and hurt only intensifies it. I often have to put myself in the other person's shoes in an effort to understand their feelings. We don't have to agree with an opposite opinion, but we must respect it. An attitude of peace is as contagious as an attitude of anger. Let's strive to follow these words that can bring harmony to our lives and those around us.

Dear Father, help me to live in peace and harmony with others. Let there be peace and let it begin with me. Help me to see each obstacle as an opportunity to reveal your love. Forgive me of my pride. Help me to love others as you love me. Amen.

76

Called To Pray
2 Chronicles 7:14

Most of us remember September 11, 2001 and can recall exactly where we were when we heard the news of the attack. 2,993 people lost their lives that day. I recall being in a meeting at my state government job that started at 8:30. Late comers kept coming in telling us what was going on. After awhile, we agreed that we were getting nothing accomplished and dispersed. Shortly after returning to my office and hearing of the tragedy,

I called my staff together because I had seen the fear and anxiety on their faces. I offered an opportunity for quiet. We held hands and prayed. None of us knew anyone in the tragedy yet there were many tears. One lady came in and asked if she could read a scripture. Everyone agreed. She read 2 Chronicles 7:14. One of my employee's grandson was born that day around Noon. We were able to experience that day with grief, hope and celebration. I am thankful to God that I can remember the day this way because I know for others it was a day of hopelessness and massive grief.

The few words in this verse are so true. God calls us to pray, to pray humbly calling his name. We must turn from our wicked ways and pray for all people to turn from evil ways. There is hope in the fact that God will hear us. He will forgive us. He will heal us. He will bless our country. Do you believe that? This is huge. We pray for daily concerns in our lives – some big, some small. According to this scripture, we should be praying for our country; praying that people will turn from their wicked ways so that God can bring forgiveness and healing. I certainly do this on days like September 11 but I can't say that I do it regularly. Let's commit ourselves to doing this. Let's stop right here and pray for our country and keep our country on our daily prayer list. I believe that God's promises are true and our obedience brings blessings.

Dear God, I pray for our country. I pray that all people will turn from evil and wicked ways. I pray all people will come to you for forgiveness. I pray that we come to you humbly, seeking your face. Forgive us and heal us. I pray for those who have lost loved ones innocently. I pray that they will turn to you for hope and peace. Thank you for your blessing upon our nation. Remind me that all things come from you. Amen.

77

The Great Commission
Matthew 28:18-20

I remember learning these verses as a GA (Girls Auxiliary) at Lexington Baptist Church. GAs met every Wednesday night with a focus on missions. We received awards when we learned Bible verses and completed projects on missionaries and their work. I have great memories of times spent in GAs and I still recall verses that I learned. I learned about the importance of spreading the Word of God not only to our local community but also to foreign countries who had very little knowledge of him. GAs was a very important part of my early years and probably the reason why this verse is still in my heart.

Jesus had recently resurrected from death and was preparing the disciples for his return to heaven. He explained to them that their mission was to preach his teachings to everyone, instructing them to live in obedience. He was granting them the authority to continue his mission. Because of his life and sacrifice, the message was for all people. In Acts 1:8 Jesus tells them that the Holy Spirit would give them power to perform this staggering task. I was taught that the explanation here meant to spread his Word to our community, county, city, state, country and the entire world. In the story of Zacchaeus, Jesus had already told them that his mission was to seek and save the lost. God's plan was for Jesus to return to heaven and extend the mission to his followers. This commission is meant for us too. We may not be called by God to go to a foreign country but we are called to spread his Word in our local community, family and friends. We should take this seriously. We often hesitate, afraid of rejection or embarrassment. Jesus gave his followers and he gives us the Holy Spirit for guidance and strength to complete his mission. Ask God for the opportunity to expand His Kingdom by spreading His Word to those around us.

Dear God, I want to follow your commission to go and tell. Forgive me where I have missed opportunities. Guide me and direct me to know what to say when opportunities arise. I want to share with others what you have done for me. I want to share the hope and peace that I receive from my relationship with you. Give me an opportunity to share my testimony of your love and faithfulness. Amen.

78

April Fools
Psalm 14:1

April Fools Day is a day some really have fun with. Over the years I have been fooled several times by untruths. When someone says something to you like, Gosh what's that on your face? and we panic to find a mirror, we feel rather silly when we see that we have been tricked. My calendar for this day says, Never argue with a fool. People might not know the difference!

God says that anyone who does not believe in him is a fool. The word fool is used many times in Proverbs and not as a compliment. A fool is someone who is not trust worthy and lives in a false reality. Anyone who does not believe that the day will come when each of us will meet Jesus Christ face to face, is headed for a tragic ending to life as we know it here on earth. Everyone will have an eternity, some with Jesus Christ and some separated from him. Some will face the ultimate fool's day. Let's be encouraged to share the truth of Jesus Christ with those around us. We must take seriously the command that Jesus gave us in Matthew 28:18-20 to preach his message to all the world.

Dear God I thank you that you are the truth and the way for me to follow. Give me courage and opportunity to share the message of your love with those around me. Help me to have a serious concern for those in this world who do not believe in you. Amen.

79

The Armor Of God
Ephesians 6:10-18

The book of Ephesians is made up of letters from Paul to the churches regarding God's eternal purpose and instructions for daily living promoting unity and spiritual maturity. The last chapter addresses the spiritual battle against evil. We are encouraged to be strong in the Lord. God has provided armor for our battles. He acknowledges that Satan schemes to undermine us and we must be prepared to stand against him. Our armor is:

The belt of truth
The breastplate of righteousness
The gospel of peace
The shield of faith
The helmet of salvation
The sword of the spirit (Word of God)

We are also advised to always be alert and to pray, pray and pray. The battle is spiritual and must be fought in God's strength, based on His Word and through prayer. We are under attack every moment of every day and must stay alert and ready. I find that the two most important things we can do to prepare ourselves for battle is to be in God's Holy

Word everyday and have a serious time of prayer everyday. I hear some people say their quiet time is listening to Christian radio driving to work and they pray all day long. Well that is well and good but I also find it a cop out. We must be willing to allow a few minutes every day for a time focused in His Word and talking to him to be truly prepared for battle. We must make a serious effort to train for battle and we must teach our youth to establish that habit early in life. If not, we will not be able to stand against the schemes of evil. Start now. Set your alarm a few minutes early every morning and spend time with God, preparing for battle. Find a notebook and start a prayer journal. Writing my prayer helps me to focus and usually eliminates distractions in my mind. Highlight verses that you find especially encouraging. Mark the date. List the name of who you pray for. Your Bible can become a prayer journal in itself. I often have the same passage marked in my Bible with several dates and several names. These marked places always catch my eye and fill me with hope and assurance when I read them again. Go back and study these verses to specifically identify your armor. Let's be prepared.

Dear Father, thank you for the armor you provide. Guide me to make time for you everyday. Guide me to teach my children to do the same thing. I want to be prepared to stand against the schemes of evil and I also want to be prepared to share your Word with others. Give me determination and help me to resist distractions that keep me from spending time with you. Amen.

80

Worthy

Colossians 1:9-14

I friend of mine was lugging the comforter from her bed to the washing machine. I asked, Will that go in the washer? She replied, If it won't, it isn't worth having. I thought that was funny. If it won't go in the washer, it isn't worth having.

In this passage, Paul is writing to his Christian brothers in Colosse. We are encouraged to live a life worthy of the Lord. We study God's Word to grow our relationship with him, gain knowledge so that we can be fruitful and be strengthened with endurance and patience. We are thankful for he has rescued us from the death of sin and offers the inheritance of eternal life. Sometimes I don't feel very worthy. But God has made us worthy through the death and resurrection of his Son, Jesus Christ. In acceptance of this gift from God, we live a life worthy of it. Of course, the only true Worthy One is Jesus Christ. Hebrews 3:3 says Jesus has been found worthy. We often sing of "Worthy is the Lamb That Was Slain". While some things are judged worthy by whether they can survive the washing machine, the Lord of Lords will judge our worthiness based on the life we live here on earth. Each day is a new opportunity to live life worthy of the Lord. Each failure is an opportunity to repent and seek forgiveness. Jesus paid the ultimate sacrifice so that we can be found worthy. Let's search our heart today for an unworthiness that needs to be addressed. Let's strive to study and grow and be fruitful.

Dear God thank you for the sacrifice of your Son and his resurrection that makes me worthy of eternal life. I want to live a life that you find worthy. Give me a committed heart that wants to grow my relationship with you every day. There is nothing else more important than my relationship with you Lord. Thank you for your forgiveness and your love for me. Amen.

81

Here I Am
1 Samuel 3:1-10

Hannah wanted a child. She prayed so adamantly to God for a child that Eli, the priest, thought she was drunk. When God blessed her with a son, she returned the child, Samuel, to full service to the Lord in gratefulness. The boy Samuel lived in the temple performing duties of service under Eli's direction. God spoke to Samuel one night telling him of discipline that was coming for Eli and his family. My point here is Samuel's response to God when He called. It was, 'Here am I' and later said, 'Your servant is listening'. Similar to Mary's response to the angel in Luke 1:38, 'I am the Lord's servant. May it be to me as you have said.'

What is our response when God calls? He calls us to simple things and he calls us to great things. No matter the call, our response should be the same as Samuel and Mary. He calls us over the tumult; over the commotion of our minds and lives. This reminds me of the old hymn, "Jesus Calls Us O'er the Tumult".

Jesus calls us o'er the tumult of our life's wild restless sea,
Day by day His sweet voice soundeth, saying Christian follow me.
In our joys and in our sorrows, days of toil and hours of ease,
Still He calls, in cares and pleasures,
Christian love me, more than these.
Jesus calls us, by thy mercies, Savior may we hear Thy call,
Give our hearts to Thine obedience, serve and love Thee best of all.

I find little to add to these words. Jesus calls us everyday to live for him and further his kingdom. Samuel and Mary were young but their faith was strong – examples for us to follow. No excuses. No hesitation. Our strength for obedience comes from God; our power from the Holy Spirit that lives within us. Let's give our hearts to his obedience, serving and loving him best of all.

Dear God, here am I. Give me opportunity to serve you. I love you more than life's pleasures. I answer your call to service. Amen.

82

The Easter Bunny
Matthew 6:1-4

I will not get into a discussion of whether we want to include the Easter Bunny or Santa Claus in our Christian lives but I did see today, an example of acts of love as we might think an Easter Bunny would do. One of the Division Directors under my supervision showed me pictures of her staff assembling Easter baskets to give to children at the homeless shelter. I had heard that they had done this over the years but never realized how big the project was until I saw the pictures. I was really impressed. There were about 40 beautiful baskets full of toys and candy wrapped in colorful cellophane. The staff had contributed their money and a couple lunch hours to make these baskets. I was so impressed by the number of baskets and they were packed full. I couldn't even imagine the faces of the kids when they discovered their basket on Easter Sunday morning. I know it was a real financial sacrifice for some of them who have small kids of their own. This act of kindness and selfless giving really touched my heart. I saw in it the true meaning of giving at such a wonderful time of year. These homeless children will hopefully learn of the love of God from the kind hearts of these strangers who were willing to give a portion of what they had to an unknown child living in tragic and unfortunate circumstances. I think this is the kind of giving Jesus was talking about in this passage. They gave quietly and they gave sacrificially. From the pictures it was obvious that they were having fun in what they were doing. I believe they will have a reward in eternity for this act. When was the last time I did something like this? I am encouraged to consider doing such an act of kindness as quickly as an opportunity arises. I know they are all around me just waiting to be done. I pray this encourages you as well.

Dear God give me a kind and loving heart of giving. I want to have the desire to give quietly and unnoticed without expectation of honor. I want to give sacrificially for you have blessed me greatly. Place an opportunity before me. I pray I will accept it with a willing heart. Thank you for how you bless me. Thank you for loving each of us the same and for loving us unconditionally. Amen.

83

Memorizing Scripture
Psalm 119:11

I learned this verse as a child but it was later in life that it was explained to me as instruction to memorize scripture. Most of us hesitate at memorizing scripture. We tend to think it is too difficult a task. I found the following note written in my Mother's handwriting in her Bible.

Memorize Scripture
Read the verse aloud 3 times in succession, 3 times a day.
Begin each study with prayer.
Ask God to open the eyes of your understanding
and lead you into truth.
Stand firm against the enemy and all his strategies
to keep you from the study of God's Word.

I do not know if the words are hers or words that she found, but they are full of truth. Hiding scripture in my heart, memorizing it, prepares me for resisting the temptation of sin. Knowledge is strength. According to my study notes, the word here refers to the promises of God. He never promises that life will be easy, but he does promise to provide ways to deal with it. Promises of his love and faithfulness to help us resist temptation. I can't think of a better verse to start with memorizing.

> I have hidden your word in my heart that I
> might not sin against thee. Psalm 119:11

> I have hidden your word in my heart that I
> might not sin against thee. Psalm 119:11

> I have hidden your word in my heart that I
> might not sin against thee. Psalm 119:11

Dear God, I have hidden your word in my heart that I might not sin against thee. Help me to commit to studying your Holy Word everyday and to memorize it so that it is in my heart. Thank you for your promises. Thank you for your faithfulness. Amen.

84

Grace
Ephesians 2:8-10

Some religions believe that we have to do certain deeds to earn eternal life. Some believe that a certain number of people will be granted eternal life. Some believe that certain laws must be observed to be granted eternal life. This scripture says that we are saved by God's gift of grace, not by our own works. Grace is divine love and protection granted by God. No effort of our own brings salvation and no one can take credit for it. When we give a gift, it is not because it was earned. An award is earned. When we grant someone something, it is given with no strings attached. God gives the same grace to each of us; no one can boast as receiving more. He has blessings for each of us. We miss out because of bad choices we make. John 1:16 says, from the fullness of God's grace we have all received one blessing after another. Grace means there is nothing we can do to make God love us more and nothing we can do to make him love us less. He always loves us. We don't have to do anything to earn his love. He gives his love freely to anyone who asks.

In this world we are always looking for something free. People are mobbed at the door of a store giving a big discount. We drive miles out of the way to save a few cents on gas. Yet, many miss out on the free gift of grace and eternal life granted by God. Some say it isn't that simple, but I say it is. People are hungry for love. It is our mission to share the love of God for them to see. Those around us should be able to see the grace in us. They should see it in our actions and in our attitudes. It's like the wind, you can't touch it but you can sure see when it's been there. God's marvelous, infinite grace pardons and cleanses us from sin. Will you this moment his grace receive?

Dear God, forgive me of my sin and grant me your amazing grace. Grant me opportunity to serve you and spread your kingdom. I pray others will see Jesus in me. Make my heart tender towards you, so I will follow you in all that I do. Amen.

85

Lost and Found
Luke 15

Have you ever lost something dear to you and found it? This chapter covers three stories of lost and found. Jesus is trying to make the Pharisees understand how much heaven rejoices when a lost person finds salvation. God has great concern over the lost and is joyous when a lost person repents. There is rejoicing of the angels in the presence of God over one sinner who repents.

The first story helps us recognize that one person is no more important than another. This theme of a shepherd caring for his sheep is familiar to us as Jesus portrays himself as our shepherd. He cares for each of us and loves us each the same. He goes after any one of us that strays. The second story relates to the loss of a material thing that was very valuable to this woman. A piece of silver could be worth an average day's wages. A lost person is of great value to God and there is rejoicing when that person repents. The last story is often called the Parable of the Loving Father. The son strays away from his father's love and protection. When he repents and returns home, the loving father is joyous and calls for celebration. The Bible says that the father started celebrating before his son even reached him. It didn't matter what the son had done. It only mattered that he had returned. Our heavenly Father calls for the same celebration among the angels when we are lost and return. He doesn't offer forgiveness according to the sin. We each find the same compassion and forgiveness. God has many of us to care for but when one strays and returns, he rejoices. The grace of God is abundant and free to all who repent.

Dear God, thank you for your compassion and forgiveness of my sin. Help me to strive to be obedient to your instruction. Help me to have a heart of forgiveness toward those who offend me. Amen.

86

The Woman At the Well
John 4:1-38

This passage has several lessons for us. Jesus is hot, tired and thirsty from walking many miles. He meets this Samaritan woman at the well who is there at an odd hour of day to avoid others because of her reputation. Jesus offers her salvation. He knows from the sin in her life that she is thirsty. She is thirsty for hope and forgiveness. Jesus reveals himself as the Messiah that she longed for, offering her abundant life. Have you ever been really thirsty? I watch lots of western movies. There are often people lost in the badlands and the desert that are found, delirious from thirst, just in the nick of time before they die. Now that is thirsty. But this thirst is no more severe than someone living without hope and a Savior. Jesus offers the water that will become in us a spring of water welling up to eternal life.

Later, his disciples return, urging him to eat. Jesus had no desire for food. He had a job to do; the job that his Father sent him to do. I think he said with excitement, 'Open your eyes and look at the fields! They are ripe for harvest!' I think he was invigorated by the experience of witnessing to the woman. He was ready to work some more, not eat. He wanted his disciples to feel the same excitement. His physical needs weren't nearly important as his mission. Do we get that excited about living for him and sharing our testimony with the lost? The last couple verses in this passage talks about many Samaritans who came to know him as their Savior not because of what they heard, but because of the change they saw in the woman at the well. Jesus doesn't just offer good teaching and advice, he offers eternal life. He offers eternal life to everyone, regardless of our past, our nationality or our reputation. He offers it to anyone who is thirsty or hungry for hope and forgiveness. He wants us to open our eyes and see the lost. He wants us to reveal him to the lost - not only tell them about him but to show them the difference he makes in us.

Dear God, thank you for this story. Help me to open my eyes and see the fields that are ripe for harvest. Help me to seek you daily, so that I am prepared to share my testimony of what you have done in my life. Put opportunity in my path to share your love to someone who is thirsty. Amen.

87

Prayer For Safety
Psalm 121

When you get ready to leave on a trip do you pray for safety? My Dad always had us pray before we left for vacation and I tried to do this when we left with our kids. We have taken several motorcycle trips with friends. We like to travel to the mountains on the bikes and ride the parkway. Once we had 8 couples going and met at a gas station. It was early November and we all had on our leather for warmth. We stood in a circle holding hands and prayed for safety. I remember as I opened my eyes and looked up, several people had stopped what they were doing and were looking at us. I felt a rush. Not only did I know God heard us and would keep us safe, I felt like we gave such a testimony in that simple act. Others could see that we were gathering for a ride and our trust was in the Lord. It was obvious for others to see.

This Psalm acknowledges that our help and comforting assurance of protection comes from the Lord, the maker of heaven and earth. My help comes from the Lord. He never sleeps. He watches over me day and night. I see him in the moon and the stars and in the radiant sunshine of the day. I know that his eyes are always on me and he is in control of all things. Such a short passage with a tremendous message of comfort and assurance. Throughout the day we can call on him for protection when we sense harm or danger. I often send up a quick prayer for protection when I sense that I need it. We should look to our Lord each day for guidance and protection and teach our children to look to him for safety in confidence that he knows our every move.

Dear Father, thank you for your love. I lift my eyes to the heavens in gratefulness. Thank you for the unfailing guarantee of your protection. My life is in your hands. My help comes from you. Watch over me and those that I love. Amen.

88

An Ordinary Day

Genesis 24:12-21

Abraham sent his servant to find a wife for his son Issac. The servant asked God to reveal the right choice by identifying a girl that was willing to show kindness to him. Rebekah was the person God would reveal. She came to the well just like she did everyday to draw water. When the servant asked her for water, she gave him water and offered to draw water for his camels. Do you know how much water ten camels can drink until they are finished? There are several lessons we can learn here from her.

Who am I when no one is looking? Who am I on an ordinary day? Does it matter how I treat someone who can't possibly help me? God often speaks and uses us in ordinary ways on ordinary days. An attitude of service on an ordinary day could change my life or someone else's, forever. When I put others first, I might be their answer to prayer. Rebekah chose to be a hard worker; she had to be to water those camels. She chose to be a servant. She had no idea how her response to this stranger would change her life. There was nothing in it for her when she chose to respond this way. There is no mention of others there to impress. She had no idea this man had anything to offer her. He couldn't even handle getting a drink of water and taking care of his camels. She took advantage of the opportunity on an ordinary day in an ordinary way. When you take a leap of faith, you can be sure God will be with you. When God opens a door, don't delay. Walk right through it.

Dear God, give me an unselfish heart of serving others, especially when there is no gain for me. Help me to be like Rebekah; to be mindful of unexpected opportunities that you send my way everyday. You have so much to teach me. I pray I never miss a lesson. Amen.

89

The Talking Donkey

Numbers 22:21-35

Sometimes God can't get our attention. In this passage, God made Balaam's donkey speak to get his attention. It's hard to even imagine that happening but I know it is true. The donkey was being resistant because it could see the angel of God. Balaam beat it. After the third beating, the donkey spoke. The donkey was trying to keep Balaam away from the angel who intended to kill him because God was so angry with him. It reminds me of the old joke about the man whose house was flooded and he prayed to God to save him. A rescuer came but the man sent him away saying God would save him. A boat came by but the man sent him away saying God would save him. A helicopter came by but the man sent it away too. The man drowned. When he faced God, he asked him why he didn't answer his prayer. God replied, I send a rescuer, a boat and a helicopter but you sent them all away.

Sometimes we are so focused on our self and our problems that we miss God's guidance or help. Psalms 84:11 says the Lord God is a sun and shade; he bestows favor and honor; no good thing does he withhold from those who seek him. When we ask for his help, we need to look and listen for him. There is a hymn we sang, "Open My Eyes that I May See".

Open my eyes that I may see, glimpses of truth thou hast for me
Place in my hand the wonderful key that
shall unclasp and set me free.
Open my ears that I may hear, voices of truth thou sendeth clear
And while the wave notes fall on my ear,
everything false will disappear.
Silently now I wait for thee, ready my God thy will to see.
Open my eyes illumine me, Spirit Divine.

Dear God, open my eyes that I may see. Open my ears that I may hear. Forgive me for when I am stubborn, driven by my own will and I miss your guidance. I know you have plans for me to prosper and your plan for me is perfect. Thank you for your mercy. Amen.

90

Dress Code
1 Peter 3:3-6

OK guys, if there are any out there. Don't put this book down. This is for everyone. It concerns me how many women and girls dress today. It especially concerns me how many parents allow their girls to dress. It seems totally acceptable for girls and women to wear blouses or tops that reveal half of their breasts, and jeans or pants that show their belly button and slip down way too far when one bends over. Now I'm not here to say that we should all wear turtle necks and long skirts but we have gone too far in the wrong direction.

Peter is clear in this passage and so is Paul in 1Timothy 2:9-10. Our beauty and attractiveness is to come from within, the unfading beauty of a gentle and quiet spirit. Why does he add unfading? Because inner beauty does not fade with age, only the outward appearance will fade. Our appearance should silently demonstrate the Christ in us. Our appearance should demonstrate our relationship with him that grows brighter and does not fade. We should dress to impress God not man. Our Christ like actions should gain the attention of those around us. Our dress should not find cause for fear or intimidation. Proverbs 3:25 says our confidence should be in the Lord. We must not believe or allow our young to believe that we gain confidence from dressing in a revealing way to attract the attention of man. Our confidence should be in our Lord and our dress should honor him at all times. I realize this is what most stores offer but sometimes a simple tee shirt or camisole fixes the problem. God will provide a way out of the temptation to dress outside our dress code (1 Corinthians 10:13). No more excuses.

Dear God, I pray that my dress, and those that I am responsible for, reveals a pure heart. Each day I will strive to impress you with my desire to have an appearance that pleases you and actions that reveal my heart for you. Forgive us where we have failed you in our appearance. Let us be the fashion setter for those around us so they will see Jesus in us and in those we love. Amen.

91

Putting Down Mercedes
Matthew 10:29-31

God created animals for us to enjoy and care for. The Bible tells us in this passage that he cares for the sparrow. Mercedes was a pony at the horse farm that provided many kids riding lessons. Yesterday, at 24 years of age and several days of illness, the vet and her owner decided it was time to put her down. Several of us were at the farm and experienced the sad sight of the owner leading Mercedes across the field to the pet cemetery where she was to be laid to rest. Seeing her stall with her name on her gate brings fond memories of her and sadness of her not being here anymore. The other horses even seem to sense her absence. It is very sad to lose a pet that we love.

God does care for the animals of his creation but he cares for us in a marvelous way. He even knows the number of hairs on my head. Too hard to grasp yet true. He loves us so much that he was willing to give his perfect Son to a cruel death as the ultimate sacrifice for our sin. When we acknowledge this and accept Jesus Christ as our Lord and Savior, he provides us a place to spend eternity with him. There is life after death for us. My Dad died in a nursing home after a long illness. When I arrived after the early morning call, he was peacefully lying in bed, like he was asleep, yet I knew that was only his body. Quickly, the thought came to my mind that he was actually with Jesus as I stood there. I could imagine the smile on his face and joy he was feeling. I could almost hear his laugh and see his wide grin. He was no longer confined to a wheelchair, confused by the days and nights. I could not be sad. I could only smile and feel excitement for him. What a wonderful way to feel even though death had come. This is available to us through our relationship with the Lord Jesus Christ. If you do not know him today as the Lord and Savior of your life, come to him now. He cares for you.

Dear God, thank you for life. Thank you for eternal life after death. Thank you for the joy the animals that you created bring to us. I praise you as my Lord and Savior. I long to be with you. Forgive me of my sin and pour your blessings upon us. Amen.

92

Restful Sleep
Psalm 4:8

A nightly restful sleep is important for a healthy life. Unfortunately, many people have trouble sleeping. Psalm 4:8 tells us to sleep in peace, without anxiety, with a confidence in our Lord. I usually talk to God when I turn out the light at night. I mentioned to a friend that it troubled me that I often fell asleep during my prayer while in bed. I felt like I wasn't giving God the attention that I should but really couldn't help it. He told me not to worry; that he couldn't think of a better way to doze off, than in the arms of God talking to him about my day. Many of us have prayed the prayer as a child, "Now I Lay Me Down to Sleep". There are many versions. The one I knew was:

Now I lay me down to sleep, I pray the Lord my soul to keep.
If I should die before I wake, I pray the Lord my soul to take.

It is important to teach our children to pray and ways to find restful sleep. Hopefully a regular prayer at night will influence their prayer life. Prayer is a very significant part of our relationship with God. I'd like to suggest that we start our day and end our day in prayer. I strive to start each day in his Holy Word, talking with God and listening to him. Matthew 14:23 tells us Jesus sought to be alone with the Father after an extremely exhausting day of preaching, teaching, and healing. The Son of God thought that the end of a tiring day was a good time to pray. The scriptures often mention Jesus retreating to a quiet place to pray. In the first verse of Psalm 4, the psalmist asks God for relief from distress and to hear his prayer. Trusting in God and maintaining a strong relationship with him should be helpful in getting a good night's sleep. We can ask God for a good night's sleep. He wants to supply all of our needs.

Dear God, help me to find the confidence in you that gives me peace at the end of the day so I can rest. Help me to find the time to spend with you each day so I can be prepared to live for you. Thank you for your words of assurance and for giving me peace in my heart. I praise you in knowing that when my life on earth is over, I will spend eternity with you. Amen.

93

Finding Forgiveness
2 Corinthians 2:5-11

Why do we sometimes find it hard to forgive? Sometimes an apology is easily accepted and we forget it. Other times, we want to wallow in our hurt and relentlessly cause the person who has wronged us pain. Satan wants to delay or even eliminate the opportunity for restoration. In the Lord's Prayer, we ask for forgiveness as we forgive others. Yet we still do not forgive. I sometimes have a desire to hang on to the pain so that the punishment can continue. If I forgive, I must strive to forget and move on without the anger. I admit in repentance that I don't want to do that. I ask

God to change this difficult situation yet I am the one that won't budge. I want that person to suffer a little longer for the hurt he caused.

I have to ask God to change my heart and help me overcome the hurt and seek restoration. It is hard sometimes as we deal with family and personal relationships. I have to accept my responsibility to forgive as God forgives me and work through the situation asking for guidance and help with each step. In my Mom's Bible, she wrote by verse 11, 'Satan's primary assaults occur in our thought life'. Now I know why she wrote that. In the situation I am in today, Satan keeps telling me to continue to prosecute the person who hurt me. That is wrong and I know it. I hope that this admission on my part helps you. Life can be unexpectedly short and we cannot carry unforgiveness in our heart, no matter how much we have been hurt or wronged. The baggage creates bitterness and resentment and separates me from God and the blessings in store for me. The wrong is for the Lord to deal with. My part is to forgive and seek peace in my heart. I will choose to forgive. I don't know exactly how this situation will work out but I find confidence in knowing God is with me in each step I take and each word I speak.

Dear God, forgive me for not forgiving as I should. You promise blessings for obedience. I seek to follow your instruction so that my actions are pleasing to you. Help me to overcome this and find peace in you. Please bring restoration to this relationship. I give you the glory for bringing peace to my thought life. Thank you that I still find encouragement from my Mother in her Bible. Amen.

94

Misleading Others
1 Corinthians 8:9-13

Sometimes I struggle with what is a sin. I was raised by very strict parents. While I know they were devoted to living a life pleasing to the Lord, sometimes I think their joy for the Lord was overshadowed by the Dos and Don'ts of a Christian. I do recognize that they taught me not to do anything that would cause someone to stumble. This scripture passage says that while we have the freedom to make our own choices, we should never let our actions negatively influence those around us. According to this, if we cause someone to stumble, we have sinned against God. I see this as an instruction to set a Christ-like example for others around us, particularly those who may have an immature faith or none at all. We should commit ourselves to a high standard as a follower of Christ so that we can affect the lives of others. So you ask, Am I responsible for my brother? I believe that Yes we are. Paul says in verse 13, that he will not do anything, even though he believes it is harmless, that could cause his brother to stumble and fall.

In Titus 2:7-8, Paul teaches Titus to set an example by doing what is good; to show integrity, seriousness and soundness of speech. Rather than thinking of something as what you can't do to be a good Christian example, think of it as a way to lead others to Christ and into a strong relationship with God by setting the example. Don't mislead, take the lead.

Dear Father, give me courage and strength to set the example of a Christ-like lifestyle in all that I do. Help me to be conscious that others are watching me and I can lead them to an abundant life in you. I need to be in your Holy Word daily so that I can learn the instruction that you give me that will set me free. Thank you for your love for me. Amen.

95

Satan's Schemes
Ephesians 6:10-18

We must be constantly aware of the schemes of Satan. The dictionary defines a scheme as a secret or devious plan. Satan is often subtly comfortable in our home. How is your language at home? Does your TV allow programs with a warning notice before starting or feature nudity, violence or preoccupation with material wealth or sex? Do you read only books that you could suggest to a Christian friend? Do your kids have friends that you do not know? Do you allow your teenage daughter to show too much skin because the other girls do or because 'pure clothes are just too hard to find'? I could go on, but I will stop here. These are hard issues for us to deal with and overcome. We live in a world where it is easier to give in. It seems easier than fighting about it or confronting it.

We are provided the armor to stand against the devil's schemes and make better choices for ourselves and our family. We have the armor and God will provide the courage and strength to overcome these schemes and devious plans to bring harm to our family. Are we in God's Holy Word everyday? Is our home a place of prayer? We must live a life of commitment to using the armor we are provided on a daily basis. I believe it will come easier as we develop habits of overcoming, rather than habits of giving in and allowing the schemes to take over and become a part of our daily life. I also believe it will take a shorter time to develop these good habits than we might think when we ask for God's help. Be encouraged to start today in making better choices in daily living. Set an example for those around you. Throw Satan out onto the doorstep and allow God back in. Sit down with your family and read these verses aloud and together make them the new rules of your home.

Dear God of Truth, forgive me for allowing Satan to be comfortable in my life and in my home. Help me to recognize him as a liar. Whisper in my ear, those things that I need to put aside. Help me to give up things that bring bad choices and habits for me and my family. Even though my children may not see this now, give me the courage to stand up against the devil's schemes. I know that I can trust you and completely believe in you. Amen.

96

Seek Him First
Luke 12:22-34

In my Bible, the heading for this passage is Do Not Worry. We are to seek God in all things. I've seen a picture hanging with the inscription, God answers all prayers, sometimes he says yes, sometimes he says no and sometimes he says, you've got to be kidding. I am sure he does. A plaque over our door says, Prayer Changes Things.

Prayer can change things. It can do many things for us. Our needs are provided in answered prayer. Hearts are changed and bodies are healed in answered prayer. Encouragement, safety and confidence come from prayer. God wants us worrying about nothing. This week, I was a speaker at an out of town conference. I had never been there. I had my trusty MapQuest printout but was as lost as I could be. I said a quick prayer, and I immediately found the street I was looking for and found my way. Coming back, I was trying to track my steps back to the interstate and got confused again. Another quick prayer...and there was the street. I laughed out loud and praised God aloud. I don't need a GPS when I have a connection to

God. Do we trust him in all things? Scripture says if we seek God first, he will provide what we need. Our ultimate quest is salvation and eternal life through Jesus Christ, but God wants us to trust him for everything from our finances to finding the right street. I believe he cares for me deeply and wants to be my provider of all things, big and small. He is preparing a place for me to spend eternity with him. People have laughed at my stories of how he helps me find my way and find parking spaces when I need one. They can laugh all they want. God loves me. He cares for me. The next time you can't find your way, I suggest you give it a try.

Dear God, thank you for helping me find my way when I am lost or confused. You are the provider of all things. You are in control. I want to praise you and serve you. I have nothing to fear with you leading the way. Amen.

97

The Strength I Need
Isaiah 58:11-12

Isaiah is one of my favorite books in the Bible. I often find strength and encouragement in these words. This passage assures me that God will always provide for me. He will give me strength when I am in a sun scorched land. There are days that I feel like I'm in a sun scorched land. Beat down, as a friend of mine used to say. While there, God provides an endless amount of water. He doesn't say he will take me out of the desert but he will provide for me while I am there. He often promises us strength and help. Read Isaiah 41:10 and 13. Mark these verses in your Bible. He promises to hold our hand to keep us from harm. We may still stumble, but God is there to help us up, brush us off and get us going again. He will help us face our fears.

I found this written in my Mama's Bible. I have no idea where she got this, maybe it is her own words, but I find it pretty good advice.

1. Ask God for guidance
2. Understand and pray on his basis - do not beg.
3. Call him by his titles.
4. Be persistent where God leads – don't whine.
5. Pray end prayers, not means prayers. Pray for and discover God's end and leave the means of achieving it to him.

6. Always be earnest in praying
7. Don't try to bargain with him
8. Remember how wise and holy God is. Don't preach to him.

Dear God, thank you for providing for me, just what I need and in perfect timing. Thank you that you don't just pluck me out of the sun scorched land, but you leave me there to teach me and provide for me while I am there. I know your way is best. You are a wise and Holy God and I praise you. Amen.

98

The Story Of Esther
Esther 2:5-7, 17, 18

I encourage you, both men and women to read the Book of Esther if you haven't. It is a wonderful story of a young Jewish orphan girl who makes the best of unfortunate situations and grows into a godly Queen. One of my very favorite books is Hadassah, One Night With the King by Tommy Tenney. It is a wonderful story of Esther based on the scriptures. There is a video but the book is better in my opinion.

It is interesting that in the book of Esther, there is no mention of God. However, it is evident, that God is supreme and is in control, directing the sequence of events of his perfect plan to save the Jewish nation. He is sovereign in all things. Life is often a roller coaster. At the blink of an eye, events can change my world. But God knows what is happening in my life, every second of every day. Whether it seems like it or not, God is always in control. Job is reminded in Job 37:11 to stop and consider the wonder of God; he controls even the clouds and the lightening. It is almost unfathomable for us to conceive that God is aware of every moment for each of us. He is our hope. I choose having that hope rather than none. When life is not at its best, we have the confidence and comfort that God is in control and he has a purpose in all that we go through. It is better to focus on what we will learn from it rather than focusing on the difficulty. That's what Esther did. She looked for the good in all the difficulties that came her way. She prayed and fasted for strength. She went from a frightened orphan girl to a Godly queen who greatly influenced her husband king to saving the Jewish nation from elimination. We can learn from her. She was willing to face troubles with a confidence in her God.

Dear God, I need to remember that you are in control and know every moment of my day. Thank you for loving me that much. Help me to remember that you are good all the time. Thank you for the wonderful story of Esther. My hope and comfort and confidence come from you. Amen.

99

Fitting In
Romans 12:1-8

We live in a world that often has different opinions from our Christian beliefs. This scripture from Paul encourages us to be different. He tells us not to conform to the ways of the world. Our whole attitude must be focused on God and his instruction. Our aim must be to exercise sound judgment at every turn; in every decision to seek and discover God's will. Everything about us should be in the honor of and for the glory of God. We are to be 'holy' in the deepest sense of the word. In 1 Peter 2:11, he calls the people of the church aliens and strangers in the world. He calls them to be such a good example that the people outside of the church would see God.

I do not think this means that we must separate ourselves from the world. Jesus came to save the sinner. He visited them, went to their home and spent time with them. He showed them that he loved them. How will they see our example if we reject them and refuse to be among them? I once heard a leader in the church tell a parent that she should refuse to go to the home of her daughter because she lived with her boyfriend. To tell her she would not step foot in her house as long as he lived there. I believe this was bad advice. I suggest that the parent be clear to the daughter that she does not condone their relationship, however she could share her love for the couple unconditionally by spending time with them and reflecting her belief in marriage, encouraging them to accept it. I know that God gives instruction and desires our obedience; however I do not recall conditions for receiving his love. I agree that there is often a fine line here but I cannot agree with rejecting and refusing to spend time with someone who has not accepted Christ. The world is our mission field. I cannot think of myself as better than others, especially better than those who do not know Christ. We are each given a gift. I believe the main purpose of these gifts is to share the love of Christ and grow his kingdom. Each gift, just like the different parts of our body, is equally important to complete his work. Sometimes God has to change the way we think to transform us into the person he can use.

Dear God, give me wisdom to know how to respond to those who do not know you or live according to my belief. Show me how to share your love in places that I don't seem to fit in. May my character and my actions reflect the message of hope and peace found in you. Amen.

100

Encouragement
Proverbs 9:10-11

We are familiar with the encouraging greeting cards of Helen Steiner Rice. Born in May 1900, as a young child she loved to preach about God's love to her family. She dreamed of attending college but her plans changed unexpectedly when her father died in the flu epidemic, the same year she graduated from high school. Instead of attending college, Helen became the family breadwinner and supported her mother and sister, creating attractive lamp shades and designing eye catching display windows. As she developed her writing skills, her simple, sincere expressions of religious truths have touched many hearts and lives. Helen believed her talent for easing human heartache was a God given gift, one through which she could share God's love. She too knew heartache loosing her father at an early age. Her husband committed suicide due to financial loss leaving her a widow at the age of 32 and shortly after she lost her mother. She became involved with Gibson greeting cards reflecting her own growing and deepening faith in God.

These verses in Proverbs give hope and encouragement. Our reverence for God is the beginning of our understanding. He gives life and blesses many with a long life. Isaiah 45:2-3 tells us that God goes before us, making a way for us so that we will know that he is Lord who knows us my name. We are grateful that God uses people like Helen Rice to give us encouragement and share his love. We should share the encouragement that we receive. Romans 12:8 mentions encouragement as a gift from God. Helen Rice had this gift and used it. Our Holy Bible is full of hope and encouragement. We can find verse after verse of encouragement and hope.

Sometimes you only have to pick it up, turn to any verse, and God will give you the words that you need. He knows our every need and responds to it. We can trust in his faithfulness and depend on his truths and grace to be sufficient.

Thank you Father that you are Lord over all circumstances. Thank you for your love and encouragement. Give me an opportunity to encourage someone today. Amen.

101

Arrogance
Romans 11:17-21

I got a lesson in arrogance recently. I had to go to Chicago for a conference but first had a short flight from Columbia to Charlotte. I prided myself in always asking for a window seat. I boarded the plane and went to take my seat, 16D. A lady was sitting in the window seat. I told her I thought that was my seat. She said no, she had 16F which was the window. It was a small plane with 4 seats across, A, C, D and F. I didn't want to make a spectacle, so sat in the seat next to her but grumbled first to her, 'I guess it is a short flight.' The entire flight I stewed telling myself to be sure and check with the stewardess when catching the flight to Chicago so I would not be inconvenienced again and hoped this lady really enjoyed my window seat. As I boarded the bigger plane to Chicago, I quickly saw the signs that identified the seats, showing A started with the window and went across. I was slapped with the thought, 'She was right. I was wrong.' I felt silly, and embarrassed with myself, as I took my seat, which was again the aisle seat. Fortunately the lady didn't know my thoughts but I recalled the verse in Psalms 94:11, The Lord knows the thoughts of man. How arrogant of me and silly to allow such a minor thing to anger me. The incident lingered on my mind all day and I really felt conviction. James 1:19 tells us to be slow to speak and slow to become angry.

Why do we do that? Why do we let such a small thing anger us and fill our mind and heart with ungodly thoughts? Pride? Arrogance? Yes and yes. I hope this lesson will stick with me and I will handle things differently the next time. I know for sure I will be reminded of it anytime I take a seat on a plane. Unfortunately, the lady on the plane probably doesn't have a very good impression of me. As I asked God to forgive me, I also asked that he would have her forgive me. I can't go back and change those few minutes. I only can learn from them.

Dear God, forgive me of my pride and arrogance. Help me to be slow to speak and slow to anger. Help me to be an example of you at all times and in all situations. Forgive me when I fail you. Thank you for loving me just as I am. Amen.

102

Fears
Isaiah 41:10

Horses are huge animals but can be very skittish. I know one that was referred to as 'Chicken' because she was afraid of everything while on a trail - the sun beaming through the trees or even her shadow. I read that a horse is only afraid of two things – things that move and things that don't.

Sometimes we are the same way. We fear uncertainty. We fear the unknown. Gods says in this verse, not to be afraid because he is always with us. Do not be dismayed or discouraged because he is our God. He is there to give us strength and help us. It comes down to trust. We must trust him. We can give our fears to him and let him provide peace in our heart. Proverbs 3:5 tells us to trust in the Lord with all our heart and not to lean on our own understanding. Sometimes it is trying to figure out why or what if, that causes our fear. I often find myself trying to figure out why something happened that caused a conflict in my life. Why someone is like they are. Why they chose to do as they do. The positive verb here is trust. That means putting all my faith and hope in God and not trying to figure it out on my own or to my own understanding, which gives in to fear. Satan loves for us to be afraid. He uses fear to alienate us from our faith in Jesus Christ. He uses fear to take away our hope. He loves to shatter our confidence in our Lord with negative thoughts and accusations. Do you find yourself having an argument with someone in your mind? And sometimes the argument in my head is about something that hasn't even happened; just a lethal suggestion from Satan trying to make me anxious. We need to push those thoughts out of our mind and not allow them to fester, causing fear. Instead, we trust in the Lord. We place our confidence in him.

Dear God, give me confidence and faith to trust in you with all my heart. You are my God and the source of my strength. Keep me from focusing on fear. Help me to ignore negative thoughts that will cause fear. Thank you for your unfailing faithfulness to help me. Amen.

103

Grace Beyond What We Can Understand
Luke 23:39-43

Dying on the cross, the criminal knew he was getting the punishment he deserved yet he pitied Jesus' suffering knowing he was being punished unjustly. The criminal couldn't fathom that Jesus was willing to accept the punishment for him. He couldn't understand it and neither can we. His belief gave him eternal life.

We don't understand a lot of things in life. It is not necessary to understand it all. We only need to understand that God loves us unconditionally and longs for our obedience and trust. He really doesn't ask for much. John 1:17 says grace and truth come through Jesus Christ. He gives grace because we don't deserve it. It would mean nothing, if we did deserve it. He paid the price for us. Through our eyes, the criminal didn't deserve forgiveness. He led a life of sin and repented only minutes before his death. We see sinful behavior and find it hard to believe that such a person would ever make it into heaven. But the grace provided through Jesus Christ is for anyone who acknowledges him. It has nothing to do with how we behave or live our life. Sin is sin. Grace is grace. There are no levels of sin or grace. We need to see those around us just as Jesus saw the criminal on the cross. Even in his suffering, Jesus gave grace. He gave the sinner a reprieve from his sin. I imagine this man had been looking all of his life for something to fill the emptiness in his heart and never found it, till the last moments of his life. We can accept that grace right now and use it to accomplish our purpose of honoring God. Most people won't get the opportunity that this criminal did. Death is not always expected; it often comes unexpected. We must be prepared and must try to prepare those around us. Accept the grace of God today. Grace beyond what we can understand.

Dear God thank you for the grace that pardons our sin. I praise you for the grace and truth that comes through Jesus Christ. Help me not to judge others' behavior but to share with them the pardon that they can receive through Jesus Christ. I pray for my community. I pray we will fall to our knees and recognize you as our saving grace. Forgive me when I fail you. Amen.

104

He Will Not Forget Us
Isaiah 49:13-15

These words from God were for Isreal at a time of restoration. They feared God had forgotten them because they had forgotten him. His answer relates to the love of a mother for her child, that it cannot be forgotten. Even if she does, God says he will not forget.

A mother's love for her child is often thought of as a strong, unconditional love that cannot be broken. We often hear stories if women who give up a child for adoption and years later, still can remember the face of the baby and could find it in a crowd. A Mother's love is the closest to total unconditional love that a human can have. Many who are in pain or danger long for their mother and will cry out for her. Nothing is stronger than a mother's love for her child. Unfortunately, this isn't always the story and a mother does reject or forget the love of her child. God knows that, therefore he was quick to add an exception to ensure a confidence in his unforgettable love for us. God speaks of this love again in Isaiah 66:12 -13 as he speaks of judgment and hope for the people of Jerusalem. He refers again to the comfort of a mother. He comforts as a mother comforts her child. This passage tells us to shout for joy and rejoice because of the comfort God brings. Burst into song about his comfort. He does not forget. He has engraved us on the palm of his hand (Isaiah 49:16). This is something to rejoice and sing about. No matter if those we love and trust forget us, God's love is unfailing and unconditional. He does not forget us.

Dear God, I rejoice and sing because of your love for me. Great is your love O God. Your love is higher than the mountains and your faithfulness reaches to the skies. (Psalm 108:4) Your Word says you will not forget me. Thank you for your love for me. Help me to share your love with those around me. Help me to strive to love others as you love me. Help me to love and comfort my children, without condition, as you love me. Amen.

105

Hiding From Our Sin
Proverbs 28:13

The story of Joseph in Genesis chapters 37-50 is an awesome story. His brothers sold him into slavery. Many years went by before the truth was revealed. I've wondered how they went about their day, for those years, knowing the sin they had committed not only against their own brother but against God as well. They were jealous of Joseph so they got rid of him. Proverbs 28:13 says that the man who conceals his sin will not prosper but who ever confesses and repents will find mercy. I imagine when the truth was finally revealed, while Joseph's brothers were embarrassed at the truth, they probably felt a relief too. While I dread addressing my sin, I do find relief in repentance. Genesis 45:14 tells of when Joseph revealed himself to his brothers. He kissed and wept over them and then they talked. What a time of restoration that was for them. God worked everything in this story for the good. He took a horrible thing and made it good.

Hiding from sin only brings grief. In Genesis 3:8-10, Adam and Eve hid from God because of their sin. It didn't take long for them to be found. We cannot hide from God. He knows our every thought and our every move. His desire is for us to bring our sin to him so that he can forgive us. He wants us to hide in him not from him. David asks God to keep him as the apple of his eye. He asks God to hide him in the shadow of his wings. (Psalm 17:8) The Holy Spirit lives within us to guide us and convict us. We need to heed the warnings and the truth of our sin and not hide.

Dear God, rescue me from my sin. I hide myself in you. Convict me of my sin so that I can come to you in repentance and find forgiveness. I am glad that I cannot hide from you. I want to hide under the shadow of your wings. I lift my voice to you for mercy. Amen.

106

In Order

1 Corinthians 14:40

This is a short little verse not very often mentioned. While it is here regarding worship, I believe we can apply it to other areas of life. I see children growing up too fast. I see very young girls in makeup and dangling earrings. Very young boys making sexual comments. Teenagers and children having babies. Teenagers and young adults living together outside of marriage. Problems with underage drinking.

I would like to suggest that God calls for us to teach our children to live life in a fitting and orderly way. Children should be children. Teenagers should be teenagers. Deuteronomy 11:19-21 tells us to teach the commands of God to our children and to talk about them all through the day, so that we and our children will have long lives. Sometimes lives are cut short because young folks have things out of order. Goals and plans are shattered because life is out of order. TV and movies often have a very negative influence on our children in these areas. Humor is used to subtly suggest and encourage sinful behavior. Do we monitor what goes into our children's ears and the things that they see? Are we willing to make that effort? It is also important to teach our children that God offers forgiveness in response to repentance when mistakes are made. Putting our lives in order at an early age should help prevent many of the difficulties we face with our young people today. Teaching them obedience to God is a must. God has plans for us to prosper and not to cage us in with a list of rules. His guidance always offers beneficial results, just as he offers a long life in this passage of Deuteronomy. We need to protect our youngsters from inappropriate behavior and wrong decisions made when our life is not in proper order.

Dear God, help us to keep our lives in order and to teach our children to live life in a fitting and orderly way. Thank you for your unconditional love and unfailing forgiveness. I pray that your plans for me and my family will come to be. I know you have a perfect plan for us. Help us to trust you every day in everything we do. Amen.

107

Just Say No
Titus 2:11-14

The book of Titus is a letter written by Paul to his co-worker Titus. I'm sure we are all familiar with the campaign for kids designed for staying away from drugs, Just Say No. That same campaign is found here in this passage. We are encouraged by Paul to Say No to ungodliness and worldly passion. We are encouraged to live self-controlled upright, godly lives in this present age while we wait for the return of Jesus Christ. We are redeemed by Christ who gave himself as a sacrifice for our sin. As we teach our kids to stay away from drugs we have a responsibility of teaching them, and ourselves, to not only stay away from sinful behavior but to live godly lives in obedience.

We are taught in 1 Corinthians 6:19-20 that our bodies are the temple of the Holy Spirit who is placed in our heart by God as our conscience and guide. We are not our own. We live to honor God. We are often taught these slogans, such as Just Say No, early in life but stop following them because we consider it kid stuff. But we can still use this in our daily lives as children and adults. A simple reminder of living in obedience - Just Say No. Say No to the peer pressures that are placed before us. Say No to filling our minds with TV and movies that suggest sinful behavior or leave lasting images in our minds that are inappropriate for godly living. Say No to being too busy to help someone in need or spend time with our family. Whatever the temptation before us, we just Say No. Say Yes to living a life of obedience in following the teachings of our Lord and living everyday to honor him. Say Yes to living a self-controlled upright life of godliness while we wait for the blessed hope – the glorious appearing of our great God and Savior, Jesus Christ.

Dear God, help me to remember the simple truths that help me live a life of obedience and in honor of you. Help me to teach my children to Say Yes to a life of service in honor of you. May my example be a witness to those around me. Thank you for your faithful forgiveness when I fail. Amen.

108

The Lord Is My Shield
Psalm 28:6-8

Horses and ponies have natural grease that protects their skin and hair; to repel moisture helping to keep them warm and dry. This protects them from the rain and snow. It is especially important if they live outdoors and not barned at night.

God is our strength and shield. He promises to protect us and help us. Our hearts should leap for joy knowing this and give thanks. Psalm 32:7 tells us we can hide in him; for he protects us from trouble. Our relationship with God gives us relief and offers a hiding place to bask in his love and comfort. Reading God's Holy Word, talking with him, sharing my troubles, provides a place for me to remove myself from worry and fear, to seek and find protection. Sometimes we find ourselves hiding from God, when we know our heart is not right. But we cannot hide from him anymore than he can avoid us; no need to. He is always there to welcome us. Our faith in God is our shield of protection from the schemes of Satan (Ephesians 6:16.) Through our daily relationship with our Lord, he will cause our fears and worries to roll off just like he provides protection for the horses and ponies from the harsh and wet weather. If God provides for them, how much more protection will he provide for me and you? Seek God today. Seek his love and protection. Hide in him under the protection that he gives.

Dear God, you are my hiding place. You will protect me from trouble. You fill my heart with songs of deliverance. Whenever I am afraid I can trust in you. Thank you for your love for me. Help me to be as loving to those around me. My community and my world need your love. Help me to share it with them. Amen.

109

Watch For Falling Rock
Matthew 26:41

Have you joked about the signs in the mountains, Watch for Falling Rock? We have wondered just exactly what are we supposed to do if we see rock falling and have considered the signs silly and useless. There were people who recently saw falling rock that changed their life forever and will take the signs very seriously from now on. On I-40 going to Knoxville, huge rocks, some the size of small houses, fell and completely blocked both lanes of the six lane highway. Thankfully, no one was seriously injured but several cars rode up on the disaster. Engineers say it will take months to reopen the highway.

There are many warning signs in life that we do not take seriously. We think serious temptation will never happen to us or we can handle it if it does. In this passage, on the night of his arrest, Jesus asked his disciples to keep watch while he prayed. Instead they fell asleep. He warned them to watch and pray so that they would not fall into temptation. This same caution is for us. 1 Timothy 4:16 tells us to watch our life and doctrine closely to save ourselves. Only God saves, but he uses us to bring salvation to others. What warning signs are you missing in your life? When we know Jesus as our Savior, the Holy Spirit dwells within us as our guide. I have learned to call it my gut feeling. I can honestly say, 100% of the time that I have not listened to my gut feeling, I regretted it. Warning signs are all around. God's Holy Word is full of warnings. Jesus asked in this passage, Could you not keep watch? He warned the disciples that the spirit is willing but the body is weak. The warning signs are there. We need to keep watch.

Dear God, thank you for watching over us and providing warning signs. Help me to take the signs of warning seriously. Your Holy Word says that you watch over us and will not sleep. Thank you for this promise. Thank you for the Holy Spirit that you provide for guidance and direction. Help me to be watchful of temptation that will come and to trust you in all things. Amen.

110

Temptation
1 Corinthians 10:1-13

The Israelites' travels from slavery to the promised land were under the leadership and guidance of God. Nevertheless, they sinned and God was not pleased with them. Many died due to the consequences of their sin. According to these scriptures, this happened as an example to keep us from yielding to temptation as they did. I think all of us have wondered at some time or another, how these people could have sinned with all the miracles in front of them and God's presence right there with them. If anyone could walk with God almost to perfection, it would have been them. Yet as we know, the story did not go that way.

I've always found verses 11 through 13 as very important verses for Christians to remember on a daily basis. We are all tempted with the same things. God will not allow us to be tempted beyond what we can bear. When we are tempted, God will provide a way out. Recognizing this, we should be standing up against the temptations that come to us. Yet, we still sin. Let's be encouraged to remember this and stand firm. There is no room for the excuse, I couldn't help it. God is there for us. He provides a way out of each situation. The most important words are in verse 13, God is faithful. Psalm 130 tells us to put our hope in the Lord. In him is unfailing love and full redemption. He himself will redeem us from all sin.

Dear God, thank you for the examples you give me. Forgive me of my sin. Help me not to find excuses but to find the way out that you provide me when I am tempted. Your love never fails. My hope is in you. O Lord, hear my voice. Amen.

111

Praying For Our Enemies
Luke 6:27-36

I was once hired as a supervisor in a unit. The other supervisor position was vacant and stayed vacant for several months after I was hired. I had settled into my position and was quite contented. Then the other supervisor was hired. She was smart and very competent; however we did not exactly hit it off. I don't recall any specifics, we just did not click. I mentioned it in my Sunday School class and my teacher suggested that I pray for her. I did and there was immediate change. We never became good friends but we did start to work well together and made a pretty good team. It amazed me how my heart changed toward her and she responded. I could not explain it. It had to be the prayer. She left before I did and I often think of the lesson I learned in our relationship.

This passage tells us that we aren't to only pray for those we love and want to help, we are to pray for those who seem against us and bring trouble into our life. It is easy to pray for people we like. It is more difficult to pray for those who aren't our friend. But it draws us to this person and develops an intimacy that we did not have before. I felt this in praying for the other supervisor. I was blessed with a better relationship which made my work more productive and comfortable in the renewed feelings we had toward each other that came from my prayer for her. It was so much better than before. Our obedience comes with reward and blessing.

Lord, help me to pray for those I do not like. Help me to recognize the renewal in relationships that comes from you. Help me to do for others as I want them to do for me and as you do for me. I don't want to be selfish with my prayers. Amen.

112

The God Of All Comfort
2 Corinthians 1:3-11

God is the Father of compassion and the God of all comfort. He comforts us in all our troubled times. The purpose of his comfort is so we will know comfort and can pass it on to others. God uses our troubles to grow confidence, patience and endurance. God is at work in our grief and difficulties. Paul proclaims in verse 9 that God allows our despair and times of trouble so that we do not rely on ourselves but on him. God is able because he is even powerful enough to raise the dead. Paul talks later in 7:6-7 about the comfort that Titus brought them because of the comfort he had received. The comfort of God passes from person to person.

God puts us in the right place at the right time to offer comfort to someone who is experiencing a problem situation that we have been through. He brings comfort to us so that we are able to share our experience and give witness to the peace he provided us. He comforts us so that we can pass his comfort on to another. Things don't just happen by chance or coincidence; there is a reason, and that reason is part of God's plan. In Hebrews 13:5-6 God says, Never will I leave or forsake you. We can say with confidence that we have nothing to fear. He knows each tear that falls and he hears when we call.

Dear God thank you for the comfort you bring. Thank you for your glorious plan to pass your comfort among us. I can live each day in the confidence of your love and faithfulness. Keep me mindful of opportunities that come my way, to share the comfort within me that comes from you. Thank you for your marvelous plans for me. Amen.

113

He Knows Me
Psalm 139:1-18

God knows me well. He knew me before I was conceived. He knows what I do, what I say and what I think. He knows my heart and my motives. He knows what hurts my feelings, when I hurt physically and my fears. He knows my desires, my hopes and my dreams. He knows my thoughts before I think them, my words before I say them and every move I will make throughout my day before it starts. He knows my secrets. I could go on. God knows me and cares about everything about me. I can't hardly imagine it. Do I really believe this? Do I really believe that if God knows that much about me, he must care about each of those details about me? In this huge world full of people and problems, how could God possibly care about such details about me? Well, there is no reason to focus on why but to simply believe. This scripture says God created me and is familiar with all my ways.

No matter what hurts, God knows and cares. He rejoices when I rejoice. I must live each day knowing that he carries me in the palm of his hand. Forgive me for repeating myself but I need to say it over and over. I am living this life and constantly in the thoughts of our God and King. I am never alone. Nothing about my life goes unnoticed. When I take my last breath, I will immediately be in his presence. I encourage you to join me in thinking on these promises today. As each moment goes by, recognize that God knows. Rejoice in this promise and do not be anxious or fearful of anything. He is with us in every moment of every day.

Dear God, I am in awe of your love for me. Help me not to wonder about it but to simply accept that you know me and care about each moment of my life. Help me to rest in this promise and put all my hope and trust in my faith in you. Thank you for your love. Amen.

114

Put It Away
Colossians 3:5-10

Has God convicted you and took away certain worldly things that you once enjoyed? Did you respond? He took soap operas and trashy novels from me years ago. At one time I enjoyed them, but at a time in my life, I lost the desire for them and they even became unpleasant to me. When I saw the lust and promiscuous behavior on the soaps, I felt such guilt when I watched them. When I read books that start describing inappropriate sexual encounters in detail, I felt convicted. Now let me quickly say, I'm not telling you these things are totally wrong, but I am convinced that God gave me the feelings of conviction because these things separated me from him. I do believe this scripture cautions us to remove things from our life that were a part of our nature before our relationship with God or that could tempt us into sinful behavior. These are things that Satan will use to subtly enter our thoughts, which often leads to sinful behavior. The scripture says to put to death, whatever belongs to our earthly or sinful nature. These things are different for me and you. The Holy Spirit will tell us what should be removed, we just have to listen and respond. We don't want anything in our thoughts or actions that separate us from living the godly life to which God calls us. I have done just fine without those things in my life now. I still love to read. I am careful about what I read. If I make a bad choice, I simply put it away and find another book. But I have learned to choose more carefully. Ask God today, what he desires to remove from your life. Or, you may already know, you just need to react.

Dear God, show me what is unclean in my life. Help me to rid myself of ungodly things that will interfere in my relationship with you and my witness to others. I gladly give them up. Help me to set my mind on things above, not earthly things. Amen.

115

Pray For All Things
James 5:13-18

Is any one of you in trouble? He should pray (verse 13). Do you have faith in your prayers? This passage says the prayer of a righteous man is powerful and effective. This passage encourages me to have faith in my prayer. It tells me that when my heart is right, my prayer will yield results. We often pray about something but then neglect to have faith in our prayer. God does answer prayer. He does not always give us the answer we want, but he answers. Sometimes he answers in silence. That is his answer. Sometimes God responds quickly and sometimes he wants us to wait. Deuteronomy 4:29 tells us if we seek the Lord, we will find him if we look for him with all our heart. We must trust that God will answer and trust that his answer is best for us. It's not that he is hard to find, our minds are naturally clouded with doubt and worry.

I've talked before about praying for the little things as well as the big things in life. We are to pray continuously. I pray for parking places and I pray for healing. Many times family problems weigh heavy on my mind. I really have to work at giving them to the Lord and then resting in the peace in knowing that he heard me and he will answer. Maybe quickly, maybe not. Sometimes I see God at work and at other times I don't realize that he has worked until I look back. God wants me to let go of the anxiousness and rest in him. This is rarely easy. I have to focus on this throughout the day so that I am not tempted to let the clouds of worry return. I have to look for God with all my heart. I have to trust him in all things.

Dear God, help me to trust you completely in all areas of my life. Forgive me of my sin and cleanse my heart so that I can seek you and find you. My hope is in you, my God and King. I praise you for your faithful promises to bring peace when I lay my worries, big and small, at your feet. I love you Lord. Amen.

116

Pass It On
1 Corinthians 15:1-4

When I was a teenager, my youth group performed songs from a musical called "Purpose". We traveled to other churches and even went to West Virginia and sang it in shopping center parking lots. It was a great time of my life. One of my favorite songs we sang was called "Pass it On". This is a great song and I still remember the words (pretty much).

It only takes a spark, to get a fire going.
And soon all those around, can warm up in it's glowing.
That's how it is with God's love, once you've experienced it, it's
fresh like spring, you want to sing, you want to pass it on.
What a wondrous time is Spring, when all the trees are budding.
The birds begin to sing, the flowers start their blooming.
That's how it is with God's love, once you've experienced it, it's
fresh like spring, you want to sing, you want to pass it on.
I wish for you my friend, this happiness that I've found

You can depend on him, it matters not where you're bound.
I'll shout it from the mountain tops. I want the world to know
The Lord of Life has come to me. I want to pass it on.

We should want to pass the story of Jesus Christ on to others. I should be anxious to pass on the story of what my relationship with him does for me. We can't just keep it to ourselves. We need to pass it on. We want others to know the strength that we find in our Lord. In this passage, Paul is encouraging his followers to pass on what they had heard and received. It only takes a spark to start a fire. We can start the spark by telling someone. Then it will spread just like fire. And others will know of the warmth of God's love and faithfulness. That's how it is with God's love, once you've experienced it, it's fresh like spring, you want to sing, you want to pass it on.

Dear God, grow in me the desire to spread your wonderful message to others. Forgive me for when I have missed an opportunity to share your story. I want the world to know that the Lord of Life has come to me. I want to pass it on. Amen.

117

I Can't Do This Alone
Psalm 62:1-8

Life is full of issues for us to deal with. Some are simple to resolve, while others seem to remain with us for a long time. Some move on quickly and some seem to grow bigger everyday. We pray and as the song says, we expect God to step in and save the day, but we say Amen and it's still raining.

The psalmist writing these words in Psalm was apparently a king who had people trying to remove him from his throne. It very well may have been David writing about the circumstances with Saul. I can almost feel his pain and anxiety reading the words. He feels threatened but his faith is strong and he is determined to trust in God as his rock and salvation. Many times I feel alone with my problems. I feel like I can't stand the pressure anymore and just want to give up. I recently told a friend that I could understand how some people just pick up and leave, never to return. But I recognize that it is wrong to be discouraged in such a way. We are not alone. If we suggest giving up, we are suggesting that God is not strong enough to take care of us. God is big enough and he is strong enough and he cares enough. He may not remove the problem but he will help us find answers. God is waiting for us to allow him to help. We must seek him and anticipate his response.

I love the ending verses here. One thing God has spoken; two things have I heard. You, O God, are strong and You, O Lord, are loving. You will reward us according to what we have done. We must not try to handle our problems alone. Our God is there to be our rock and our strength. We will not be shaken. In obedience, we must seek strength and restoration from him.

Dear God, I trust in you. I pour out my heart to you. You are my refuge. I hide in the shadow of your wings and wait for you to bring peace. Thank you for your wonderful promises. In obedience, I trust in you. Amen.

118

Integrity
Isaiah 29:15

It is difficult to fathom however it is very true that God knows every thought and every move we make. When we are alone, we think no one sees, but God does. We have no secrets from him. This scripture says woe to anyone who tries to keep secrets from God. My dictionary defines woe as misfortune, grief or sorrow. None of these sound good. Colossians 3:23 tells us to do everything as if working for God. He knows our heart. He knows when we do wrong and he knows our intention. We can hide from others but we can't even hide our thoughts or unspoken intentions from God. He knows what we do and why we do it. He knows our heart.

Our integrity is important to those around us and it is important to God. I have been deeply hurt by someone close to me who had a sinful habit in secret. When it was revealed, it caused us grief and sorrow. But that person hurt not only me but also hurt their relationship with God. Integrity was shattered. Thankfully God brings restoration after repentance. Let's be encouraged to be especially careful of what we do that no one sees. Let's make sure our integrity is true. Romans 2:16 says that God will judge our secrets. In Psalm 139:23, the psalmist cried out for God to search his heart and show him anything offensive within. He asked for God to judge his integrity and keep him honest.

Dear God you know my inner thoughts and intentions. Search me and show me anything in my behavior or thoughts that are offensive to you. Forgive me and help me to change and correct my ways. I want to honor you in everything I do, seen and hidden. Thank you for how you love me and your never ending faithfulness and mercy. Amen.

119

Giving In Secret
Matthew 6:1-4

I love giving to the needy and helping those in need. I get so excited when I hear someone mention something that they like or want, and I am able to give it to them for their birthday or Christmas. We are thrilled at receiving a special gift that we really wanted. One of the girls in my Sunday School class complained that her dog chewed up her favorite flip flops. At her birthday, I spoke to her Mom and was able to replace them exactly. She was very surprised that I had remembered. It is also exciting to hear of someone in need and anonymously filling their need. But sometimes, we have the desire for others to know when we help meet a need. We may want praise and recognition for what we contribute. We like to give the best gift for others to admire our giving.

This passage offers a word of caution in our giving. Jesus spoke these words. He taught that giving should come from the heart and should never be done for others to see. I see this as service without thought of a reward. My Bible study notes indicate the acts of righteousness as giving, praying and fasting. We do these things from the heart, in praise and obedience to our Lord, not for something in return or for recognition. If these acts are done for man to see or hear, or even for God's favor, we lose our reward. Our reward comes for selfless giving. Only God truly knows our heart.

Dear God, help me to keep my giving in secret and not desire recognition. Help me to give truly from my heart with a desire only to act in obedience to you. Help me to listen when you suggest someone in need. Help me to respond quickly and cheerfully. Thank you for the blessings you have given me, especially my salvation and promise of eternal life. Amen.

120

Thanksgiving
Psalm 100

It is easy to be thankful at Thanksgiving. Even those who do not know the Lord recognize the special day each November to be thankful. I cannot read this Psalm without lifting my hands to God in gratitude for his blessings. It is hard for me to read it to myself. I want to read it out loud. This short passage sums up exactly who God is and what he does for us. This call for praise is for everyone. All the earth is to know that he is God and we are his people, the sheep of his pasture. God is good and his love for us is forever.

We should have an attitude of thankfulness every day, regardless of whether or not it is Thanksgiving Day. Yes, it is hard to be thankful in the hard times. It is hard to praise God when things are not going well for us. However, his love and faithfulness never change with our situation. He doesn't love us less when times are hard, even when it is our own doing. His love endures forever and his faithfulness continues through all generations. We must be thankful in the good times and in the bad times. We are to praise God in the easy times and the hard times. Stop right now and read this Psalm out loud and raise your hands in thanksgiving!! It is Thanksgiving everyday when we know Jesus Christ as our Lord and Savior, no matter what the calendar says.

Dear God, I shout for joy and worship you in gladness. You made me and I am yours. Thank you for your love and faithfulness. Forgive me of my sin. Cleanse me and use me today. It's Thanksgiving Day because of you. I love and adore you. Amen.

121

The Solid Rock
Psalm 71:1-3

Scripture often refers to God as our rock. Rocks are hard and solid. Our hope and confidence in God is solid. There is an old hymn I remember singing in church, "The Solid Rock".

My hope is built on nothing less than Jesus' blood and righteousness.
I dare not trust the sweetest frame, but wholly trust in Jesus' Name.
When darkness seems to hide his face, I
rest on his unchanging grace.
In every high and stormy gale, my anchor holds within the veil.
When he shall come with trumpet sound,
oh may I then in him be found.
Dressed in his righteousness alone, faultless
to stand before the throne.
On Christ the solid Rock I stand; all other ground is sinking sand.
All other ground is sinking sand.

When we put our faith and confidence in anything other than our Lord, we are placing our future onto sinking sand. Nothing and no one is more solid than our Lord Jesus Christ. The world wants to suggest other things that we can trust and depend on, but nothing can contend with God's unchanging grace. My daughter once had a pet rock. She could not break it and it never moved. It was always there. Its painted smile never wore off. It was to remind her that God is her rock. He is solid and cannot be broken or dissolved. Place your trust in God alone. He will return at the sound of the trumpet and take us to the place he has prepared for us for eternity. A solid promise you can believe in and depend on. A promise that will not be broken.

Dear God, be my rock of refuge to which I can always go. You are my rock and my fortress. My hope is in you and I praise you. I never need to fear, for you are solid and will never stray from me. You are my Lord and Savior. Amen.

122

Our Foundation
Matthew 7:24-27

The wise man built his house upon the rock
and the rain came tumbling down.
The rain came down and the floods came up
and the wise man's house stood firm.

The foolish man built his house upon the sand
and the rain came tumbling down.
The rain came down and the floods came up and
the foolish man's house washed away.
So, build your house on the Lord Jesus Christ
and the blessings will come down.
The blessings come down as your prayers go up, so
build your house on the Lord Jesus Christ.

Our foundation is important. When a tall building is under construction, the foundation takes many days to build. Building the foundation of our children is just as important. Our church ministers to a prison in our area. We take homemade cookies and have a time of devotion, prayer and singing. Because we visit the psychiatric ward, we have to stand outside their doors. We can hear them but can only see them through the small window on the door. It has often amazed me when they sing along or speak scripture with us. I believe they had some type of Bible teaching in their foundation. Granted it may not have resulted in obedience, but it is still evident and likely to mean salvation. In this passage of scripture, Jesus is saying it is wise to practice his instruction and foolish not to. Our foundation must be based on Jesus' teachings in order to withstand the rain and storms of life. A foundation without Jesus will bring our life crashing down around us. A parent has a great confidence in knowing a child has had a Biblically based foundation and has trusted Jesus Christ as Lord and Savior. No matter what path that child takes, their salvation cannot be taken away. So, build your house on the Lord Jesus Christ and see the blessings come down as your prayer goes up.

Dear God thank you for this good example of how we should build our foundation. Help me to build my life on the solid rock of your instruction and not on the sandy earthly standards. I thank you for the songs and stories that I learned as a child and still remember. I praise you for my parents who knew the importance of my foundation. Thank you for your everlasting love and faithfulness. Amen.

123

The Lord Is My Shade
Psalm 121:5

This is a powerful Psalm and is also written into a wonderful song. I love hearing the Brooklyn Tabernacle Choir sing it, "My Help Cometh from the Lord". These comforting words provide assurance that our help comes from the Lord and he is our shade. You know what it is like to be outside on a hot sunny day and you find a shade tree or cover to block the sun. The relief is immediate, especially if there is also a breeze. And think about if you walked into your house at night and none of the lights or lamps had a shade. The light from the lite bulbs would be harsh and offensive to our eyes. These thoughts come to my mind when I read how the Lord watches over me and is my shade. The sun will not harm me by day nor the moon by night. Isaiah 25:4 says God is our shade from the heat.

God protects us from this harsh world that we live in. His protection is like the cool of that shade tree we find on a hot day, providing comfort from the offensive light or heat. He watches over us without ever sleeping and knows every hurt, pain or concern that each of us experiences. He is the only constant dependable source of help. He will not let us down as others can. He is our shade. Lift up your eyes and experience the wonder of this magnificent promise. The Lord is my keeper. The Lord is my shade. All of my help comes from the Lord.

Dear God, you are my Heavenly Father. You are my shade. I lift my eyes to the heavens and praise your everlasting name. Protect me from all harm. Watch over me and restore me like the cool of a shade tree. Forgive me of my sin and use me today in a special way to serve you. Amen.

124

God Is My Shield
Psalm 3:3

Yesterday we looked at Psalm 121 and saw God as our shade. Today in Psalm 3:3 we see that he is a shield around us. Psalm 7:10 says my shield is God Most High. Proverbs 30:5 says he is a shield to those who take refuge in him.

People who we love and trust can let us down. They can commit sin that betrays our trust in them. While we can forgive, it is often difficult to reestablish the trust and allow the relationship to move forward. We often build up a wall of defense in an effort to protect our self from getting hurt again. The shield that we put up causes fear and anxiety that can consume us until we almost can't function. It can be crippling. This shield can delay the victory that we can receive in Christ over troubling situations. God is our shield. He will shield us. Others may let us down once and then again, and maybe even again but God is there to provide refuge and strength. I do not have to build barriers to shield myself. He is my shield. My own shield portrays mistrust in God. How dare I think I can protect myself better than my Lord! My shield comes from the Lord, the maker of heaven and earth. He will not let my foot slip and he never sleeps. Let's tear down any shield created on our own and allow our Lord Jesus Christ to place his shield around us. We trust him in relationships that he has joined together.

Dear God I trust in your unfailing love. I will praise you forever for what you have done for me. In your name I will hope, for your name is good. Shield me from harm as you've promised. Help me to tear down shields of mistrust that I create on my own. You are my refuge and strength. Amen.

125

Crossing Over
Matthew 18:21-35

Psalm 3:8 says deliverance comes from the Lord. Built up anger is disabling. God can deliver us from it. It is only God himself that moves within me to help me take the step to cross over from hurt and unforgiveness to the freedom that comes from letting go. I cannot be like the unmerciful servant who refused to forgive but expected forgiveness. His master called him wicked. When we pray the Lord's Prayer (Matthew 6:9-13) we ask for forgiveness as we are forgiven. How do we cross over? His grace is sufficient and his power is perfect in weakness.

Crossing over is taking the step into the garden of fresh air, leaving behind the stifling smothered feeling on the other side. Crossing over brings relief. Relief from the wickedness I feel when I refuse to let go of anger and resentment. I know that God knows when my heart is not clean and when

I hold on to the stuff that causes me to be unclean. I feel unworthy to even call his name. After taking that step to relinquish the sin in my heart, I no longer feel separated from God because of things in my heart that didn't need to be there. Not only is the burden I carried removed but I can praise him with delight in a feeling of obedience and achievement. Whew! We made it across. Yes, we did the right thing. Freedom rings! John 5:24 says whoever hears the Word and believes, has eternal life and has crossed over from death to life. Don't be afraid to cross over. You will be so glad that you did. Believe me, I am witness to it. My life is not problem free but I can relax easier and sleep better when I let go. Take the step and cross over into life. Life without unresolved anger and unforgiveness.

Dear God thank you that you are Lord over all circumstances. Help me to trust you even in the difficult places. I want to be obedient. I want you to smile when I choose to do the right thing. Forgive me when I am stubborn. Thank you for your love for me. Help me to be willing to forgive as you forgive me. Amen.

126

God's Love and Compassion
Psalm 103

Praise the Lord, O my soul. The psalmist starts reminding me to praise the Lord with my heart and soul. Not just because I might be happy today, but with the joy that comes from within me. Be reminded of the blessings we receive from him. He forgives. He heals. He rescues us from our sin with unconditional love and compassion. He gives us the desires of our heart. He strengthens us as strong as an eagle, which is known for power and speed. He does not discipline us as we deserve. He forgives us and forgets our confessed sin. He separates us from our sin, as far as the heavens are above and as far as east to west. Our eyes cannot see or measure this nor can our minds truly imagine it. He gives mercy to those who respect him and live in harmony with his will, and he will bless our children's children. He knows everything about me before I was formed and when my body will return to dust. He cares about every minute of my days here on earth, yet these days are only a whisper in the wind. He cares so deeply yet this life is only a fragment of his plan. It just hit me – this is huge. This life is so insignificant compared to God's eternal plan for us yet he still is aware of every second with love and compassion. Stop and think on this for a moment. He has established his throne in heaven and rules over everything. Praise the Lord. O my soul. Everyone and everything, praise him.

Dear God, thank you for your love and compassion for me. Help me appreciate the small specific ways you bless me. I praise you with my heart and soul. Show me unconfessed sin so that I can confess it and reap your blessings. I praise your Holy name. Amen.

127

Do Not Be Anxious
Philippians 4:4-7

I have been anxious about several issues in my life. Yesterday, I felt physically ill from the worry and anxiety I felt. I had to go to bed. Later in the day I took my prayer journal and made a list of the issues. I knew I was not to be anxious. I knew I was to give my burdens to my Lord. I prayed over the list, asking God for help. I realized that the anxiousness was not coming from God. We are instructed in this passage, not to be anxious about anything; to present our requests to God. 1 Peter 5:7 tells me to cast all anxiety on him because he cares for me. Proverbs 12:25 says an anxious heart weighs a person down. So, I said to myself, this anxiety is not from the Lord. If God tells me not to be anxious, why would he make me anxious about my issues? I realized that the anxiety was from Satan – the father of lies. He was trying to take my peace and my confidence. He was lying to me, that I had to handle all these issues alone and quickly. After reading these scriptures and praying I felt such a relief and release. The issues are still there but my confidence has returned knowing that God knows about each thing on that list and he will help me resolve them, one by one. I can praise him and worship him while I wait, taking one step at a time with him by my side. I must resist and fight the temptation to let Satan do that to me again. I have my list and I will wait patiently for God to help me with each one. I know that the day will come when each thing is checked off and resolved. I imagine there will be more added in time but I hope I can handle things better from here on. I hope that you find this encouraging.

Dear God forgive me for allowing Satan to put anxiousness in my heart. Give me courage to resist his lies. I give you all my cares and concerns because I know you care for me. I will praise you and worship you while I wait. Thank you for your love for me. Amen.

128

Follow-up To Yesterday
Romans 15:13

Yesterday I told you about my experience with anxiousness. Today I came across a verse that brings me to tears. Tears of thanksgiving and hope. God shows us exactly what we need to hear in His Word.

May the God of hope fill you with all joy and peace as you trust in him, so that you may overflow with hope by the power of the Holy Spirit. Romans 15:13

My hope comes from the Lord Jesus Christ. Nothing else or no one else can give me hope like this. There is no where else to find it. Right now I am listening to the Brooklyn Tabernacle Choir sing, "O Happy Day". God taught me how to watch, fight and pray. He taught me how to live rejoicing everyday. O happy day when my Jesus washed my sins away. God's Word is full of words and promises of hope. We just need to seek them everyday and hold on to them with everything we have in us. Let's stop right here and read this verse aloud praising God for the hope he gives and his everlasting unfailing love.

May the God of hope fill me with all joy and peace as I trust in him, so that I may overflow with hope by the power of the Holy Spirit.

Dear God of hope, fill me with all joy and peace as I trust in you, so that I will overflow with hope by the power of the Holy Spirit. Thank you for the hope I have in you. Forgive me when I doubt you. Help me to resist Satan's lies. Thank you for my salvation in Jesus Christ. Please use me today to share this promise with someone else. Thank you for the joy and peace you bring to my heart. Amen.

129

Psalm 32

I am blessed because my God forgives me when I sin. The price has been paid in advance to cover my sin. When he forgives me my sin is forgotten and wiped out. God does require that I am honest and do not plan to sin again when I ask for forgiveness. I must have a true heart of repentance. He knows my heart. When I sin and do not ask for forgiveness, I feel ill just like the drained feeling after being in the sun and heat all day. I hurt and I complain during the day and do not sleep well at night. I can no longer ignore my sin. I must confess to the Lord and he will forgive. I must encourage others to confess to receive forgiveness. Problems will come and temptation comes with them. Me and my fellow believers need to know this. We must not wait until our sin separates us from God. He delights in our confession and repentance. He will protect us. He sings over us. We can hide in him. He will give us guidance and direction. If we do not seek him we don't know which way to go. We would become like a horse needing a bridle and bit to be controlled because we are at such a point of misunderstanding. Do not let shame keep us from God's grace. Life is full of the wicked who tempt us to wickedness but God will protect us when we stay close to him and trust in his protection. This is a great promise. Rejoice in the Lord and be glad. Sing to the Lord. Be glad knowing his promises. Stay in his Holy Word and clear your heart of sin.

Dear God thank you for your promises. Forgive me of my sin. Cleanse my heart and use me for your glory. Search me and show me unconfessed sin. Protect me from wicked temptation. Help me to stand firm. This is what I pray. Amen.

130

Hospitality

Hebrews 13:1-2

It is easy to love those that we enjoy being around. Entering a room of people we immediately seek out those we know and move to be near them and in their company. But there are those, even in our circle of friends and family that we don't enjoy being around. Some people are difficult to deal with for different reasons. And then there are strangers. How often have you been in a crowd and could not pick out a person that was familiar?

There are stories in the Old Testament where people actually experienced seeing and talking with an angel sent by God. I find it very possible that God still sends angels among us to influence us or help us through a time of need. I can recall where someone came out of nowhere to offer directions when I was lost or said something of encouragement that I really needed to hear. This verse tells me that I may even be tested on how I treat a stranger that really is an angel. This verse may be here for no other reason than to caution me to treat everyone with love regardless of whether I know them or like being around them. I find a similar warning in Colossians 4:5 that instructs me to be wise in the way I treat outsiders. We meet and pass strangers and outsiders everyday. If they drop something, do we pick it up? Do we hold the door for them as they approach? Do we speak to them while standing in the check out line? Or do we only do these simple acts of service when we know the person or the person appears friendly or of my kind? Do I turn my head because they are of a different color or race or aren't dressed as nice as me or they aren't in my circle of friends? The next time, we should consider this instruction. Not only are we commanded to love everyone, it just very well may be an angel unaware.

Dear God, forgive me when I think I am better than others. Forgive me when I limit my smile and acts of service to only those I see as deserving. Thank you for your unconditional love for me. Give me opportunity today to share your love with a stranger. Amen.

131

Sin Of Omission
Matthew 25:31-46

We usually think of sin as bad behavior, thoughts or words. We seldom mention the sin of omission. The sin of neglecting to do the right thing. We can sin by doing the wrong thing but also by not doing the right thing for the right reason. Jesus is speaking here of a time of judgment that will determine the believers and the unbelievers, the obedient from the disobedient. The sheep will be separated from the goats.

We have opportunity everyday to feed the hungry, give drink to the thirsty, welcome a stranger, clothe the needy, minister to the sick or visit the imprisoned. I do not believe Jesus only means giving food or water or an overnight stay or clothes or a visit to a hospital or in a prison. In addition to these things, there are simple acts of service to those in need of knowing him and experiencing his unconditional love through us, that we miss. I know I neglect these opportunities everyday. Sometimes it is as simple as smiling at a stranger on the street. God created us to share his love to others, even to the 'least'. I don't think God focuses here on the act. Be reminded that we are not saved by our works (Ephesians 2:9). He is interested in our heart. When we serve the least of those around us, we are serving him. The fact that we love others and serve them without thought of a reward or recognition. Often it is time and patience that we have to surrender in addition to monetary giving. Let's ask God for an opportunity today to serve him. Will I be a sheep or a goat? I hope to be placed on his right with his sheep.

Dear God, forgive me when I have failed to serve you. Forgive me for being too interested in getting a reward or recognition than serving the simple who are in need. Forgive me for thinking I am better than those I see in need. This world is full of opportunity. Many are living behind bars and don't see them. Show me today how I can serve you. Amen.

132

The Rich Fool
Luke 12:13-21

In this passage, Jesus was teaching the people, using stories or parables to help them understand. Apparently, in the middle of his preaching, a man came and asked Jesus to help him with a dispute with his brother over their inheritance. Do you recall talking with someone trying to make a point and they interrupt to ask a question, indicating that they clearly missed your point? I imagine this is exactly how Jesus felt. The man had obviously not been listening. Jesus was preaching his plan of salvation and eternal life and this man's concern was money.

The parable here is about a rich man whose main concern was gathering and storing up as much goods as he could, thinking this wealth gave him assurance and confidence of many years of a good life. Little did he realize that he would not live to enjoy his gathered wealth. He never used his wealth to make an eternal impact on someone else. He let it gather in the barns rather than using it for glorifying God. For many of us, status is money. We measure our accomplishments on how much is in our bank account. Some will sit on money and die of malnutrition or freeze from the cold. People have been found in shacks with no electricity sleeping on a mattress covering thousands of dollars. God does not frown on the wealthy, he frowns on how the wealthy use their wealth. When we know Jesus Christ as our Lord and Savior, we are rich. When God blesses us with many material things it is important to keep our perspective in the proper order. We need to ask God to help us keep our life in perspective so that our main focus is always on him.

Dear God thank you for the many blesses you give me. Forgive me when I put my faith in my material belongings. Show me how to keep my life in perspective so that my focus is always on you. Give me opportunity to share my wealth, for I am rich in you. Give me opportunity to share your love with others. Amen.

133

Just Enough For Today
Exodus 16

A month has passed since the exodus out of Egypt. The people didn't know where food would come from. God provided a daily amount of manna. The flakes of manna literally fell from heaven. He told them to collect only what was needed for the day. God was angered when they tried to collect extra to store for the next day. It angered him that they did not trust him day by day. The dictionary defines manna as something of value that someone received unexpectedly. The manna was for their body. God's provision was for their soul.

God still gives the true bread from heaven which is eternal life through Jesus Christ. In John 6:32-33, 35 Jesus says, I am the bread of life. He is not the means to get the bread as the crowd saw their ancestor, Moses. They suggest in verse 31 that Jesus' act of feeding the 5,000 was little compared to Moses providing for the Israelites for 40 years. The manna came from God in heaven, not from the hand of Moses. Jesus is the bread. He provides what we need and promises eternal life for our belief. Daily interaction with him gives us just what we need for the day. We can't store it up to have enough for tomorrow. We are to seek him daily and trust him for provision enough for the day.

Father above, one day at a time sweet Jesus,
that's all I'm asking from you.
Just give me the strength to do everyday what I have to do.
Yesterday's gone sweet Jesus and tomorrow may never be mine.
Lord help me today, show me the way, one day at a time. Amen.

134

What Am I Thinking?

Philippians 4:8-9

How often do you think about what you think about? Our thoughts affect our whole attitude. When my mind is focusing on the wrong things, I am miserable. And when I am miserable others see it and experience it. What we allow into our minds will affect our actions. Sin usually begins with just a thought. Negative thoughts can separate us from walking with God. We are not aware of his presence when we allow our minds to obstruct our focus.

Paul is instructing us to keep our thoughts praiseworthy. Keeping our thoughts pure and lovely and following what we have heard and taught will bring us the peace of God. 2 Corinthians 10:5 tells us to take captive every thought to make it obedient to Christ. Capture any thought that is misleading, lock it away so that it is out of mind and will not obstruct our joy and obedience to Christ. We can mostly control what we allow into our minds – TV and movies we see, books we read, music we choose, places we allow ourselves to go, people we choose to be with. All of this affects what our thoughts will be. It is our choice. We play a big part in what goes into our mind. Our relationship and daily focus on him allows us to fight against and remove what improperly enters our mind. Examining our thoughts and being constantly aware of what we allow into our mind will surely result in a life of obedience to God. Let's examine our mind and clean up our thoughts.

Dear God, search my heart and my mind and help me to remove anything that is not praiseworthy. Help me not to be wrapped up in misleading thoughts that will separate me from you. Help me to be aware of your presence and not allow anything into my mind that will separate me from you. Amen.

135

Do Not Be Afraid
Exodus 14:13-14

At a time when I was afraid, God gave me this. Do not be afraid. Stand firm. And you will see the deliverance the Lord will bring you today. The Egyptians you see today you will never see again. The Lord will fight for you; you need only to be still.

The Israelites were preparing for battle and God is reminding them that the victory would come from him. He fought their battles for them. They needed only to stand firm and do as he told them. We have 'Egyptians' in our life that we battle. We all have our enemies and we all must deal with Satan, the father of lies. When we face these battles in fear, it is because we are fighting in our own way, in our own strength, and we should be prepared to lose. Instead, we must allow God to fight the battles for us. We must allow him to stand against our enemies. The enemy could be a person, a habit, a decision, a health problem, a financial issue – I could go on. We each know what our battles are. God will fight for us and we will never see it again, we only need to be still. There is so much we can learn from the stories of the Israelites. God was present and he led them to restoration. He fought their battles for them. He is here and available to do the same for us. We just need to let him. 1 Samuel 17:47 tells us that the battle is the Lord's. We need to lay our battles at his feet and allow him to take them from us and fight for us.

Dear God protect me from unnecessary fear. Help me to realize that fear means I don't trust you. Help me to find the confidence to allow you to fight my battles for me. Victory comes from you. Thank you for loving me enough to want to fight for me. Amen.

136

Letting Them Go
1 Corinthians 6:19-20

One of the most difficult things in parenting is letting our kids go. This passage tells us that we are not our own. We are of God and have been paid for with a price. Our children are not our possession. They belong to God. We have been entrusted with their care and as they mature, we have the responsibility to relinquish them to form their own life. Just like the mother bird that naturally sends her young to fly away, we relinquish them at different times and in different ways throughout their life, whether at a young age, teenage years and even as adults.

This has been easier for me since it has been explained in comparison to God's parenting of us with loving care and instruction. He does not force his way into our heart. He does not force our obedience. He longs to bless us but allows us to choose our way. Our bad choices and rebellion grieves him but he allows the consequences that teach us the value of obedience. He never abandons us.

So it is with our children. We must allow them to choose their way, love them unconditionally and support them. But we must let them go. We all know of situations where parents continue to be directly involved in the lives of their adult children therefore the 'adult' never grows up and never allowed to build their own life. We must give our children back to the Lord when our task is completed. We must let go and allow God to take control. It is never easy to let them fend for themselves and watch them do things their way instead of how we want. They will make bad choices and hopefully learn the value of obedience. Do we recognize this as exactly the way we are in our relationship with God? He allows us to fend for ourselves and do things our way. He longs for us to learn obedience so that he can bless us. We want that from him and we want it for our children.

Dear God help me to recognize that I am not my own but I belong to you. Thank you for paying the price for me. Thank you for loving me unconditionally. Help me to relinquish my children when appropriate, whether young or old. I want my children to fly away and build their own life based on the Biblical instruction I ensure that they receive. Help me to allow you to be in control. Search my heart right now and show me anything that I need to give back to you. Amen.

137

Time With Jesus
Matthew 26:36-38

When reading this the very first time, you might think that Jesus asked the three men to watch with him for protection. They could have watched and alerted him when the soldiers were coming and they could have hidden and avoided Jesus' arrest. But Jesus wasn't looking for a guard because he already knew God's plan. He was looking for companionship. He wanted them to spend time with him in these final hours of his life. He asked a very small thing of them. But instead they fell asleep. They did not take him seriously or they wouldn't have been able to sleep.

Jesus wants us to spend time with him. He doesn't need us in the same way we need him but he desires our companionship. We view our time with Jesus as being for our benefit only. He waits for us to meet him in prayer. How our perspective changes when we consider that our Lord longs for us to be with him because he wants to be with us as much as he wants us to seek him. Our time together works both ways. My daily quiet time is very important to me. I often fall asleep thinking about what I have to say to him in the morning. I anticipate the morning, writing in my prayer journal because it is a very special connection to God for me. Now I consider that he also anticipates the time with me. This brings a very warm feeling in my heart. He wants to be with me. He longs for my companionship as much as I long for his. He delights in our fellowship. Let's be encouraged to avoid making excuses in spending time with him daily. Establish a place to meet him each day. He will be waiting there for you. Let's not keep him waiting.

Dear Jesus, how easily I can be distracted from meeting you each day in a special time together. It warms my heart to know that you desire my companionship and wait, in anticipation, to spend time with me. You long for me to know you. May I be faithful to keep watch with you. Thank you for wanting me as your companion. Forgive me when I fail you, especially when I find other things to do in place of seeking you daily. Amen.

138

Depression
Psalm 6

Refuse to allow depression into your life. I am not speaking of a chemical imbalance that requires medication and treatment. If you need medication or treatment seek professional help or follow the directions of your physician.

We may become depressed because of bruised feelings or a current situation in our life. Negative feelings come easily. I believe that Satan encourages negative feelings and remember that he lies. I am speaking of a wounded feeling that requires the healing touch of our Lord. Feeling bad about myself or my life and feeling hopeless can make me depressed. The knowledge of the truth of God will set us free from the feelings of hopelessness that can make us depressed. God doesn't want us to live this way, not for a short time or a long time.

In Psalm 6, the writer is ill or possibly depressed. The symptoms are there - faint, agony, anguish, worn out, groaning, weeping, weak, sorrow. I can identify with that. I have felt this way when someone hurts my feelings, when I have a financial crisis, when I have unrepented sin in my heart or when I have to deal with a problem that seems hopeless. Shall I go on? Let's not. Let's talk about verses 8-10. When we cry out to the Lord, he hears us and will remove those negative feelings from our mind. God may not always quickly fix the problem completely, because he works in his own time and usually has something for us to learn. Know that he will bring peace and it will come quickly. Peace and joy like no one or nothing else can bring. Sometimes we feel trapped by these feelings and the 'bad mood'. God wants us to ask him to help us out of it and he will. Whatever the burden, take it to God. Tell him exactly what's bothering you. Give him your heart. Pour it all out to him. Give it all to God and he will help. It always helps me to pull out my prayer journal and make a list of what is bothering me. As 2 Corinthians 1:3-4 says, God is the Father of compassion and the God of all comfort who comforts us in all our troubles.

Dear God forgive me when I get caught up in negative feelings and a bad mood. I bring to you my problems and concerns and ask you to give me the peace and joy of knowing and loving you. I pray that I will not give in to negative feelings and sulk. I raise my hands and praise you as the Almighty God and the Prince of Peace. Amen.

139

What God Requires Of Us
Micah 6:8

This is a very simple verse that we probably don't come across very often. It tells us what God requires of us; which is to act justly, love mercy and walk humbly with him. Deuteronomy 10:12-13 offers similar requirements of us. It says we are to fear the Lord, walk in his ways, love him, serve him with all our heart and soul and observe his commands. This passage adds that these requirements are for our own good. In a nutshell, his desire for us is a personal, honest relationship of obedience with him. And as is true for all other laws and rules, it is in our best interest to meet these requirements. Why? First, to keep us out of trouble and second, to receive blessings.

We teach our kids that the rules and requirements we establish for them are to keep them safe and out of trouble. Rules are also to establish structure and boundaries of expectation. Some people have problems with rules. They see them as obstacles that take away their freedom. Not true. Where would we be without rules? There would be total chaos.

God establishes requirements of us to protect us from moving in the wrong direction and into temptation, resulting in sin. He still allows us the freedom to make our own choices however we have to face the consequences of our mistakes when we choose not to follow what he desires of us. We miss out on his blessings awaiting our obedience and good choices. In Micah 6:1-7, God is stating his case against Israel for their rebellion and disobedience. The people are miserable and groan at his rebuke. Yet God offers them forgiveness and hope. His offer is the same today for you and me. Spending time with him daily helps us stay on track. Let's be reminded of what God requires of us and seek his help in obediently meeting his expectations so that we receive blessing rather than misery.

Dear God, you require me to act justly, love mercy and walk humbly with you. I want to be obedient and follow your ways. Forgive me of my sin. My desire is to spend time with you daily, so that I am strengthened and prepared for the daily battles of temptation. Thank you for your forgiveness and hope. Amen.

140

Roots
Jeremiah 17:7-8

Why do plants and trees have roots? Why are healthy roots necessary? Roots provide nourishment. Roots provide support. A deep root system keeps the very tall trees from being top heavy and falling over. Roots seek out and store nourishment and water deep in the ground to prevent thirst and starvation. Roots normally are not seen but they are real and evident.

I have seen cement sidewalks and asphalt roads ripped and torn by roots that slowly grow and push aside whatever is in the way.

This passage advises us to develop a root system that is anchored deep in the Lord. Our trust in God brings us confidence like a tree whose roots spread out to provide nourishment and water. The tree has no fear or worry of drought or failure. Our life can be just like that confident tree planted by a stream when we trust in the Lord. Psalm 1:3 offers the same encouragement and promise of prosperity. The psalmist calls a man blessed when he meditates daily and delights in the law of the Lord. We are encouraged to develop a habit of drawing near to God. A habit of trusting him and living in confidence. In this, we will develop a deep root system that will provide us nourishment, support and stability regardless of what obstacles come before us. A root system that will spread deep and strengthen as we grow our relationship with the Lord Jesus Christ. This reminds me of 2 Corinthians 4:8-9 that says we are hard pressed on every side but not crushed, perplexed but not in despair, persecuted but not abandoned and struck down but not destroyed. The tall trees are able to withstand strong winds, hail, rain, snow and even man's construction crews; they are not easily pushed over or taken down because of their strong deep established root system. The same root system that you and I need to withstand temptation and sin. The root system anchored deep in the Lord.

Dear God, thank you for hope and trust that comes from you. I want to develop a habit of drawing near to you. I want a deep root system that is anchored deep in the confidence of knowing you as my God and Savior. Forgive me of my sin and help me to keep my roots nourished by your Holy Word and fed by the living water that you bring me. I put my hope and trust in you, my God. Amen.

141

Helping the Homeless
1 Thessalonians 5:14-15

I witnessed a very interesting thing today. Arriving at work, I came up behind a man entering our building pulling a cart of several bags and carrying two other large canvas bags. It didn't appear to be heavy but awkward to maneuver and it was raining. I did not know him but had seen him before. An older man with a gentle and kind face, I remember thinking. As we got on the elevator together, I mentioned that he seemed to have his hands full. He smiled at me, directed his attention to the load he carried and said that he and his wife fed lunch to the homeless in the park across the street, twice a week. I asked if it was a function of his church. He said no, he and his wife had the vision and started one day a week and now was doing it two days a week and hoped to continue until they did it five days a week. I asked him if anyone helped him with the cost. He replied, some from time to time but they mostly managed on their own – God had provided. He said, it wasn't much, just a sandwich, an apple, a bottle of water and a homemade cookie. As he reached his floor, he stepped off and told me to have a good day. I thought about him all morning with the Bible verse, Be ye kind, ringing in my ear. Believe it or not, I stepped out to run an errand at lunch and as my elevator went down, guess where it stopped and who got on. Yes, it was him again. This time he was bundled up in a rain coat and hat and gloves, pulling the same cart and carrying the bags. We exchanged a smile and said, here we meet again. I said that I hoped it had stopped raining. He said the rain was OK, he just hoped it wasn't too cold. He got off on the Mezzanine and I went on my way. As I left the building, it was raining and I was glad that it wasn't very cold.

He has been on my mind all day. He and his wife are actively showing God's love in a very special way. Sacrificing their time and money, and in the rain!! How many of us are willing to do that? I'm not sure what I will do with this or how God may prod me to move, but I stand in awe of this precious couple's love for Christ and willingness to serve less fortunate strangers. I encourage you to ponder this and ask God to show you what you should do in response.

Dear God, I pray in a special way for this couple. I pray you will provide them the strength and the resources to continue and further their vision. I thank you for their obedience and how it has touched my heart. Forgive me for being too busy to serve you. Help me to always try to be kind to others. Amen.

142

In All That We Do

1 Corinthians 10:31-32

Our Praise Team is discussing worship. We were talking about how our worship and praise of God should be a part of everything we do throughout our day. In this verse, Paul used examples of eating and drinking to illustrate how our most common and everyday activity can and should bring glory and honor to our Lord. Our actions and our choices should never cause anyone to stumble. Non-Christians watch Christians. When we think on glorifying God in everything we do, that shouldn't be a problem. Living to glorify God will result in doing what benefits others, not ourselves.

We have opportunity to give glory to God in more ways than at Sunday worship service. Sometimes we forget that we are to glorify him in all that we do. We can glorify him at home or school or work. Our simplest and most common tasks can bring honor and glory to God. Our attitude should reflect our worship. Attitudes are so contagious, whether positive or negative. How we enter the classroom or meeting speaks an attitude of worship. The way we greet a stranger can reflect our love for God. The way we speak to our friends and family reflects our relationship with God. Let's think about that throughout our day today.

Dear God help me to glorify you in all that I do today. I pray that my attitude and my actions will reflect my relationship with you. I pray that my actions today will not influence anyone negatively or cause someone to stumble. Help me to focus on you in every task today. Amen.

143

Envy
Genesis 4:1-6

Cain was jealous of Abel. It angered him that God favored Abel's offering over his. It was because of Cain's heart that God favored Abel. He could have corrected it but he chose to be envious which turned to hatred which turned to murder and sin. Cain wanted what Abel had and he killed him for it and he suffered for the rest of his life.

Nothing good comes out of envy. Envy leads to anger and to hatred and then to sin. The dictionary defines envy as a feeling of discontent and resentment aroused by another's desirable possessions or qualities accompanied by a strong desire to have them for oneself. James 3:16 says that where there is envy and selfish ambition, there you find disorder and every evil practice. We can't allow such thoughts as... *I wish I was....I wish I was like....I wish I could be...If only I had....If only I was like him....* God created us individually for a reason. He has a plan for each of us. We can't focus on what others have and what others are like until we become totally dissatisfied with ourselves, our family or our life. That dissatisfaction will turn to hate and resentment. Everyone has good qualities. We must remember that goodness comes from the heart not our outward appearance. Changing ourselves for the better is one thing, but being envious of others is wrong. Many young people's lives are ruined because they are determined to be like someone else. God loves us just as he created us. We must not bring unnecessary unhappiness and dissatisfaction into our life because of envy. Proverbs 14:30 says that a heart at peace gives life to the body but envy rots the bones.

Dear God forgive me when I am envious of others. Help me to be content with myself. Help me to find the peace of knowing that you created me like I am for a reason and you have plans for me to prosper. I want to refuse to be envious of others so that I will not become restless and hateful. Thank you for your love for me. Amen.

144

Success
Joshua 1:6-9

Do you want to be successful and prosperous? Of course we do. The answer to being successful is in God's Word. He sets his expectations and reveals the results for us. After Moses died, God put Joshua in his place as the leader of the Israelites. He tells Joshua how to be successful. He commands it.

- Be strong
- Be brave
- Obey all the law
- Read my Word
- Meditate on my Word day and night
- Do what my Word says
- Do not be afraid
- Be confident
- Don't get discouraged

God says to do these things to obtain our inheritance and be successful. These verses clearly tell us what to do and what we get out of it. Find these verses in your Bible and underline them. Prior to these verses and in closing

God says, I will never leave you nor forsake you, the Lord your God will be with you wherever you are. He promises to never leave us and to prosper us if we follow His commands. Have I not commanded you?, he asks. He told Joshua and he is telling us the key to success.

Dear God in heaven, I want to reach the success that you plan for me. I want the inheritance that you prepare for me. I want the prosperous life that you have in mind for me. Help me to be strong and confident in your strength. Thank you for the promise that you will never leave me. The desire of my heart is to keep your commands. Amen.

145

Asking For Wisdom
1 Kings 3:11-12

In this passage King Solomon asked God for a discerning heart to govern his people and to distinguish between right and wrong. He asked for wisdom. My dictionary defines wisdom as the understanding of what is true, right and lasting. This was Solomon's desire. What do we ask God for? Is God pleased with our requests? God was pleased that Solomon asked for wisdom rather than a long life, wealth or victory over his enemies and blessed him with great wisdom. 1 Kings 4:29-34 speaks of Solomon as having great insight and understanding and wiser than any other man. Much of Proverbs was either written by Solomon or linked to his teachings and has much to say about wisdom. He was certainly the expert on wisdom. Proverbs 8:11 says wisdom is more precious than rubies. Proverbs 3:13 says blessed is the man who finds wisdom and 4:7 says wisdom is supreme. Even today many folks still refer to or repeat the proverbs and wise sayings of King Solomon.

God's Word is full of wisdom. The more familiar we are with the scriptures, the better we will understand God's direction regarding what is true and lasting. As we encounter questionable situations and problems that we have no idea where to start in addressing, we should ask God for wisdom.

1 Corinthians 12 speaks of wisdom as a spiritual gift. Certain people are given the gift of the Holy Spirit to wisely discern situations and advise on proper direction and action. We should be careful of where we seek advice to ensure we are listening to the right person and not seeking a certain answer.

Let's ask God for daily discernment and wisdom. If we don't feel very wise ourselves, we have God's Word to advise us and Christian leaders and friends with the gift of wisdom to advise us. Wisdom that is supreme and more precious than rubies.

Dear God I seek you for wisdom and knowledge. Thank you for the wise proverbs that you gave to King Solomon. Help me to realize that following what you say as true and lasting is far better than my own understanding and knowledge. Thank you for being ever present to help me when I seek you for wisdom. When I need personal advice, guide me to those who have the true gift of wisdom from the Holy Spirit. Amen.

146

We Are Not Home Yet
Revelation 21:1-8

These verses give us a glimpse of heaven. We are not home yet. The best is yet to come. Our future is in God's hands. It is believed that John wrote the majority of Revelation. He writes fully convinced that Jesus Christ will triumph over Satan's forces at work. He informs us that we are to be encouraged because the showdown between God and Satan is coming and Satan will be defeated.

I copied these words awhile back in my Bible – author unknown:

Since the fall in the Garden of Eden, we all inherited a sin nature and our tendency is to rebel. But when Jesus returns, he will restore order to a world that has been in chaos against our Creator almost since the beginning. Our only hope must be in someone bigger than ourselves and that hope lies in salvation through Jesus Christ.

As Christians, we will leave this earth to live with God himself for eternity. He prepares a place for us as a bride prepares herself for her groom. There will be no more tears, death, crying, mourning or pain. He will make everything new. However, unbelievers are doomed to eternal suffering. This promise is trustworthy and true.

This week, a 28 year old young lady in our church went to be with the Lord. She suffered with Batten disease. Over time, children with this disease suffer mental impairment, worsening seizures, and progressive loss of sight, speech and motor skills. This was true for Amanda and she loved the Lord. When able, her mother brought her and her sister to worship services. She is with God now in her new body, seeing her Lord face to face with no tears or pain. Praise God. This is what it is all about. Yes we will miss her but we are also very glad that she is with God and we rejoice for her.

Dear God, thank you for your words that are trustworthy and true. I long to be with you. To see you face to face and spend eternity with you. I pray my life has been a blessing to others here on earth that reflects my relationship with you. You are my God and my Savior and I give all praise, glory and honor to you. Amen.

147

Ananias and Sapphira
Acts 5:1-11

What an alarming story. God dealt harshly with these two. He did not tolerate their deceit. Ananias and Sapphira literally dropped dead in their tracks for stealing money from the Lord's work. I can hardly imagine witnessing such an event. It was horrible. This story says a lot about how God feels about a deceitful heart.

In 1Timothy 6:6-10 we are instructed to be content with what we have. A strong desire to get rich quick can lead to destruction and sin. An eagerness for money sends us in the wrong direction which leads to grief. There are two old sayings of truth in this passage that we have all heard – We bring nothing into this world and we can't take anything out with us. And, the love of money is the root of evil. Both statements were certainly true for Ananias and Sapphira. God expects us to work for what we have and to obtain it honestly. I have worked in the social services field for 35 years and there are times when people need a helping hand from the government and there is nothing wrong with that for those who qualify. But we all know that there are those in this world who are willing to cheat or lie to get a few extra bucks or free assistance.

Matthew 6:21 says our heart is where our treasure is. Where is our heart? Is it a heart of faith in God for provision, a heart of honesty, a heart of being content with what we have? Or is it a heart of trying to find a quick way to get rich? Is there a willingness to be jealous and deceitful from discontent with what we have and a strong desire to get what others have? Some people spend part of their weekly pay on the lottery. I'll not get into my belief on gambling but I have heard that a person has a better chance of getting struck by lightening than winning the lottery. Why not take that extra money each week and set it aside in a savings account and watch it add up? Why not ask God to help us spend wisely and provide for us when we have a need? That could be a better plan.

Dear Lord thank you for how you provide for me. I want to have a heart of honesty and contentment. I want to trust you for my needs. Help me to teach these truths to my children and set an example for those around me. When I need something extra, help me to trust you for the answers and not trust quick schemes. Thank you for your blessings. Amen.

148

I Can't Do That
Exodus 4:1-17

God has a plan and chooses Moses to carry it out. Moses tries every excuse he can think of. Much of this task included public speaking and it does appear that Moses had some type of speach impediment. It appears they actually get into an argument over Moses' ability and God got angry with him and offered Joshua to help. But we know the story of the roller coaster ride they took for 40 years and were eventually successful through the leadership partnership of God, Moses and Joshua. God's plan was good and perfect.

Do you recall the book you may have read as a child, The Little Engine that Could? I grew up with the 1954 version by Watty Piper. This story comes to my mind. The story of the little engine has been told and retold many times. The underlying theme however is usually the same. Only the little blue engine is willing to try something that neither he nor others thought they could do. While repeating to himself, I think I can, I think I can, he overcomes a seemingly impossible task.

Apparently it didn't occur to Moses at the time that God would be with him and would help him complete the task. When God asks us to do something, he does not desert us. He works in us to accomplish his plan. He provides the strength when we are weak. He is at our side providing the knowledge, ability and resources we need to accomplish the task, whether simple or big. Let's be encouraged that when God whispers a plan to us, that we listen and respond like the little engine. I know I can with God's help. I know I can with God's help. Anything is possible when we join God in accomplishing his plan. Ask God today what you can do for him.

Dear God forgive me when I am hesitant and reluctant to respond to you. Use me to accomplish your plans for today. I am not weak because you are strong. Forgive me when I have failed you. Offer me something to do today that will honor and glorify you. Amen.

149

False Prosperity
Psalm 73

This psalm of Asaph is very relative to today. We see people who do not live in obedience to God obtain wealth and achieve successful lives, while it sometimes seems like those of us who live the Christian life just can't seem to get ahead. Asaph envied the success of the wicked. It appeared to him that they had no struggles, were strong and had healthy bodies and were free from common struggles and burdens. We see the rich and famous, smiling for the cameras without a care in the world. Many of us, especially our youth, want to be just like them. Asaph felt like his efforts of obedience and righteousness were in vain. He was really letting it get to him and eat at him. Then, in verse 17 he turns his focus back to God and has a complete change of attitude. His thoughts were depressing and disturbing until he entered the sanctuary of God. He realized that the wicked lives were without foundation and recognized how easily they would fall. He reminded himself that God was the strength of his heart and his relationship with God was worth more than earthly things had to offer. He decides that he is very glad to be near to God and again recognized God as his refuge.

Sometimes we let negative thoughts take over our mind and we lose our focus on the truth. The truth is that those who do not believe and recognize God as Lord and Savior may be getting ahead temporarily in earthly value but will eventually be destroyed and swept away. Their success and earthly wealth will not save them when they meet their Maker. As Asaph says, my flesh and my heart may fall but God is the strength of my heart and my portion forever. Let's lock onto those words - my flesh and my heart may fall but God is the strength of my heart and my portion forever. The Lord gives us life. He is our life. Don't let the smiles and flashy glitter fool you. Our Lord will return. Every knee will bow and confess him as Lord. Every unforgiven sin will be addressed one at a time, person by person. Do not let Satan convince you that your life of obedience in Christ is in vain. My flesh and my heart may fall but God is the strength of my heart and my portion forever.

Dear God forgive me when I desire earthly success and wealth as the wicked have. Help me to keep my focus on you and your promises and throw out negative thoughts from my mind. It is hard when I struggle and others never seem to have problems like I do. You are my strength. I come before you and bow to you as the Lord of my life. You promise blessings for living in obedience. My desire is to live to please you. Amen.

150

The Cost Of the Gift
Luke 21:1-4

Many of us learned this Bible story as a child in Sunday School or Vacation Bible School. God is not as impressed with the size of the gift as he is the cost. God knew the heart of the rich man's gift. He knew that the amount he gave was a small sacrifice to pay out of his wealth. I was taught as a child, that when the rich man placed his offering in the treasury box, probably made of brass or metal, he made sure it made a lot of noise to get the attention of others. The small coins that the widow gave were probably most of what she had and were given with a humble heart. God knew that in her heart she was willing to make a great sacrifice knowing that the Lord would provide for her.

How much of a sacrifice are we willing to give the Lord? Do we give the best of what we have or do we give what is left over? I've heard someone say that they can't give because they have nothing left after they pay their bills. I personally believe that if the offering is paid before the bills with faith that God will provide, there would be enough left for an offering **and** to pay the bills. It's not the amount but what it costs us. The widow gave out of her poverty not her wealth. My father taught us that we were to give the Lord the first portion of our earnings, not what was left after what we needed or wanted. God wants a gift from the heart. He wants a gift from a heart of faith and love and obedience. Let's think about it the next time we have an opportunity to give. Let's ask ourselves, what did this really cost me?

Dear Lord thank you for the many blessings you give me. Help me to give from the heart. Help me to give to you an offering of an honest sacrifice. I will search my heart for what you would have me give and I will give it cheerfully and in humble faith like this widow. Amen.

151

God Stays the Same
James 1:17

This is a great passage but let's focus on a few words in verse 17. God the heavenly Father does not change like shifting shadows. We change. Some days we're up and some days we're down and some days we're not sure. Yes we change and our relationship with God each day sometimes depends on how we feel that day. God feels the same everyday. He loves us and is there for us everyday regardless of how we feel. He does not change. This is a wonderful promise full of hope and trust. God remains faithful. He does not lie and does not change his mind about us.

Hebrews 13:8 says that Jesus Christ is the same yesterday and today and tomorrow. The story is old but it never changes. So if you think God has changed and stepped away from you, think again. You are the one who has changed and stepped away. Draw near to God and seek him. His promises are true and can be trusted. Lamentations 3:23 provides the words for the hymn we love, "Great is Thy Faithfulness". I often keep this song in my head throughout the day to remind me of my faith and hope in God.

> Great is thy faithfulness, O God my Father.
> There is no shadow of turning with thee.
> Thou changest not, thy compassions, they fail not,
> as thou hast been, thou forever will be.
> Great is thy faithfulness! Great is thy faithfulness!
> Morning by morning new mercies I see. All I
> have needed thy hand hath provided;
> Great is thy faithfulness, Lord unto me!

Dear God forgive me when I step away from you. Forgive me when I let go of my trust in you. You are the same yesterday and today and tomorrow and my hope rests in you. Help me to capture negative thoughts and throw them away. Help me to focus on the promises of truth in your Word. Thank you for your unfailing love for me. Amen.

152

That's What It's All About
Philippians 4:6-7

I saw a bumper sticker one morning that made me laugh out loud. It said, What if the Hokey Pokey is really what it's all about? Do you know the song, the Hokey Pokey? It is a very silly song that many kids sing and maybe adults as well.

….You put your hand in, you take your hand out, you do the hokey pokey and you turn yourself around and that's what it's all about…..

There really is not much to the song except an opportunity to move around and have fun. Is that what life is all about to some of us? I am afraid so. I am afraid that is what it is all about for someone who does not have faith and hope in our Lord Jesus Christ.

When we know Jesus Christ as our Savior we can rejoice in all things. We are gentle in spirit. We are forgiven. We don't have to be anxious about anything because in prayer and thanksgiving we can give all of our concerns and needs to the Lord and not worry about them anymore. By this, we are blessed with peace that rises above all understanding that will guard our hearts and minds. This is available to anyone who accepts it. Freedom and peace. Some days I am better at living this than others. But the promise never changes and will never be rescinded. I may change based on how I feel but God's promises never change. This is what it is all about.

Thank you Lord for your many promises. You are good to me all the time. My hope and trust is in you. Remind me every day of the joy that comes with my salvation and that I should live it every day. Forgive me when I allow thoughts of hopelessness and fear to enter my mind. You are a gracious God of provision and I love you. Amen.

153

Our Hope Is An Anchor
Hebrews 6:13-20

An anchor is a heavy object attached to a vessel by a cable and cast overboard to keep the vessel in place. An anchor must be strong and heavy enough to hold the vessel in calm or stormy waters. On the aircraft carrier

USS Dwight D. Eisenhower there are two anchors. Each anchor and chain weighs a total of 735,000 pounds. You wonder how the ship floats with such an anchor aboard. Verse 19 in this passage says that we have a firm and secure hope as an anchor for our soul. Like an anchor holding a ship safely in place, our hope in Christ holds us safely in place. Instead of going to the water's depth, our anchor reaches to the heavenly throne of God where Jesus awaits the time to return for us.

You know how I am about old songs. There is a song that is fitting here, "The Anchor Holds". The chorus goes something like this:

The anchor holds though the ship is battered. The
anchor holds though the sails are torn.
I have fallen on my knees as I face the raging seas;
the anchor holds in spite of the storm.

We can picture here, our lives which are battered by problems and difficulties of life, facing the raging storm. Like a torn sail we struggle and feel battered. We fall to our knees seeking God's guidance and acknowledge him as our Lord and Savior. Our anchor of faith and hope holds, in spite of where we are. Our anchor in Jesus Christ provides security and stability and is strong enough to hold us whether the waters are calm or stormy. Praise God for his promises. Hold on, though your waters may be raging. Your anchor is strong and unmovable. We have a hope as an anchor for our soul, firm and secure.

Dear God thank you for the anchor you provide. Thank you that I will hold firm though the storm rages. I can face anything with you by my side, holding me firm and steady. Your promises are marvelous. In you I place my trust forever. Amen.

154

Time For Confession
1 John 1:5 - 2:6

Different things move us to confess but it needs to be a daily thing and a regular part of our time with God. Are we serious about our confession? I'll admit that I often say in my prayers, Please forgive me of my sins and move on to something else. I think we need to take time to be more serious about confession of our sin. Much of the time we know when we have done wrong, didn't do what we should have or allowed a sinful thought into our mind. We often go through our day so routinely that we aren't conscious of a sinful deed. The psalmist in Psalm 139:23-24 asks God to search his heart and show him the sin in his heart. When there is unconfessed sin in our life and unresolved issues with those around us, our relationship with God is not what we claim it to be. We must never think at the end of the day that we have gotten through it with no sin to confess.

The good news is that God is faithful and will forgive our sin when we bring it to him. It is important for me to ask God to help me focus on repentance and find ways to submit myself to obedience, striving to not commit that sin again. Sometimes we struggle with the right words. More good news. We can ask Jesus to speak to the Father for us and in our defense. He knows our heart. He knows when we are being truthful and honest with him. We can hide nothing from him. So to sum this up here are a few suggestions:

1. Confess continually. Thank God for His faithful forgiveness.
2. Ask God to search our heart and remind us of unconfessed sin
3. Be honest. Hold nothing back.
4. Talk to God about the things that are difficult to deal with.
5. Know that Jesus is available to help with our confession.
6. Ask God for help in living obediently after confession.
7. Let it go. There is no condemnation.

Dear God thank you for your grace and mercy. Help me to be serious about confession of my sin. Search my heart and show me my sin. Guide me in spending time with you daily in prayer and confession. I want my relationship with you to be honest and true. Thank you for your love for me. Amen.

155

Authority

Romans 13:1-7

This passage of scripture is written by Paul regarding submission to authority. He tells us not to be tempted to claim allegiance to Christ only and be disrespectful of authority. Government is ordained by God. Authority exists to bring order and protection. As Christians we must respect authority.

When we rebel against authority, we rebel against what God has ordained. Rebellion brings judgment.

Presidents Day, officially known as Washington's Birthday, is a federal holiday and is celebrated on the third Monday of February. Although it has become known as a great weekend for sales, it is a time to honor our current and past presidents and pay tribute to America's most famous leaders. After Washington's death, our nation began celebrating his birthday as a way to remember his life and how he contributed to establishing America's independence. In 1865, America began celebrating Abraham Lincoln's birthday on February 12th. President Richard Nixon combined the two holidays into one and ever since we have honored all past presidents on this day.

It is not always easy to respect authority whether it is our president or our supervisor or our parent. I believe many community problems come from people who do not respect authority or don't want anyone telling them what they can or cannot do. We do not have to agree with authority but we must respect it and we must teach this respect to our youth. Is the example we set, one of respect and honor regardless of how we feel? Let's be encouraged to do what is right and recognize respecting authority as respecting our God.

Dear God, thank you for those who govern me to protect me and bring order to my country and my community. I may not agree with rules or decisions but help me to respect authority as I respect and honor you. Help me to be a good example especially to young people around me. May my attitude toward authority be of gratitude and reverence. Amen.

156

Jesus Understands Loneliness
John 16:32-33

Jesus knew the disciples could not withstand the fear and stress of his coming arrest, trial and death. He knew he would be left alone, however he also knew that his Heavenly Father would be with him. Jesus knew he would have victory over the pain and death. His Word assures us that we will have troubles. But not to worry Jesus says, for he has overcome the world. When we trust in his victory, we will have peace and victory in our own lives. Jesus assures us of victory when we follow God's plan for us.

When we have problems, one of the first things we feel is loneliness. Jesus knows how this feels. He went through the suffering all alone. We can draw to him and ask for his comfort and peace. We never need to say, no one else knows how we feel. We can speak directly to him, telling him of our problems and fears. He longs for us to share our burdens with him and allow him to work through them for us. Jesus has suffered just as we have. He knows rejection, he knows sadness and he knows grief. Psalm 62:5-8 reminds us that we can find rest and hope in God alone. He is all we need. Yes, we also have hope in our friends and family but I have learned that by first putting my trust in God, I can find the peace that I need to get through life's struggles. Through my trust in him, I can learn to trust those around me who I need to trust. We can depend on him to answer our requests. Be encouraged today to tell Jesus what concerns you. Don't tell him how you want it resolved. Let him do that. Tell him all about it and sit back and watch him work. Jesus came to earth to save us but also to experience life as a human to give us assurance that he knows and he understands what we have to deal with. Trust in him at all times. Pour out your heart to him, for he is our refuge.

Dear God thank you for caring for me. I lay my fears at your feet and ask for you to resolve them for me. I will accept your way as best. I cannot do this alone. I need you to guide me and to show me the way. You are my hope. You are my refuge. I thank you now for how you will deal with these fears and show me your perfect plan for me. Forgive me when I doubt you. Thank you for your love for me. Amen.

157

Contentment
Philippians 4:12-13

Yesterday I got a lesson in contentment. My husband and I decided to go to the mountains for the week end. As usual I did the packing and gathered everything in the den for my husband to load in the car. I always complain about having to do all the packing but then I am the person who has to have everything and anything I might need when I travel. I take everything I could possibly need. I had put most of our stuff, everything of mine, in a larger suitcase. I put his extra jeans and sweaters in a smaller bag. We get to the rented cabin and start unloading. I notice that the only suitcase in the bedroom is the small one. I asked him where the other one was and he was not aware of another one. Obviously the other suitcase was still at home. We stood and glared at each other. We had left that large bag at home. He immediately offered to make the 3 hour trip back home to get it. I sat down for a minute and pondered the situation. That would give me six hours of reading time alone. Yes! It was his fault that everything did not get in the car, right? He went into the bathroom. I sat on the couch and said, Lord what do we do? I had nothing but the clothes on my back and my bag of books and computer. We decided to make a list and go to the store to purchase what I really needed. We can always use an extra pair of underwear and socks, right? Besides, it was a holiday week-end and everything was on sale. As I sit here this morning and ponder yesterday, I am thankful for several things.

I am thankful that he offered to drive 6 hours to get me my things. Granted he needed a few things but he had clothes, I did not. I am thankful that we were wise enough not to allow this to erupt into a finger pointing argument and ruin our trip. I am thankful we purchased almost everything we needed at half price. I am thankful we were financially able to make that unexpected purchase. I am thankful that these bedroom shoes that I found on sale for $3 are more comfortable than the ones in the suitcase sitting at home.

Life changes direction everyday. Some changes are heart shattering and others are minor but seem huge for a moment. Romans 8:28 tells us that in all things God works for the good of those who trust him. Sometimes life calls for flexibility and God will have something for us to learn in it. God is in control. We should be content in all situations and thankful for what comes our way. There is always something to be grateful for. God will not allow more than we can bear. He is always with us. He never sleeps and he never turns his head from us. We simply need to be mindful that God knows what we need and will provide for us. He gives us the strength to move through any situation and we give him the honor and glory.

Dear Lord thank you for the way you provide for me. Thank you for the strength you give me to live each day in your promises of provision. I can do all things in your strength. I love you Lord and I praise your name. Amen.

158

Do Not Be Afraid
Deuteronomy 7:17-26

The Old Testament is full of wonderful stories and promises. Some people lean on the New Testament, which is fine, but I love the Old Testament. It always applies to us in different ways even though the stories took place many years ago. The people long ago had trials just like we do. They had enemies just like we do and they had temptations that often misplaced their trust. Look through this passage. Who are the nations, the people, the trials and wild animals that we fear? We can face them with the promise that the Lord our God is among us and he is great and awesome. What do we have to fear? Do we keep our eyes on God or do we allow fear to consume us? Maybe we have allowed other gods into our lives that distract us from the One who can help us. Maybe material things have become too important to us and this passion impairs our vision and the truth.

Look at verses 7-16 earlier in this passage. God chose us because he loves us and wants to bless us and the generations that come after us. God is faithful. Each time he gives us a law it is an opportunity for a blessing. He knows what is best and offers it to us. He chooses us. He wants to love us. He wants us to trust him and live in obedience. He offers blessing for obedience. He knows that it is for our own good that he commands us not to have other gods before him. When our eyes and our focus is on something else, it is not on him. Trust him today. Trust him in everything. As verse 12 tells us, the Lord will keep his covenant of love when we focus on him and do not fear.

Dear God thank you for your faithfulness. Thank you for your truth and your blessings. We love you and adore you. We choose your way and your promises. Forgive me when I stray from you and your truth. Help me to fear nothing. You are all I need to get through these days. Thank you for your unfailing love for me. Amen.

159

God Is Good
Genesis 1:31

I sit here in our rented cabin and I think to myself, 'It doesn't get better than this. God is good'. We still don't know where that suitcase is but it is a beautiful morning and I have everything I need. It is very cold outside and a few snow flurries yet the sun peaks out brightly and shines through my window. My husband is asleep in the chair but atleast he has made it out of bed!! A fire is burning and the coffee is good. I sit in my new pajamas with my Bible, doing what I love best, writing of my love for my Lord and sharing it with you. Oh yes, there are still family issues and other problems we left at home but God is good. He is right here with us, closer than ever in these glorious mountains. I can think of no where else I would rather be. I am content with this day and praise my Lord for it.

Stop for a minute and look around. What do you have to be grateful for today? Be thankful. God sees what he has made and it is very good. Isaiah 26:3 tells us that God brings peace to those whose mind is certain of him and trusts in him. He made everything about this day. He made the things that we find marvelous in his sight and he knows of the things that bring us concern. When we keep our focus on him, he brings peace. A peace that nothing else can match. Look around you and see the goodness of our Lord. Feel the peace and warmth in your heart because of his promises and his faithfulness. God sees what he has made and it is very, very good.

Dear God thank you. Such simple words for a tremendous God. You are just and you are faithful. You bring peace we can find nowhere else. You are the maker of all things and it is good. I give you my heart and I ask for your forgiveness of my sin. I love you Lord and I praise your name. Amen.

160

Facing the Consequences
Acts 5:17-42

To start out for those of you who have read the past couple days, the suitcase was in the bedroom right where I left it as I was packing. I never zipped it up. I guess I was distracted and never took it to the den. Oh well. I certainly will remember this when packing again.

We all make decisions everyday. Some greatly affect us and some are minor. Some will affect the rest of our lives while others only affect the next few minutes. Sometimes I tire of making decisions. After a long day at work, I don't even want to decide where I want to go for dinner and I say, 'just take me somewhere. I don't want to make another decision.' Do you feel that way sometimes? I think we often make it harder on ourselves than it has to be.

Every decision we make has consequences. I heard yesterday on a TV Bible study that when we take our decisions to God and follow his guidance in obedience, the consequences are his. When we make our own decisions the consequences are ours.

This is a cool story. In this passage, Peter and the apostles had a decision to make. They were released from jail by God and were told to continue their preaching. They were in jail for preaching to start with. There were consequences for their decision. If they continued to preach as God told them to, they would face the consequences of the high priest. If they decided not to preach anymore, they would face the consequences of disobedience to God. God had a plan. Peter and the apostles knew that obedience to God would bring them under his protection and blessings. Yes, they may suffer by the hand of men but they knew that obeying God would bring blessing and favor. Gamaliel was so right when he said that if their purpose was from God, it couldn't be stopped anyway. The apostles rejoiced in their experience and opportunity to please God.

Even when wrong decisions are made, God still has a way to accomplish his purpose. He longs to guide us and help us with our decisions. He will always answer. Sometimes the answer comes quickly and sometimes the answer is to wait but the answer always comes. Peace always comes. In my experience, when I ask God for guidance, the consequences are favorable and praiseworthy. When I rely on myself the outcome is not as favorable. Let's be encouraged to seek God's guidance first, in all our decisions and follow him in obedience. Let's think of the consequences before making a decision on our own. I believe God's consequences are worth waiting for.

Dear God I know you have a plan for me and have a desire for me to prosper. Forgive me when I rely on myself when making decisions. I want to rely on you in all things. I know that the consequence of obedience to you brings blessing and favor. I want to live my life within your will for me. Thank you for your love for me. Give me a heart of commitment to read your Holy Word each day and stay near to you. Amen.

161

An Earnest Request Of God
Psalm 25

I often pray Psalm 25. A few years ago, I started marking scripture that touched my heart, with the date that I read it. Since April 2003 I have this passage marked eleven times as a prayer for someone in my family. Today I prayed it for other issues in my life that are overwhelming and cause me anxiousness. This passage is my earnest request of God and it always, always brings me peace. It helps me put my hope in the right place. Only God can release me from the snares of worry and frustration. As I finish the passage, I do not understand why the issues are here nor do I have an answer from God as to how he will deal with them but I do have a peace and hope in knowing that all his ways are loving and faithful. We have many enemies. Most of the time the enemy is Satan trying to bring confusion and hopelessness. Sometimes the enemy is the consequences of bad decisions made on our own. Decisions made quickly without seeking God's guidance and following in obedience. Sometimes the enemy is illness or exhaustion. God can rescue us from anything. God is our refuge. The last verse ends my request with, My hope is in you O lord. Redeem me O Lord, from all my troubles.

God is waiting for our requests of him. He longs to be our refuge and our help in times of need. What a marvelous hope we have in him. Be encouraged to read this passage out loud. Pray it to our Lord. Speak out to him your individual needs and troubles within the passage. Make it your own request of God. He is waiting. He is listening. He is our hope.

My hope is in you O lord. Redeem me O Lord, from all my troubles. I know you are faithful and all your ways are loving. You know my needs before I even speak them but I know you want to hear my requests and the desires of my heart. Guide me in your truth. I lift up my soul to you and in you I trust. Amen.

162

Our Appearance
Isaiah 58

This is one of those passages that steps on our toes. While God is rebuking the people for their half hearted fasting, it reminds me of our general appearance, inward and outward. We can apply this to honorable fasting but I see it also applicable to our lifestyle and unspoken desires and thoughts that are not hidden from God. He knows our heart. It is easy to make a good outward appearance but we really have to work hard on our inward appearance that God sees and knows.

How do others see us? Do those around us know that we are a Christian? Does our language, our actions, our lifestyle reflect our love of God? Verse 2 makes me cringe to hear God suggest that we may *seem* eager for his nearness. Seem? While subtle, it is harsh. God sees the inside and the outside. The inside is what worries me. Do my prayers and my actions only *seem* to be honest and obedient? Do we fast or commit to him yet do as we please (verse 3)? And does God mumble at our commitment saying, Is that what you call…..? (verse 5). Let's stop here and search our heart. God longs for a heart of truth and honesty and actions that show his love to others. We ask him to search our heart. We better be careful when we ask that of him. We might need to do some heart cleaning before we ask.

As usual, God is faithful with his promises of blessings like a well watered garden and a plentiful inheritance. He always has a consequence for us. We reap blessings from obedience. We find joy in obedience and commitment. The darkness we feel turns to the brightness of the noon sun. Great is the faithfulness of our God. His forgiveness and mercy is everlasting.

Dear God guide me in a search of my heart and my actions. Show me what I need to get rid of. Show me what I need to do. I want to be obedient and pleasing to you. I want you to find favor in me. Forgive me of my sin and help me to be constantly aware of the thoughts I allow into my mind and the desires of my heart. Help me to be loving and kind to those around me. I want my commitment to you to be true and honest. Amen.

163

Giving It Up
Genesis 22:1-18

This is one of those stories that is often difficult for us to understand. Why would God ask Abraham to give up his only son? A couple things in this passage touched me today just when I needed it. In verse 12 God stops Abraham. God realized that Abraham was not withholding anything from him. He was willing to act in total obedience regardless of what he may be losing. God did provide the sacrifice in place of Issac. Verse 14 tells us that Abraham named the place The Lord Will Provide. How I would love to go there and touch the ground. God did provide and he promised to bless Abraham for his obedience. Not just blessings, but blessings that none of us can even imagine. Blessings that would out number the stars in the sky and the sand on the seashore. And Abraham's blessing would affect many people after him.

Today I struggle with a problem that I thought was resolved but it comes to surface again. I ask God, Why?. My daily Bible reading led me to this passage. I thought I had drawn closer to God during these times of trouble but I see that there is more I can give. I can spend more time with him. I can seek his advice more. I can act in obedience and not in my own way. I search my heart today and ask God to reveal what more can I give. What am I withholding? Am I allowing him to be in control? No matter what I have to give up, God will provide. He will make a way for me. Some might say that God asked too much of Abraham. Will God ask that much of me? Go back to the passage and read the whole story. Whatever God asks of us, he will provide and promises blessings in response to our obedience. Blessings that provide more than we had before. We have nothing to lose when we follow God and are obedient to his calling. We only have something to gain; more to gain. I have a magnet on my refrigerator that says, God never closes a door without opening another. That is exactly what he did here for Abraham and is willing to do for us.

Dear God show me what more I can give. I do not want to withhold anything from you. I want to live in obedience. Give me strength and confidence to trust you with everything. Help me to be just like Abraham, willing to act in total obedience without fear of what I could lose. I believe your promises and I commit my life to you. Show me clearly what I need to do. Thank you for your love for me. Amen.

164

Peace
Proverbs 2:6-8

Worry, anxiousness and confusion come unexpectedly. When it comes, I find it hard to focus on anything and want to crawl in bed under a blanket. Today instead, I go to the Lord and seek his wisdom. I find confidence in his promises. Verse 7 says he holds victory in store for those who trust in him.

I also look to Job 27:2-6. If anyone knew worry, anxiousness and confusion, it was Job. Even his friends encouraged him to give up his faith and confidence in the Lord. When I read these verses, I can see him standing with his eyes to the heavens, fist clenched, speaking with a voice as strong as he could muster. Then again, maybe he said it quietly with conviction in a whisper. Sometimes we listen more to a quiet voice than a loud one. Job was basically saying that he would not deny his Lord. We need to exhibit the same firm stand with a convicted confidence in God and his sovereignty. Satan will try to convince us that we should give in to our weakness and lose our hope in God. But Satan is a liar and a looser for sure. Our confidence comes from God and we should stand firm and not give in to the worry, anxiousness and confusion. Hold on to the promises in Proverbs 2. Strive for Job's confidence in chapters 27 and 28 of Job. Peace will come. We can anticipate it and welcome it. Peace that comes only from our Lord.

Dear God help me to ignore the worry, anxiousness and confusion that life can bring. Help me to ignore Satan's lies and confusion. Help me to trust in you in all things. You promise victory for me and I believe you and find confidence in your Word. Forgive me when I allow thoughts contrary to your promises to enter my mind. My hope is in you. My strength comes from you. Help me to hold fast and stand firm to my belief. Amen.

165

A Still Small Voice
1 Kings 19:11-12

I have been dealing with a family relationship for the past year. We have greatly benefited from six months of counseling, learning how to communicate and work through the simple things and the difficult. Just when I thought we had crossed the finish line and were home free of the problem, it came up again. Last night I went to bed with a very heavy heart, worried about the situation.

When I woke this morning, I anxiously got up, made coffee and went to my quiet place for time with the Lord. My devotion led me to this passage. I wrote in my prayer journal my frustrations with the situation. Why do I have to be the one that makes the effort? The other person had withdrawn and just was not trying. No sooner than I wrote the words, God spoke to me quietly. He said very clearly, You don't have to handle this, give it to me and let me handle it. Trust me, he said. I went back and read the passage again. Frustration and fear had come because I was allowing my mind to focus on fixing the situation myself rather than giving it to the Lord. There was too much noise and worry in my head to hear him. Only when I went to him in a quiet way did I hear the gentle whisper from God. Elijah did the same thing. He was focusing on the problem and his fear, rather than talking to

God about it. It was in a quiet whisper that Elijah and I found the peace that only God can bring. My Mom's Bible calls it a still small voice. I later came across Psalm 31:15 that assures me that my times are in God's hand. My day then started with hope and confidence that God was in control. If I had done this before I went to bed last night, I imagine I would have slept much better. I will sleep well tonight.

Dear God thank you for wanting to handle my problems for me. Thank you for the peace and hope that you bring. Forgive me when I give in to fear and lies of the enemy. I trust in you and find my hope in you. Amen.

166

Who Are You, Lord?
Acts 9:1-6

Chapter 9 of Acts is the story of Paul's miraculous conversion. I say miraculous because it was something that only God could do. Paul's life changed from a commitment to kill and persecute as many Christians as he could, to preaching God's plan of salvation to as many people as he could. Instead of persecuting the Christians he encouraged Christianity. Paul's life took a different direction. I am challenged to ask the same question Paul did, Who are you, Lord?. In Psalm 71:19, the psalmist asks, Who O God is like you?.

Life is hard. Problems come and go and often resurface again. We come to a crossroad just as Saul did. Which way do we go? Which way do we turn? The answer is the same for us as for Saul. Get up and listen for direction. Maybe we need to change direction; maybe even as drastic as for Saul or maybe not but we must be willing. We need to be willing to listen for instruction. Willing to follow in obedience. God did not immediately tell Saul what the plan was. We must be willing to wait as well. Saul knew he was in the presence of something far beyond what he had imagined. He recognized the truth. He was willing to follow the light from heaven. He was willing to change direction. Am I?

Dear God show me the direction I am to take. Help me to trust you completely with everything. I want to have a willingness to change direction if I need to. I want a willingness to wait for your instruction. Who are you, Lord? Who O God is like you? Show me the way. Show me the truth. Amen.

167

Favor With God
Luke 1:26-33

The angel told Mary she had found favor with God. There are others in the Bible that heard the same message – Noah, Abel, Samuel for a few. Does God find favor with me? We profess Jesus Christ as our Lord and Savior and we live as close to his commands as we can. But is there more? Have I asked God, what can I do to find your favor? What can I give up? What can I do more of? What have I neglected to do? In Psalm 90:17 the psalmist says, May the favor of the Lord our God rest upon us and establish the work of our hands. The work of our hands cannot give salvation however the work of our hands can earn us a crown in eternity and help us find favor with God.

This morning there is a desire in my heart to ask God what I can do for him. I come before him with my requests yet today I praise him and seek his favor. I search my heart and ask what can I do? What can I give? Today I change my focus from what God can do for me to how can I find favor.

Dear God I praise you today as Lord of my life. My desire is to find favor with you. Search my heart and show me your desire for me. I humble myself before you. Give me courage to hear you and follow you. There are things I selfishly want to keep but my desire is to please you and follow your will for me, not for blessings but for favor. Thank you for your unfailing love for me. Amen.

168

Learning To Love
Matthew 7:7-12

At a community re-entry facility in Rockwell City, Iowa, neglected animals and prison inmates soon to be released are helping each other prepare to return to society. Rescued horses are rehabilitated by prisoners to get healthy and to have their faith restored in people after suffering neglect and abuse at human hands. In return, the inmates are given the opportunity to learn selfless character by adopting responsibilities of caring for someone other than themselves and forming bonds of compassion, with human and animal, teaching each other to care.

The Golden Rule says we are to treat others the same as we want to be treated. We often fall into the hands of those who cause harm leaving scars that make it difficult to trust others and often turn their victim into a hateful person. While the program in Iowa is a wonderful idea and opportunity to help man and animal, we can find healing and learn to love through a relationship with our Lord Jesus Christ. In our busy lives, anger can come quickly. We often miss opportunity to treat someone as we want to be treated and allow them to see the love of Jesus Christ in us. Look at verse 1 in this chapter. We often treat others poorly because we think they are less than us and of little value. That's probably why those horses were mistreated but people are treated that way too. God loves us each the same. We must strive to love each other and treat everyone as the Golden Rule challenges us.

Dear God thank you for this simple truth. Our world would be so different if everyone followed the Golden Rule. I pray for this program in Iowa. I pray that it thrives and I also pray for the inmates; that someone will cross their path and teach them of your promises of love. Give me courage today to treat everyone that crosses my path as I want to be treated. Give me an opportunity today to show someone your love. Amen.

169

Sharing With Those In Need
Hebrews 13:15-16

The January 12, 2010 Haiti earthquake measured 7.0 on the Richter scale which identifies it as a major earthquake that would cause serious damage over large areas. This earthquake caused severe damage and casualties in the Port-au-Prince area. It was felt throughout Haiti and the Dominican Republic, in Turks and Caicos Islands, Cuba, Jamaica, Puerto Rico and the Bahamas and as far as Tampa, Florida and Caracas, Venezuela. Many of us watched the devastation on TV however still cannot imagine the magnitude of the loss and suffering. What can we do in such situations and what can we learn from it? First we can give. I have been convicted to go through my closets and give the clothes that I don't need or wear anymore.

I am embarrassed to say that this task resulted in three large trash bags of clothes and shoes. Yesterday I was in a book store and at the checkout I heard the clerk asking folks if they wanted to give to the Red Cross for the Haiti earthquake. As I waited my turn, I looked down at what I had. There was nothing there that I really, really needed. I was convicted to give as much as I was spending. The clerk was shocked and said I was the first to give that much. I was again embarrassed. Why? Because I have so much and live here in my world of few serious problems, never having experienced such a disaster as these people. This scripture says, do not forget to do good. I should not forget that there are many in need. I should not have to be reminded to share what I have with others. I should be sharing with others all the time not just in the time of a disaster. I plan to look for ways to share with those around me in need without waiting for the conviction to come.

Secondly, there is something else to learn from this. 2 Peter 3:10 says the Lord will return like a thief. In other words, the Lord will return when we least expect it. Those folks in Haiti who lost their life, never knew they would not see another day and now they stand before our God. Are we ready? Is our relationship with the Lord where it should be so that we are prepared for his unexpected return? Are there things we need to do? Are there things we need to surrender? This brings an opportunity for us to search our hearts and evaluate our commitment to our Lord. Let's not let it pass us by.

Dear God help me to give up selfish ways and be willing to share with others. Give me opportunity to share. I pray for a heart of compassion for others. You have blessed me in so many ways and there is so much I can give. I pray my relationship is right with you. I pray I am prepared to meet you face to face. Forgive my sin and show me what I need to surrender so that I am fully committed to you. I love you Lord and I thank you for your love for me. Amen.

170

He Cares For Me

Naham 1:7

Today I felt overwhelmed by life. Family issues, a hectic job and a medical problem (not serious but uncomfortable). I couldn't seem to work anything out and got to the point that I was in a panic. Everyway I turned was a brick wall. I had to stop and pray. I cried out to God, I can't handle this. I need you. The words of my prayer came easily.

God I need you. I know you love me and I know you care about me. This day is now out of control and I need to let you take control. Please help me take this day minute by minute trusting you.

I went out on the back porch and sat down in the rocking chair. I immediately felt a sense of peace. A couple thoughts of direction came to me and I followed them. I had already planned lunch with my sweet daughter who seemed to sense my mood. Our time together was simple and just what I needed. We later strolled through a gift shop and chatted. I came across a beautiful painting of birds in a tree captioned, His eyes are on the sparrow.

It was God who delivered me this morning. He provided the refuge that I needed. The family issues are still here, the job is still busy and the medical issue is still with me (but I do now have drugs for it). I have a peace in knowing that God cares about me and he is in control. He does not make life perfect but he walks with me through the day and helps me to handle it minute by minute. God is good and he cares for those who trust in him. Take this as a witness, cry out to God and let him take control. He cares for us when we trust in him just like he cares for the birds in the trees. He may not immediately fix all our problems but he cares how we feel and he does not want us in a panic. He wants to control each minute by providing the peace and contentment that we need for the day.

Dear God, thank you for the peace you bring. Thank you for caring for me. You are my refuge in times of trouble and when I am in need. Help me to trust you in each minute of every day. Amen.

171

Tug Of War
Ephesians 3:16-21

Tug of War is a great outdoor game for a group. We played tug of war or the tug rope game at youth events, usually boys against girls. And the boys didn't always win. It's a fun way to encourage teamwork, break the ice, or just have some good old fashioned fun. Each team tries to pull the other team across a mark. The team that gets pulled over the mark loses. It occurred to me today that I often play tug of war with God. Sometimes I allow him to be in control and others times I pull away on my own. Sometimes I trust him and other times I trust my own plan. Sometimes I hold on to things I shouldn't and other times I submit them to him. As I said, we play tug of war with him.

Psalm 56:4 says, I trust the God who I praise; I will not be afraid. We can rest in the peace of knowing that God wants to be in control of our lives. We can stop pulling on the tug rope, cross the mark and follow his lead. There is no need to tug and pull or strain to gain control or struggle to gain level footing. It's like trying to drive a car with a foot on the brake and a foot on the gas. Just like I've been known to ride a horse. The difficult ride gets us nowhere really fast. God wants to carry our burdens. He wants to lead as we follow. Our strength comes from him. Things may not always flow smoothly but God is with us all the way and brings an awesome peace as no one else or nothing else can bring. God is our peace. Psalm 32:10 says the Lord's unfailing love surrounds the man who trusts in him. Put down the tug rope and follow him.

Dear God thank you for your love for me. I long to trust you in everything but sometimes I try my own way. Forgive me when I hesitate in following you or try to trust myself. You are the truth and the way. I praise you and I trust you. Amen.

172

I Will Not Fear
Psalm 23

Our church offers Upward Basketball to kids. At each game there is a time of devotion during half time for parents and friends attending the game. Tomorrow is my turn to provide the devotions for the afternoon games. You probably think this is very easy for me as I write these devotions. I can simply pick one. But I want to be sure that I speak what God wants these folks to hear. This evening as I prepare, I ask God what they need to hear. The answer comes quickly. God wants these folks to know that he is our shepherd, he is with us and we have nothing to fear. There will not be one person there, myself included, who doesn't have a problem, fear or worry on their mind. Some do not know Jesus as their Lord and Savior and have no hope.

I read quietly through Psalm 23 and my heart is full. The Lord is my shepherd. He leads me. He restores me. He guides me. He comforts me. I have no fear for he is with me. Because God is my Savior, I will dwell with him forever. Life is hard. Life has many difficulties and troubles. But the Lord is our shepherd. We need nothing else and have nothing to fear. Our hope and our trust is in God. No matter what you face today, God loves us and longs to be our shepherd. Read through this psalm and absorb the love and care of your shepherd.

Dear Lord thank you for being my shepherd. Thank you for caring for me. Give me courage to face each day knowing that I am under your protection. Lead me. Restore me. Guide me. Comfort me. I have no fear for you are with me. Amen.

173

We Are His Sheep
Psalm 23:1-4

I am still on Psalm 23. We rarely hear today of someone having the occupation of a shepherd, at least not in the Midlands of South Carolina. David appropriately describes the Lord as our shepherd. A shepherd lives with this flock. He knows each one and can identify his own even when mingled in with another flock. He provides for them and he protects them. He will leave the flock to find a lost one. The sheep know the shepherd's voice and will run to it when called. Did you know that sheep aren't very smart animals? One will follow another anywhere, over a cliff or into a ditch. They eat when they aren't hungry and what they shouldn't. They are easily frightened and run away, often toward their predator. A sheep can lay down a certain way and can't get up on its own. The shepherd has to watch for a 'cast down' sheep and help it back onto its feet. Sheep need a shepherd. Does any of this sound familiar? Can you identify with these sheep? I think we are alot like sheep. We sometimes do some really dumb things.

The Lord is our shepherd and we are his sheep. In John 10:27, Jesus says that his sheep hear his voice and he knows them each one. We all need a shepherd. We must recognize the Lord as our shepherd. We must recognize that we need shepherding. We need his protection from the many predators in our world, mainly Satan. The Lord will lead us by the still waters and protect us through the dark valleys. We need shepherding just like those not-so-smart sheep. Ask the Lord to be your shepherd. Let's read it one more time.

Dear God help me to recognize your voice and follow you as my shepherd. I trust you to provide everything I need and protect me from predators. Surely goodness and mercy will follow me and I will dwell with you forever. Amen.

174

Specific Requests Of God
Jude 1:17-25

I heard someone say today, Specific requests are God's specialty. That has stuck with me all day. What do you pray for? Do you only pray for big things? Do you sometimes feel like you bother God with your many requests? This statement reminds me that God is interested in every detail of my life. He longs to hear my specific requests and concerns. Think about your best friend and how you talk freely, sharing your secret desires and needs. Specific requests are God's specialty. God is our best friend. He gave his Son as the ultimate sacrifice so that we no longer have to offer a sacrifice for forgiveness or have the priest enter in his presence and speak for us. We now have an open line to God and he wants to hear from us. He wants to hear our secret desires and needs. He wants to hear specifics.

Dear God thank you for your presence in my life. Help me to speak to you specifically as a friend, even though you are the King. Help me to trust you with my desires and needs. I know that you provide for me and take an interest in the details of my life. Help me to trust you in all things. Amen.

175

Setting Standards
Proverbs 4:20-27

This morning I read a brief article about two parents that made the decision when their son was fifteen, he would not be allowed to have single dates with a girl. They decided if he became interested in a girl, he was to first bring her home for meals, games or outings with them. Then they could possibly move to group outings with friends but except for special occasions he was not to spend time alone with her. These parents spent many hours in prayer about this decision and then sat him down and explained it to him. While he was resistant at first, six months later he complied and brought a young lady home for pizza and a movie.

When I first read this I thought, Gosh, how strict and difficult for the son. Then I thought on teen pregnancies, drugs, underage drinking, DUI, etc., and with shame realized my original thought was that of the world. These parents could be saving their son's life as well as his girlfriend's. It came to my mind that these folks were doing just what this passage advised. They took time to consider God's guidance, the truth of the world we live in and were bold enough to develop rules for their family in an effort to live a life of obedience and in safety. This process that they established and followed would be remembered by their son when he had his own family and hopefully he would do the same thing.

So often, things just happen without our even giving them thought. Our son or daughter comes home one day and says, I have a date tonight and there has been no time for planning. We need to take the time to pay attention to God's guidance and find ways to keep God's directions in our heart and make them a part of our daily life. We should be in daily prayer asking God for guidance in the daily happenings of our life, whether routine or big issues. As verse 26 says, make level paths for your feet and take on ways that are firm. Do not swerve from the right or the left; keeping our feet from evil. This is how we guard our heart from bad decisions that were not first considered in prayer. And how many times do we change our decisions because of what those around us are doing. I think this couple had it right and suggest that we try to follow their plan, not in just the dating thing but in daily routines. We must be willing to take the time to seek guidance, follow through with our decisions that we first bathed in prayer and then be willing to take the time to stand firm and implement them.

Dear Lord, give me courage to make firm plans and decisions for myself and my family according to your guidance. Help me not to be swayed by worldly ideas or what those around me may be doing. I want to have a heart of obedience and protection for myself and my family. Thank you for your words of instruction. Help me to study your Holy Word and talk to you daily so I can make better decisions. Thank you for your love for me. Amen.

176

The Sabbath
Exodus 31:12-17

Is the Sabbath the same as any other day for you and your family? In this passage, God was very serious about keeping the Sabbath holy. In fact, God directed that anyone who worked on the Sabbath should be put to death. There are several scriptures that reference God's desire for the Sabbath: Exodus 20:8, Deuteronomy 5:12, Isaiah 56:6, 58:13, Jeremiah 17:21-22. In Genesis 2:2, God blessed the first Sabbath and called it a day of rest after he spent six days creating the heavens and the earth. I have mentioned before that as a child, this day was very different from other days for my family.

We have six days of work and then need rest. Not only do our bodies and minds need rest but we need spiritual rest as well. As we rest our bodies, we can focus on our relationship with our Lord. Not only through worship service and Bible study at our church but actually spend time focusing on God as we set aside other routine functions for the other days of the week. We can ask God to search our lives and speak to us, how he wants us to treat this day. I imagine there are many things I can do differently. While I still remember the teachings of my parents, I have strayed away from how I was raised and don't treat the day as different, as holy as I should. This is something we need to teach our children and set the example for those around us. It was once mentioned in our church that we should not have meetings on Sunday but schedule them on others days of the week. There are many things we can identify and change. Let's feel challenged to observe this command, yes command, of God and try to live it as he desires for us.

Dear God forgive me where I have failed you in this. Help me to acknowledge the Sabbath as holy and change the way I go about it. I know there are things I need to change. Convict my heart and give me courage to follow your example of resting after the six days of work. Thank you for the blessings that I know I will receive for my obedience and how I can affect the lives of my family and others around me by following your command. Amen.

177

Giving In To Anger
Proverbs 29:11

I love watching old episodes of *Gunsmoke*. This afternoon I was watching an old sheriff friend of Matt Dillon's who had harbored anger for years toward an outlaw who had turned on him and destroyed the use of both his hands which of course ended his career as sheriff. This outlaw was finally released from prison and returning home. The sheriff had turned into a very angry person and had planned for years to kill him. When the outlaw stepped off the stage, he apparently had suffered a stroke while in prison. He had long snow white hair, no use of a hand and dragged a leg as he walked. His face was aged and gnarled and he didn't even remember any of them. The sheriff crumbled to the ground in agony as he realized that he could not harm him now and had lost and wasted years smothered by his anger. Matt Dillon who of course always saves the day, was able to encourage him to return to a life with his son and daughter-in-law who welcomed him back, renewed as he had finally let go of his anger.

Proverbs 29:11 says a man is a fool when he allows anger to consume him but a man is wise when he controls his anger. We all experience different levels of anger. Sometimes anger leaves us in a few minutes and other times it lingers and dwells in us. If we aren't careful it can consume us.

1 Corinthians 13:5 says love is not easily angered and does not keep a record of wrongs. How quick are we to anger? How soon do we forgive and forget? It is not wrong to be angry but it is wrong to allow it to fester. I have experienced times when I allowed anger to linger for days and it not only made me miserable but it made me feel separated from my relationship with Jesus Christ. I cannot truly focus on Christ when I allow anger to linger. The anger changes my whole outlook and my relationship with everyone around me. When I take my anger to the Lord and ask for his help in releasing it, he saves the day and brings peace that only he can. Anger will weaken my defense and give Satan an open door to tempt me. Ephesians 4:26 says not to let the sun go down while I am still angry and give the devil a foothold. Is there anger in our heart today that we need to let go? Let's take it to the Lord.

Dear Lord thank you for your forgiveness. I am glad that you are slow to anger with me. Help me to follow in your way and be slow to anger and help me not to keep record of it. I need to forgive others as you forgive me. I don't want to do anything to negatively impact my relationship with you. I love you and I need you. Amen.

178

Resisting Confrontation
Genesis 3:8

Why do we resist confrontation? Even though some of us enjoy a debate we generally resist confrontation. We cringe when we see a police car behind us especially if the blue light is going. We are uncomfortable with the authority watching us. It is difficult to face the fact that we did something wrong and it is being pointed out to us. Why is it that when we get a ticket we blame the officer and the cars around us?

Adam and Eve sinned in the garden. Once they realized what they had done, they hid. Knowing God as they did, could they really hide from him? Of course not but they wanted to delay the confrontation as long as they could. Their paradise was now a place of fear and hiding. They could only imagine what was coming next.

We deal daily with confrontation. Someone rejects us or says something we didn't like or points out a fault or mistake. Or we reject someone or speak unkindly or point out a fault. Most of us then retreat and want to go into hiding avoiding the confrontation. I'd like to suggest that we deal with this as sin. First we ask God to help us deal with the situation. Remember that he is there for us for minor things as well as the major situations. We must seek his guidance. Then we confess, admitting the truth. We ask God to forgive us of our wrong doing and ask the one we offended or offended us for forgiveness. Then we repent of what we confessed. This is a change of heart. This is all difficult for us because we expose our self. We must openly admit what went wrong and work graciously to resolve it. Don't put it off. Focus on the refreshment that comes afterwards. We will feel clean, relieved and refreshed. We are freed from the bondage of carrying the dread of the confrontation. Proverbs 22:11 says, He who loves a pure heart and whose speech is gracious will have the king for his friend.

Father, give me the courage to address confrontation graciously knowing the freedom that comes with it. Help me to forgive as you forgive me. May the words of my mouth and the meditation of my heart be pleasing in your sight, O Lord. You are my Rock and my Redeemer (Psalm 19:14). Amen.

179

Our Legacy
Joshua 4:1-9

This scripture relates to the Israelites crossing the Jordan. The Lord instructed them to leave stones as a reminder to their children and the generations to follow, of the miracle of their crossing. The passage ends with, And they (the stones) are there to this day. A legacy is often thought of as money or property. A good friend of mine died several years ago after a short illness leaving behind a 5 year old son and husband. When her grave stone was put in place it said, Be happy. Her husband described her well with those two words. How will people remember you? We should leave a legacy of faith. Our life should leave a positive reflection of our faith in God.

Our pastor once said, We are always going into a storm, in a storm or coming out of a storm. Take a minute to recall how God has parted waters for you. Which Jordan has he held the waters back for you to cross? Use those experiences to leave a legacy of faith for those you leave behind.

Dear Father, Thank you for this reminder of how we should live our lives so that our legacy is one of faithfulness. I pray my legacy will be honest and true and will remain as those stones have. Search me and know my heart. Amen.

180

Outstretched Arms
Deuteronomy 7:17-19

According to www.dateandtime.com practically every day is a holiday. June 29th is Hug Holiday Day. This special day was created by the Hugs for Health Foundation. This foundation is founded on the notion that hugs, friendship and volunteer support are vital components to the overall senior care plan. These folks encourage us to give hugs to those who need them. On this day, volunteers of the organization go out to give hugs at senior citizen centers, hospitals, and other places. The focus is mainly on the elderly, sick and invalid, lonely people and anyone who needs the warmth, cheer, and love that a hug provides. What a great idea. We all need a warm touch and hug of encouragement especially in difficult times but we don't need a special day to be willing to give a hug. Hebrews 3:13 instructs us to encourage each other daily.

Chapters 6 and 7 of Deuteronomy speak of God's love for us and his desire for us to love, respect and obey him. He led the children of Israel out of bondage with a mighty hand and outstretched arms. He does the same for all who love him. Verse 9 of chapter 7 encourages us that the Lord our God is God. He is faithful in keeping his promises to a thousand generations of those who love him and keep his commands.

Dear God we thank you for your love for us and how you love us with a mighty hand and outstretched arms. Help me to love others as freely as you love me. Help me to be willing to share hugs of encouragement and the message of your salvation and promise of eternal life in your presence. Give me an opportunity today to share your love with someone in need. Amen.

181

Living and Active
Hebrews 4:12-13

This is a passage that I have read many times but today when I read it the words pierce my heart. The word of God is living and active, penetrating, judging my thoughts and attitude. Nothing is hidden from God. My Mom's Bible which is the King James version says all things are naked and open unto his eyes. Does this touch you? It really speaks to me of how consuming God's Word is. It should consume my every thought and stay constant in my every spoken word. I find it difficult to put this into words. It has been on my mind all day. Today my life is a mess but this brings warmth and comfort and confidence. I am naked before God. He wants his Word to be alive and active in me just as he is. He sees right through me knowing my thoughts even if my actions and words conflict. He truly knows why I do what I do. At one time in my life I may have found this frightening or embarrassing but today it warms my heart and makes me want to seek and know him more. I want to kneel before him and melt into his loving arms. It urges me to search my heart for any forgiveness I should seek from him or give to someone else. It prompts me to take every concern and decision to him, waiting patiently and obediently for his guidance and direction. Nothing else matters. He calls me his child. I am a child of the King. If this doesn't move you I suggest you either check your pulse or drop to your knees. God is the Lord over all circumstances. Praise to God for a living hope (1 Peter 1:3-9).

Dear God I pray I have expressed to my readers how close this scripture brings me to you and I want the same for them. We need you God. We need you in every breath, every thought and every word. I fall before you and recognize that my inner being is known and seen by you. Thank you for this marvelous promise. Forgive me of my sins and show me how to draw closer to you in all that I do. Amen.

182

In Remembrance
2 Timothy 2:8-26

I saw a church sign that said, Is what you do in remembrance of him? We are familiar with the scripture (1 Corinthians 11:24-25) regarding the last supper. Jesus said, This is my body which is for you; do this in remembrance of me. The cup is in remembrance of Jesus as well. This scripture also warns us that when we partake of the bread and drink in remembrance of him we are to examine ourselves first to resolve any unforgiven sin in our life. It must never be taken in an irreverent or self-centered manner. He commands that we recognize the significance of remembering his death and resurrection. We must also recognize it as a privilege.

Aside from the Lord's Supper, is what we do in remembrance of Jesus? This passage in 2 Timothy instructs us that we are to do our best before God and allow nothing into our life that we would be ashamed of, upholding the truth of God's Word. We do this in remembrance of Jesus. Our daily actions and words should be done in remembrance of his death and resurrection. Accepting Jesus Christ as our Lord and Savior, we died with him when he died for us and are therefore assured that we will live with him in eternity. When we strive to live according to his word even when it means suffering, we will be rewarded when he returns for us. We strive to live in remembrance of Jesus Christ.

Dear Jesus Christ, help me to take very seriously the fact that you suffered and died for me. Help me to be strong in living according to the instructions of your command, recognizing it as a privilege. I want to live a life in service to you completely and faithfully. Forgive me for the times I have failed you. Thank you for your forgiveness and your love for me. Amen.

183

The Drive Thru Difference
1 Timothy 6:17-19

A local Christian radio station in town has a program called The Drive Thru Difference. Folks are encouraged to share the love of Jesus in tough times by paying for the order of the car behind you in the drive thru line. The idea is to leave a note with the cashier saying 'you don't know me but I just paid for your order...signed the stranger in the car in front of you'. The station offers a note to use or you can write your own. Of course the idea is to get folks listening to the radio station which offers Christian music and words of encouragement and salvation. What a great opportunity to share the love of Jesus. I believe when God sees things like this happening he will put just the right person behind or in front of just the right person. He can use a good deed such as this in a mighty way. Both cars are blessed but we know of course that it is more blessed to give than to receive (Acts 20:35). The Bible teaches us to be rich in good deeds. We live in a world full of hopelessness and suffering. A simple act of kindness can change a bad day to a good one and can also change a life forever. Acts of kindness such as this are treasures in God's eyes and are the kind of thing we can take with us to heaven and we will be recognized for them in heaven. Maybe you know of other ways to help those around you today to see and experience the love of Jesus through an act of kindness. It seems extra special when done for a stranger. Let's be encouraged to ask God to reveal to us today someone who needs Jesus. Be aware of an opportunity that is placed before you and be ready to act. A quote on my calendar this week said, You may be only one person in the world but you can be the world to one person.

Dear Jesus thank you for your love for us. Give me opportunity to share your love with someone today. Help me not to be bashful but to be ready to act when you send someone my way. Provide whatever I need to do this. Make me willing to sacrifice and let go of a few dollars if I need to. Help me to see those around me through your eyes. Thank you for the opportunity you will send my way. Give me strength and courage to continue these acts whenever I see a need and I pray that this willingness will be contagious to those around me. I pray that others will see you in me. Amen.

184

The Best Boss
Jeremiah 9:23-24

Today I had opportunity to attend a luncheon for a young man who was leaving our agency and going to another job. His supervisor was very upset at his leaving not only because he was a great employee but he had become a good Christian friend. She was struggling in a difficult time working full time, helping tend to an aging sick mother and parenting a young child. She felt a real loss when he gave his resignation. At the luncheon she tried to be very brave but as she stood to speak, she broke into tears. Those of us around the table took over and starting giving him send off words of encouragement to help her out. As we finished, he stood and thanked us and then pulled out a plaque that he had ordered for her, honoring her as the Best Boss. Many joked saying, 'Who are we honoring here?'. It was really neat to see this special relationship especially at the work place. I know them both and believe their relationship stemmed from their personal relationships with God. Proverbs 18:24 says a man of many companions may come to ruin, but there is a friend who sticks closer than a brother.

My study note for this passage says, ultimately only God and our knowledge of and love for him are worthwhile. God exercises kindness, justice and righteousness and he delights in them. While we don't always understand the happenings in our daily lives we know that God is in control. I love the song that says, God is too wise to be mistaken and too good to be unkind. Sometimes we just have to trust in his kindness, justice and righteousness. Sometimes we just have to trust God's heart. He cares for us and knows our every need. Today's luncheon was special for me. I was encouraged to be thankful for the close Christian relationships that are in my life. I thanked God for my relationship with him and for his daily comfort and guidance. I was honored when asked to bless the food and I prayed a true prayer of thanksgiving from my heart. I am amazed how God shows up in the most unexpected places and times.

Dear Lord thank you for your kindness, justice and righteousness. Thank you for the blessing of special relationships. I cherish my relationship with you. Thank you for saving me. I know that one day you will come for me and take me to live eternally in your presence. How awesome are your promises. I praise your name and adore you. Amen.

185

Freedom
2 Corinthians 3:16-17

There is a song we sing at church that is based on this passage.
Where the spirit of the Lord is there is freedom.
There is peace. There is love. There is joy.
It is for freedom you've set us free.

Do you feel free? We live in a free country although we don't always agree and feel that way. But compared to other places that we could live, yes we are free. What is most important is that we have freedom in Jesus Christ. He allows us to make our own decisions. He offers an alternative of taking our burdens on himself and providing wisdom for our decisions. He offers freedom. We have freedom from sin through his forgiveness. We have freedom from guilt. We have hope. And Jesus Christ offers blessings for our obedience in accepting the freedom that is available to us. It doesn't get better than that.

I challenge us to be thankful for the freedom that we have living in the USA. It was won with a price. Many have lost their lives to ensure and protect our freedom. Jesus Christ paid the price to ensure our freedom through forgiveness and the gift of eternal life. As we celebrate our freedom and the birthday of our country, let's also celebrate this freedom in Jesus Christ. Let's be sure to share this knowledge with the lost ones around us. Many don't realize that the price has already been paid.

Dear God thank you for my freedom. Where your spirit is, there is my freedom. Thank you for the sacrifice of your Son as payment for my sin. I pray I do not take my freedom of living in this great USA for granted. I pray I do not take the freedom of my relationship with Jesus Christ for granted. Thank you for your blessings. Thank you for your love for me. Help me to be committed to share my story of freedom with those around me. I pray I do not miss an opportunity that you put in my way. Amen.

186

Praying For Our Country's Leaders
1 Timothy 2:1-6

We are fortunate to live in a democracy. Our judicial system is established as a democracy. You may say, what democracy? Compared to other countries, yes we are fortunate to live in a democracy. While I understand deceit and sin of many of our leaders has tarnished our respect for our country's leaders, we still must maintain a spirit of respect for our country's leaders. Life is full of votes and opinions. We vote in our families, in our churches, in our communities and for national leaders. Does our opinion and our vote always win? Of course not. Isn't that what democracy is all about? We must accept the outcome and respect it. Isn't that what we expect when our vote or opinion wins? I suggest that we first of all pray for our community and country's leaders. Secondly we pray about our vote; that we properly research and listen to the nominations and ballot decisions and we follow through with a vote. Third, we respect the result and continue to pray. I am from South Carolina and there have been a few embarrassing moments for our state this year. Sinful behavior and disrespect for our leaders caused the embarrassment. God mandates authority and requires respect for authority. We don't always have to like what we see or hear but we are to pray and we are to respect. Do you write to your leaders or do you think it isn't worth the time? If God has a message for them, be assured he will see that it is received.

I have worked in state government for 35+ years and many of those years in management positions. God has blessed me in my career. I have had opportunity to work for Christian supervisors. I have had opportunity to respond to many letters from concerned citizens. Many times, changes in policy and procedure were made because of the constituent contacts and requests that we received. I believe I was in certain situations and positions to help people that God sent to me. I have experienced good times and proud moments, and I have experienced disappointment and embarrassment. I had to learn to pray and roll with the punches. Sometimes I did not like what I saw or heard but I was brought up to respect authority and that is how I have tried to live. Being the boss is not easy. We often see only one side of an issue, our side. We may unfairly challenge and disagree with decisions that are made. I wonder what difference we would see if we and our Christian fellowships earnestly committed to regular prayer for our community and national leaders?

Dear God thank you for the country that I live in and the freedom that I have. Forgive me when I take it for granted. Forgive me when I miss opportunities to make a difference. Help me to be a good example for my family and others around me. Please help me to remember to pray regularly for those in leadership positions. Help me to respect authority that you ordain. Amen.

187

Haste Makes Waste
Proverbs 19:21, 21:5

This common saying, Haste Makes Waste, means that if you try to do something quickly without planning, you're likely to end up spending more time, money, etc., doing it. God has a purpose for us. As we make daily decisions and choices we should seek his guidance rather then moving quickly on our own. It seems we are always in a hurry. I never understand why some morning drivers stay bumper to bumper, moving in and out of lanes at a fast pace on the way in to work. What is the hurry? I understand going home but why to work? Are they that anxious to get there? I love my job but usually the drive in is the most peaceful time of my day. I am in weekly counseling as I deal with family issues and she is always telling me that life doesn't work like the work plans that I use on my job. In serious situations and decisions, we can't set goals to be reached on a certain day insisting that certain steps and decisions will take place on a schedule that we set. It may work for accomplishing tasks at work but not in our daily lives. It is more important and our accomplishments will be more successful when we seek God daily and move at his pace rather than our own. In most situations, there will be waiting periods. I believe God often does this to help us to trust him and not ourselves. When we move on our own we will usually make hasty decisions and as the saying says, we are likely to end up spending more time or more money. Or we will have regrets and after the disaster, we seek God not only to fix the mess we made but to deal with the original problem. The Bible says that plans of the diligent lead to profit. I'm not sure if this refers to rash actions or a desire to get rich quick but I'm sure we get the picture. Hasty decisions are wasteful in our lives. Seeking God's guidance brings profit and blessing. Let's agree to slow down today and spend the day continuously in conversation with our Lord, seeking his guidance and instruction in everything we do.

Dear Lord, help me to slow down and give my heart the desire to seek you in all things. Lord I trust you with my life and I need to recognize that you have plans for me to prosper and you have control of every detail of my life. Forgive me when I think I can make decisions on my own and do not need your help. Forgive me when I move on my own and create disasters in my life. I want to be in your Holy Word everyday and spend time in conversation with you daily. I love you Lord and I thank you for your love for me. Amen.

188

The Fear List
Psalm 27

I teach High School Girls Sunday School. Today I asked them what their biggest fears were. They listed public speaking, death, falling, failure and bad decisions. I told them about an article I read of a survey of people's greatest fears. The survey results listed public speaking, blindness, heights, serious illness and death. It was interesting that both lists revealed some of the same fears and a couple different ones too. We all have fears. Fear can immobilize us and actually make us physically sick. Often our fear is linked to questions of 'What if?'. I get so frustrated with myself when I get worked up over something that hasn't even happened. God understands that we have fears but doesn't want us to live in fear. He wants us to trust in him without fear. Satan will use our own individual fears to pull us down in an attempt to destroy our trust in God. Today in class, we studied Psalm 27. In this psalm David speaks of evil men, attacking foes, war and armies who bring trouble and conspire to destroy him. My girls have enemies of their own – peer pressure, decisions about college, school studies and projects, drama in relationships and family issues. We studied these verses for encouraging words that bring us victory and confidence when we face problems and our enemies of this world. The Lord is our light, our salvation, our stronghold, our confidence, our rock and our helper. He provides shelter and safety and is the source of our blessings. We can have victory over our fear when we place our trust in God and do not give into the lies and hopelessness that they bring. What is your fear today? What is your enemy today? Be confident and see the goodness of the Lord in our world. Wait for the Lord, be strong and take heart and wait for the Lord.

Dear God I do not want to be afraid. I want to trust you completely. Give me confidence and a willing heart to be in your Holy Word everyday. I lay by fears at your feet and wait for your control over them. Help me to recognize the lies that Satan sends and throw them out of my mind. You are my light and my salvation. I have nothing to fear. Amen.

189

Lost

Isaiah 48:17-18

My son is getting married next month. My daughter and I were trying to get to a church this afternoon where they were having a bridal shower. We got dreadfully lost and were over an hour late. We stopped twice and asked for directions but got more lost. As we finally arrived, we laughed thinking we were grateful we were not trying to get to the wedding because we would have missed it. As I sit here tonight I think about the many times in my life I have been lost or got bad directions or bad advice. It is a terrible hopeless feeling. But once you find your way, a great feeling of relief comes and the lost feeling is quickly forgotten. Once we arrived at the shower, the frustration and yes, a little anger was easily forgotten. We enjoyed our time together and it was a beautiful day for a ride in the country.

This passage tells us that God teaches us what is best for us and directs us in the way we should go. Paying attention to his commands brings peace and righteousness. Psalm 119:133 asks of God, direct my footsteps according to your word and let no sin rule over me. Following God's directions puts us on the right path. Sometimes we take a wrong turn or veer off the path and get side tracked and lost. Looking to him for directions we can find forgiveness, get back on the right path and back on track. I travel a good bit in my job and often use the mapping tools on the Internet. Usually they are pretty good but sometimes the slightest wrong turn and I find myself lost. That's a bad feeling when you're alone in an unfamiliar area and trying to get somewhere at a certain time. I have stopped and asked a stranger for help and they get me more confused.

There have been times that I pulled over and prayed and quickly found my way again. Life can be this way. We can trust in the wrong person for directions. The good news is that we can be totally confident that when we ask God for help and seek his direction, we are guaranteed that we will get the help we need and he will get us back on the right road. Let's make God our navigator as we drive the roads of life. When we keep our eyes on Jesus Christ, we will not get lost. We will find peace and confidence, living under the shelter of his safe keeping.

Dear God thank you for caring for me. Help me to keep my eyes on you and not veer off of the path that you have made for me. I love you and I thank you for your love for me. Direct my footsteps according to your word and let no sin rule over me. Teach me what is best for me and direct me in the way I should go. Amen.

190

The God We Have
Hebrews 4:14-16

People serve many religions and many gods. I feel sorry for those who worship wooden, metal or ceramic idols or gods who are dead. How do they find hope in a hopeless god? This morning I read this passage of scripture and became overwhelmed with thanksgiving for the God we have. We do not have to go through a priest; we can speak directly to our God and if we don't know the words to express, we have the Holy Spirit to intervene for us. Our God knows loss, frustration and anger. He knows the traps of temptation that are set by Satan. He has assured us that he will always provide a way out when we are tempted. He allows us to come before him without needing his permission. Remember the days of the king when a person could be killed for entering the king's presence without his permission? Be grateful that we don't need God's permission to approach him. He is available to us day and night. He never sleeps. He never goes away. He is here. He loves us unconditionally and has an individual plan for each of our lives. Verse 16 says we can approach the throne of grace with confidence so that we may receive mercy and find grace to help us in our time of need. The King James version says we come boldly unto the throne. We approach our God boldly and with confidence and we find what we need. Let's not take this for granted. We serve a marvelous God who loves us, provides for us and protects us. He will return one day and take us to live eternally in his presence. Never have we had to ask his permission or fear of him being unapproachable. What a mighty God we have. We don't thank him nearly enough.

Dear God forgive me when I take you for granted. You never slumber or take a rest. You are always available to me and love me unconditionally. I want to serve you with a heart of commitment. Forgive me when I fail. You are a mighty God and I love you. Amen.

191

Changing the Way We Think
Romans 12:2

I was challenged today to change the way I think. Does your preacher or Bible study leader or even God step on your toes sometimes? The world has a lot of strange and corrupt ways. At times, we don't stand up to our own opinion or the opinion of the Word of God because of the influences of the world. How many times do our kids say 'everyone else is …' and we give in. I think it is time we study God's Word, seek his advice and develop our own way of thinking. I get so frustrated with staff when we're discussing a problem and their response is 'but that's the way we've always done it'. Maybe that's the problem. This verse challenges us to no longer conform to the patterns of the world but to be transformed by the renewing of our mind or change the way we think. This can cover many areas of our life – our spending, time spent with the Lord, time spent with our family, what we allow our ears to hear and our eyes to see, what we allow our kids to do and where we allow them to go, the way we dress…..I could go on. My challenge today for you and me, is to spend quiet time with God and ask him to reveal what areas in our way of thinking needs to be changed. He will reveal it in a loving, constructive way. I say this because Satan will quickly be at work as well, so be prepared for his lies and resist the confusion he will try to bring. Let's read Romans 12:2 aloud to God and ask him to reveal his truth. Then ask him for confirmation. Get out that prayer journal and pencil and let's get to work.

Dear Lord, reveal to me the opinions and way of thinking that I need to change. I do not want to live by the patterns of the world. I want to live by your truths. I desire to be transformed by the renewing of my mind. I am prepared to listen. I am ready to let go of opinions that will corrupt me or separate me from your way. Thank you now for how you will change me. Amen.

192

Go To the Ant

Proverbs 6:6-8

Ants are very interesting. I remember having ants in a jar filled with dirt when I was young, watching them work at their tunnels. They are always at work. You do not see them on a warm rock sunning. The ant is always busy going about its business ignoring anything in its way. As a child we would use leaves or sticks to try and divert them but they found a way around, over or through any obstacle. Ants are determined little things. I read that some of their tunnels can go 15 feet into the ground. They can break a large bug into many pieces and carry it below, stored for later. They prepare daily for tomorrow. These verses in Proverbs say we are to consider the ant as wise. Just from the couple things I have mentioned, I can see why. Many of us live for today never thinking of what tomorrow will bring. We purchase houses, cars and run up credit cards because we can afford it today. When life changes tomorrow, we wonder what happened. We often forget that we need to save for the rainy day and only remember when the rainy day comes. What about our relationship with Jesus Christ? Are we determined? Are we prepared for his return if it is tomorrow? Do we allow obstacles to keep us from opportunity to share him with those around us?

I think there are two lessons for us from the ants. We need to be good stewards of the blessings God gives us. We need to spend wisely and properly save because we do not know what tomorrow brings. There are good Christian financial counselors who can teach us how to stay out of debt or help us get out of debt. Secondly, we are challenged to live our relationship with Jesus Christ in a determined way, ignoring the obstacles that the world puts in our way. We need to live in preparation for his return, storing up treasure in heaven rather than material treasures on earth. Notice too, that we rarely see one ant. There is usually a trail of them. We are better at accomplishing this when we seek Christian fellowship of other believers. It is hard to work alone. Don't try to go it alone. Consider the ways of the ant and be wise. Ask God what he wants you to learn from the ant.

Dear God I seek your wisdom and long to live a life that pleases you. Help me to learn from the little ant that you created. Reveal to me how I can live wiser. Help me to live prepared for tomorrow both financially and in my relationship with you. Show me your desires for my life and help me to trust you in all that I do. Amen.

193

Spiritual Poverty
Luke 12:16-21

I recently heard that the point of this story is spiritual poverty. This man was wealthy and highly valued his material possessions. I imagine his friends and neighbors thought he had it all and maybe even envied him. It never occurred to him that tomorrow could be different from today. It never occurred to him to place his value on our Lord and Savior instead of his belongings. He valued himself. He lived in spiritual poverty. God called him a fool.

The world we live in considers our value based on our job, our house, our car, how we look or what restaurants we favor. The world considers our value based on things that don't matter. We are valuable when we are a child of God and have a future in eternity with our Lord. We may live in poverty or less than middle class but we are wealthy when we are rich in Jesus Christ. Satan lies to us telling us we are of little value. We live dangerously when we place a high priority on our material belongings and live above what we can afford. Life can change in a minute. We can quickly get into debt trying to live up to the values of the world. Rather we should live within the financial means that God has given us. We must place our value on our relationship with him and focus on the status of our heart rather than the car we drive or the neighborhood we live in. This man thought he had it made because of the riches he owned. He was in for a rude awakening when God took his life. We can't place our trust in what we have. We must place our trust in what we believe.

Dear God thank you for how you have richly blessed me. I am rich in you because I am your child and I will inherit eternal life, living in your presence. Help me not to value what I have here on earth. Help me to value what I believe and my life in you. I do not want to live in spiritual poverty. Thank you for your love for me. Thank you for showing me the truth. Amen.

194

The Wedding
Genesis 2:23-25

Last night my son got married. I never saw a more handsome groom or lovely bride. I will never forget the extraordinary feelings as he walked me down the aisle to light two candles in memory of my father and in honor of my mother who could not be present. As he seated me, we shared an embrace of a lifetime and he turned away to prepare to greet his bride. As I watched them give their vows, they stood as if no one else was around. There for a moment it looked as if they both would tear up and I was thankful to see that they were serious about what they were doing. As we went about the ceremony, pictures, the reception and their driving away, I was thankful. I was not sure what emotions I would feel as this time approached. My son has had his share of adolescent and teen issues. When he first told me he was ready to marry this young lady who had stolen his heart, I was somewhat alarmed. But I saw a new person in him as we planned for this event. And last night I saw it for sure, he had grown into a fine young man. For that I give all the praise and recognition to God. As many folks commented to me that I had a fine son and had done a great job in raising him, my mind often went to Proverbs 22:6 that says, train a child in the way he should go and when he is old he will not turn from it. I have not been the best parent but I do know that he and his sister are saved and are children of God. Knowing that brings peace and comfort. I would rather live knowing this than having a child who has never given a day of trouble. My children will spend eternity with our Lord. This morning as I think on this week-end's events, I have not lost a son but have gained a daughter. I release them to live as one and will pray for them daily. I do not feel sad for I know while one chapter in our life as ended another begins.

Adam explains it all in these verses of Genesis. My study notes call this the divine intention. God has a plan for male and female. The intention of marriage is that the two no longer live under the guidance and protection of their parents. They establish a separate unit and live as one. The intention is that the parents raise them as best they can according to God's instructions and then send them out on their own. Thus the ceremonial wedding and 'send off' that we experienced last night.

Thank you Lord for my precious son and this lovely new daughter you give me. I pray that you will watch over them and guide them as they start their new life together this morning. I pray that they will never doubt the importance of living a life focused on you. I pray they will keep a relationship with you strong and alive in their new family unit. Provide for them and may they remember daily that all things come from you. Help me and her parents to recognize and accept our role of letting them go. Thank you for the lovely ceremony and how you answered all my prayers throughout the event. Amen.

195

While He Is Away
Philippians 2:12-15

Paul sent word to his church encouraging them to continue to work out their salvation through spiritual growth and development. He tells them to obey as if he were there and even more so while he is away. As a child I was always expected to be obedient and on good behavior but I was especially expected to behave myself exceptionally well when I was away from home. I got in more trouble for misbehaving away from my parents than when I was home. It struck me as I was reading this passage that we are to be on good behavior while God reigns from heaven as we wait for his return. While he can see and hear more than our parents could, he still expects us to live in good behavior in preparation for his return. He has left instructions and guidance for us to follow as we prepare for our home in eternity. He expects us to continue to work out our salvation as Paul instructed his church members. My mother's King James version says to work out our salvation with fear and trembling. I don't think this means in an anxious way but of a serious, reverent and determined manner. We live a life of obedience as we did as a child in fear of our father and his expectations of us while he was away. We are expected to do everything without complaining or arguing so that we are without fault. We are to shine like stars in the sky. Think of a night sky with many stars that change the darkness of the heavens to sparkling bright lights. We are to stand out as the stars stand out in the black sky as children of God waiting for his return.

Dear God help me to shine in this troubled world as a star in the dark sky. I want those around me to know that I am a child of God. I pray my behavior and obedience to your teachings reflect my relationship with you. Forgive me of my sin. Forgive me for my complaining and arguing. Thank you for your love for me and the eternal place that you prepare for me. Amen.

196

Complaining
Numbers 11:1-3

The Israelites were complainers. They started complaining at the waters of the Red Sea three days after leaving Egypt. They complained about not having food, about the manna God sent them to eat and about not having water. Their complaining made God angry.

Do you know people who are never satisfied and complain about everything? I have said about a few people I know, 'if they were to get a million dollars on a silver platter, they would complain about the shape of the platter!' Do you know people like that? Complaining can be very contagious. It is easy to get caught up into complaining. Ephesians 5:18-20 offers advice on behavior quite the opposite of complaining. The passage tells us to be filled with the Holy Spirit, speaking to one another with songs, singing and making music in our heart, always giving thanks. If we follow this instruction there will be little time or room in our heart for complaining. God our Father provides all of our needs. We should encourage those around us to spend our thoughts and words in song and thankfulness rather than complaining. No matter what our situation, we have many things to be thankful and grateful for. Let's be encouraged to remember how complaining will anger God. We want to live according to his instruction with a heart of gratefulness and less complaining.

Dear Lord, forgive me for my complaining. Forgive me when I forget how I am blessed not only with material things but with your gift of salvation and eternal life. Help me to offer encouragement to those around me and set a good example with thankfulness rather than complaining. Give me courage to discourage complaining. I pray that my actions and words will reflect my relationship with you and your love for me. Amen.

197

Unexpected Opportunity
Philemon 1:4-7

I have a friend at work. We work together almost daily and recognized quickly that we are both Christians. I knew that her Mom had been very sick, her job is very fast paced and she has a very young one at home. I have been dealing with a difficult situation in my life and decided the other day when we were working alone, to share my situation with her. She was of course sympathetic and immediately gave me a hug. She then shared that she was dealing with a very similar situation and it had been especially difficult for her because her Mom was the one she usually shared with. We had an awesome time together praying for each other and sharing. It amazes me how our God works. Our opportunity for encouraging each other was mutually shared and we walked out of that room more confident than ever of our faith in the Lord Jesus. And I know our relationship will never be the same. We now love each other in an intimate way because of our mutual faith and that special opportunity together. God knew when we both awoke that morning how this unexpected opportunity would affect us.

We are told several times throughout the Bible to encourage each other. We are told to encourage so that we can be encouraged. I can look back over my life and see several opportunities that I have had to help someone because I experienced the very same thing. It is always encouraging to know that someone truly understands. God knows and he understands our troubles. He encourages us to use our experiences to encourage others. Unexpected opportunity can arise at any time. Let's not miss any of them.

Dear God thank you for the experiences in my life that equip me to encourage someone else. Thank you for the hope we have because of you and your promises. Give me opportunity to encourage others. Give me a heart of committed prayer so that I can lift up those who I know are in need. I pray that my life will reflect your love for me. Amen.

198

The Outward Appearance
1 Samuel 16:7-13

God sent Samuel to anoint the next king to follow Saul's reign. He sent him to Jesse of Bethlehem who had eight sons. As the sons passed in front of Samuel for his inspection, he looked over each of them very closely but never felt led by the Spirit to choose one. God told Samuel not to focus on the outward appearance but to be concerned about the inner disposition and character. God chose David, the tenderhearted shepherd boy as king.

Each of us is unique in appearance. While we carry consistencies through our family line, we are still very individual. Even identical twins have something about their outward appearance that is unique. When you ask a young person to describe their idea of the perfect mate, they will quickly start describing their appearance. Unfortunately, we judge a person by outward appearance often before we even meet them and certainly before we get to know them well. How unfortunate for us. Paul preaches in Galatians 2:6 that God does not judge by external appearance. I want people to judge me by my character and inner self rather than how I look, especially more so on some days than others. However I must be careful that my inner self is reflected in my appearance and my actions. God focuses on our heart and we should do the same in our daily encounters with those around us. We should be concerned about our own inner disposition and character. We should teach this to our youth. We should reflect this in our daily interaction with others.

Dear God forgive me when I treat others as I perceive their outward appearance. Forgive me when I have judged someone on how they look or dress. Help me to remember that I will be judged as I judge others. Thank you for your unconditional love for each of us and that you love us equally. Help me to live with the same love for others in my heart. This world can be so harsh and difficult. Help me to avoid negative actions of others and to set an example that reflects my relationship with you. Amen.

Endurance

Romans 15:1-13

Amigo, an endurance horse, was given a slim chance of survival following surgery to remove a tree branch which had penetrated his chest and snapped two ribs in a riding accident. An endurance horse is trained and conditioned for 25, 50 or 100 mile rides or rides up to 275 miles over a couple days. Amigo fought life threatening conditions while being cared for at an animal clinic at the University of Tennessee but pulled through all of them. He was nearly lost during surgery to clear an abscess but again bounced back. His recovery has been monitored by more than 6000 fans on Facebook. Clinic staff report that he is spending time outside and is pulling at the hay net, eating all the grain given him and tipping over the feed bucket for more. It is believed that his endurance training contributed to his strong stamina.

From where do we get our stamina? How do we train and condition ourselves for life threatening accidents? The Scriptures were written to teach us, so that through endurance and encouragement we will find hope. God's Word is available for us to gain strength and courage and build our endurance. Paul tells the Thessalonians in 1 Thessalonians 1:3 that our work is produced by faith, our labor prompted by love and our endurance inspired by hope in our Lord Jesus Christ. We need to train and condition ourselves for the long rides, long days and unexpected set backs of life. In 2 Thessalonians 1: 4 Paul applauds the Thessalonians for their perseverance and faith in all the persecutions and trials they were enduring. He encouraged them that God is just and brings relief to their troubles. A daily thriving relationship with Jesus Christ prepares our endurance and gives us hope. We can't wait for the difficulties to come or the accidents to happen and then try to build our relationship. We need the training and conditioning of Amigo the endurance horse to be an endurance Christian.

Dear God help me to trust you in all things. Help me to be committed in my relationship with you. I need to talk with you daily and study your Holy Word every day to build my endurance. Thank you for the hope and encouragement that you give me. Thank you for your promise of eternal life when this life on earth ends. Thank you for your enduring love for me. Amen.

200

The Dollar Menu
Luke 18:9-14

My good friend often tells me about the great sandwiches she gets for a dollar at one of my favorite fast food restaurants. I decided to try one. I was highly insulted when the sandwich that I got was not as good as the one for full price and told her it was a rip off. As I drove away from our conversation, I was strongly convicted by God. I cringed as I heard myself arrogantly saying that the dollar sandwich was not good enough for me. I had to have the full price sandwich and how dare them give me less. As soon as I could, I texted my friend and apologized for my arrogance. She laughed and graciously accepted but I was really embarrassed. I immediately thought of this passage of scripture. For everyone who exalts himself will be humbled and he who humbles himself will be exalted. Arrogance is a terrible ugly monster that prowls among us. It can catch us before we realize we are acting it out in word or deed. And oh how the conviction penetrates and humbles us. I praise God for the humbling affect that comes from my relationship with him. 1 Peter 5:5 says that God opposes the proud but gives grace to the humble. While I stumble and fall daily, God convicts me and forgives me transcending peace and hope.

Dear God have mercy on me a sinner. Forgive me for my arrogance and the hurtful words that can come from it. Forgive me when I think I deserve more. Thank you for friends who easily forgive. Thank you for the peace and hope that you bring me. I desire to live a life that pleases you. I adore you. Amen.

201

Chosen
2 Thessalonians 2:13-17

One of my favorite books is <u>Chosen by a Horse</u> by Susan Richards. This is a tender story about a rescued horse, Lay Me Down, who came to live with her and her other horses Georgia, Tempo and Hotshot. It's one of the best true horse stories I have read. While she had picked another horse to rescue, Lay Me Down climbed up in her trailer and chose her. This loving bond soon taught her how to embrace the joys of life despite her troubles and enriched her life immeasurably, showing her how better to love people.

God created and chose us. His desire is that all will know him as Lord and Savior. The psalmist writes in Psalm 42:1-2 of longing for God as a deer pants for water. He writes, my soul thirsts for God, for the living God. This speaks of a personal, intimate relationship; a bond of love that cannot be broken. The time that we spend with our Lord is precious. God longs for us as well. We experience the joys of life and the dangers of living. We do not have to experience them alone. God is with us and longs to have a personal relationship with each of us. We only need to accept his call and experience him. He is our friend and our provider. We trust him in everything. God is our refuge and our hope. Seek him today. Accept his call for the chosen.

Dear God I long for you. I long for the loving relationship that you desire for me. Forgive me of my sin and allow me to draw near to you. My time with you is precious. I will meditate on your words all day long. I will trust in you in all things. Amen.

202

Accepting What We Have
Matthew 25:14-30

Thomas Kinkade was born in 1958 and grew up in the foothills of the Sierra Mountains in a small town in California. From the age of four, his calling as an artist was evident. When Kinkade was five years old his parents divorced which was rare. He recalls it as being a time of embarrassment, shame and poverty. The one thing he had from an early age, something the other children didn't have, was his art. By the age of 16 he was an accomplished painter in oil. He married his childhood sweetheart, Nanette and later they began to publish his paintings together. Bridges and steps or grassy inclines leading upward or through a gate are his favorite subjects as well as symbols of his Christian faith. Some of his paintings are visuals of Bible verses such as his A Light in the Storm, taken from John 8:12, I am the light of the world. He frequently pays loving tribute to his wife and daughters by hiding their names or initials in his paintings. Looking closely you can make out the initial N for his wife which he works into all his paintings. Thomas Kinkade made the best of what life handed him. He accepted and thrived on his talent for art, developed his Christian faith and learned to love and laugh.

Jesus teaches us to honor what has been handed us. When we do not grow and thrive on what we have, it may be taken away. We often miss opportunity to grow and expand. We often have our eyes on other things or consider ourselves worthless based on what we don't have and think we need, or sit still in discontentment. Let's be good stewards of our place in life. Let's be good stewards of what we have. Jesus will give us opportunity to grow what we have regardless of our circumstances. He expects us to thrive and requires that of us. I believe we will have responsibilities in heaven and will be assigned based on how we managed what we have while on earth. We want to meet Jesus face to face and hear him say that we did well. Discover what you have. Praise God for it and use it.

Dear God thank you for the blessing you give me. I pray that I will use what I have wisely for your honor and glory. Give me strength and courage to grow and thrive. Close my ears and heart to words and thoughts of failure. I know you have plans for me to prosper. Thank you for your love for me. Amen.

203

The Lord Gives Us Success
Genesis 39:1-6

Most of us are familiar with the story of Joseph and his difficulties in his early years (Genesis 37 and 39). This is one of the many inspirational stories in the Bible of how he rose from being thrown into a cistern to success. God was with Joseph and brought him success. Joseph's employer, Potiphar saw that the Lord was with him and that the Lord gave him success in everything he did. Abraham was promised that his offspring would be blessed and successful. In Exodus 35 and 36 where Moses is instructing the people on building the tabernacle, he refers several times to the worker's skill coming from God. Our skills and our success come from God.

When we think of someone being successful, the first thing that comes to mind is our job or employment. Some positions are seen as successful and some are seen as not. I believe that when we seek God's guidance when planning our adult life and career, he will place us according to his plan. No matter how high up the career ladder we go, God has a plan for our success. Stay at home Moms can be successful in what they do as well as presidents of large corporations can be successful. We can succeed in many areas not just in our job. Our skill is God given and our success is according to his plan for us. We should never judge each other according to our idea of success. The King James version of Psalm 75:6-7 says that promotion comes neither from the east nor from the west nor from the south but God is the judge; he putteth down one and setteth up another. God gives us our individual skills and he controls our promotions and our success.

Dear Lord thank you for your plan for me. I seek your guidance for my life and long to live within your will for me. Forgive me when I set out on my own and leave you behind. You are my solid rock and my strength. Thank you for the successes you have given me. Help me to remember that all good things come from you. Amen.

204

Jesus Wants Me For a Sunbeam
Matthew 5:14-16

It's funny how we remember songs from our childhood. I recall many. I remember singing, "Jesus Wants Me For a Sunbeam".

Jesus wants me for a sunbeam, to shine for him each day.
In every way try to please him at home, at school, at play.
A sunbeam, a sunbeam, Jesus wants me for a sunbeam.
A sunbeam, a sunbeam, I'll be a sunbeam for him.

Jesus is the light of the world and he wants us to shine for him. Just like another song I recall, "This Little Light of Mine", we need to share his light with others. We can't hide it. We must not keep it to ourselves. Do people around you see the light of Jesus in your heart? Matthew 5 is Jesus' sermon on the mountain also known as The Beatitudes. The dictionary defines beatitude as supreme blessedness or happiness. Jesus sets a standard of living for us in these verses. Some may see it as impossible to achieve and I agree if tried in our own power. We must have the light of Jesus in our heart and the strength of the Holy Spirit within us to achieve this calling. And as we know, obedience brings blessings. 2 Corinthians 4:6 says God makes his light shine in our heart to give us the knowledge of his glory. The darkness of sin is overcome by the light.

You may think these childhood songs to be silly. I see them as wholesome foundations of my relationship with God. Whether you came to know him as a child or as an adult, the standards he set are for all of us. We all have the same source of power from the Holy Spirit. I don't think he makes one stronger than another. I believe one seeks the power more than others. Let your light shine for all to see. Jesus wants us for a sunbeam, shining for him each day.

Dear Jesus thank you for the standards of living you set for us. Thank you for the power you give us to achieve them and the forgiveness you give when I fail. I pray that others will see your light within me. I want to shine for you. I want to be your sunbeam. Amen.

205

How Do We Do It?
Philippians 2:13

God works in us according to his will. The psalmist in Psalm 40:8 says I desire to do your will, O my God. Your will is in my heart.

Our desire and God's will should be in accord. How do we do this? Matthew 7:7-8 says that we ask, seek and knock. We often look back over time and see the trials that we have come through. At the time we felt hopeless but looking back we stand in awe at God's plan and purpose that was accomplished. It is in times like this that a prayer journal can give marvelous testimony and encouragement. There is no better compliment than for someone to notice how we came through a difficult time, standing firm in our faith without a doubt that God had a plan and it would be accomplished. This is how we get through the daily bumps in the road. That's what faith can do. I pity those who do not know the Lord as Savior and have to stumble through life's difficulties alone. We should never let an opportunity pass by when we see them. God encourages us so that we can encourage others. We should always be ready to answer the question, How do you do it? I have a simple reminder written in my Bible, Every flower that bloomed had to go through a lot of dirt to get there. We often have to push up through the dirt but Jesus Christ awaits us when we bloom. Be encouraged today.

Dear Lord and Savior of my life, thank you for your plan for me. My desire is to do your will. You are my God and I long to see your plan for me. Thank you for the encouragement of your Holy Word. Give me opportunity to share my faith and experiences with someone who needs hope. Amen.

206

Instead Of Fear
2 Timothy 1:7

Worry and fear can be the same. I worry about tomorrow and I fear what tomorrow will bring. The past year has been difficult for me. Some days my fears are easily let go and other days I can't seem to overcome them. God does not want us to be afraid. He wants us to feel empowered because of his love and faithfulness. My Mom's Bible marks this verse, 'instead of fear'. We must trust God with confidence in spite of our fear.

It is difficult sometimes to understand what God is speaking. At times I hear him clearly and at other times I feel like he has me on hold. Either way I must trust him completely. I must stay alert to his whispers in my ear and to my heart. I must speak cautiously in an effort to allow him to speak through me. When I do this the fear subsides. I replace the fear with faith and hope. I try to be content in this knowing I will get through it and will learn from it, growing from it. Right now I am sitting at my desk. Yesterday was a very rainy, dreary day. Today the sunshine is beautiful, looking at me through the window. I see the sunshine as God's assurance that he is with me and offering a brand new sunny day. The difficult issues are still with me but so is he and he is strong. He knows my fear. I must continue to trust in him absorbing his power and strength like the warmth of the sunshine streaming through my window. This life is only in preparation for my eternal home with God. He allows the rain and he sends the sunshine. I will trust in him looking past today and looking forward to tomorrow when I will be with him for eternity with nothing more to fear.

Dear Father, I feel your presence. Help me to be content in knowing that you feel my fear and offer your unfailing love for comfort and peace. Help me to trust in you and reject the lies of fear and worry. My hope is in you. Amen.

207

The Psalms Of David

Psalm 150

I have a book of my mother's, <u>The Psalms of David,</u> illuminated by James Freemantle. According to the inscription it was a gift to her. It is a rather strange book. Apparently Mr. Freemantle was not a religious man but worked on the illustrations of the Psalms as a testament to his love for his wife. According to the Foreward written by his son it took almost 30 years for his father to complete the illustrations. As I read this I hoped to learn that his father came to know the Lord as he worked however there is no mention of it. Yet it is beautiful work. I don't know if he ever acknowledged that his talent was God given. It's hard to believe that he studied the Psalms for years, these wondrous Words of God, yet misplaced it on is wife. So often even as Christians we misplace our praise. I can see that my mother enjoyed it because of the notes and underlining she made. I'm sure she read the Psalms in praise of her Lord.

I was particularly drawn to the last Psalm. While the page is not decorated with flowers and color as some are, he boldly highlighted the words, Praise Him, ending with Praise ye the Lord. The End. Psalm 150 is a song of praise. It begins with the fact that God must be praised, follows with where he should be praised, why he should be praised, how he should be praised and then who should praise him. The word praise appears 13 times in the 6 verses. Let everything that has breath, praise the Lord. And this is certainly not The End but only the beginning. Our day should start in praise and end in praise. Every morning brings praise. Every night fall brings praise. No matter what life hands us we must praise our God. He is worthy of our praise as we enter the storms of life, ride the storm, come out of it and prepare for the next. Praise is as necessary as our heartbeat. We can't live without it. And we must be sure that our praise goes to him and it isn't misplaced.

Dear Lord, when I don't know if I can carry on, I praise you. Help me to remember that you hold all things in your hands and you are here to strengthen me and give me joy. Amen.

208

The Work-aholic

Exodus 34:21

Do you know or are you a work-aholic? We all know them. I was one for awhile and I have worked for a work-aholic. We get so wrapped up in our job that it becomes our life. No one else works as fast or as much as we do and we are sour towards them. We want to be the first to arrive and the last to leave. We ignore breaks, we ignore lunch hours and get frustrated with those around us trying to enjoy a holiday season. It is miserable but we don't know it at the time. This verse instructs us to rest on the seventh day even during the busy times. I believe it recognizes that some times in our lives are busier than others but we still rest wisely and practically. Rest is different for each of us. Working in the yard can be restful for some while it is work for others. Reading can be restful for some and a chore for others. Normally productive labor is not restful. When we strive to follow God's instructions we know what is rest and what is not. Some of us may have to work at finding something that brings rest other than a nap but it can be done. We may even need to ask God to show us. We also know when our job is consuming our life and becomes more important than anything else including our witness to those around us and our relationship with our Lord. Nothing is more important than this. Many relationships are unnecessarily strained and drained or even destroyed because of the work-aholic. Genesis 2:2 tells us that even God rested on the seventh day from his work of creation. Do you think he really needed the rest? I think not. He set an example for us. The same example we are to set for those around us. Deuteronomy 5:14 says that even the animals need rest from work. My friend who is a trainer and runs a horse farm sees that her school horses rest on Sunday. We need to be mindful of how we set the different priorities in our lives especially when it comes to our jobs and career. We are to work as if working for the Lord himself but he sets boundaries even when working for him. Let's be sure our job and career reflects our Christian living example and our devotion to our relationship with Jesus Christ.

Dear God help me to seek your guidance in setting the priorities and work standards in my job and career. Help me to put you first. I do not want to be consumed by my job so that it becomes the most important thing. Forgive me where I have failed in this and guide me in setting standards that you approve. My desire is to live a life that pleases you and to set a proper example for others that will reflect my relationship with you. Amen.

209

God Is Our Friend

Genesis 3:8

God walked in the garden with Adam and Eve before they sinned. I can imagine that the three of them spent time together walking and talking among the animals and birds in the beautiful place that God designed just for them. Maybe we cannot literally walk with him but he is our friend as he was to them and he walks and talks with us. I love the old hymn "He Lives" that speaks to this.

He lives, he lives.
Christ Jesus lives today. He walks with me and
talks with me along life's narrow way.
He lives, He lives, salvation to impart.
You ask me how I know he lives. He lives within my heart.

One of my Mom's favorite songs is "In the Garden" that speaks to walking with Jesus in the garden. At my aunt's burial a friend played the guitar and sang this song. It was beautiful in the quiet of the cemetery.

And he walks with me and he talks with
me and he tells me I am his own.
And the joy we share as we tarry there, none other has ever known.

Jesus taught in John 15:14 that he is our friend when we follow him. Romans 8:15-17 tells us that we have received the spirit of sonship and we can call God, Father or Daddy. Isn't it thrilling to know that we can have such a relationship with the King of Kings? God calls us his friend. We are his children.

Dear Father thank you for the special relationship we have. Thank you for calling me friend. I am thrilled to be your child. I pray I never need to be reminded that we can walk and talk together. My relationship with you should be daily in the good and bad times. I know you have a plan for me and it is perfect. Help me to share this news with those around me. This is such good news for the world that we live in. I long for your return so that we can exist in your heavenly presence together. Amen.

210

Very Good Advice
Proverbs 23:17-19

Sometimes it seems like we'll never get ahead. We're either going into a storm, in a storm or coming out of one. Sometimes it seems like those who appear to have no trust in our Lord achieve more than we do. These verses offer encouragement and remind us of the hope we have and the future that is held for us. God is well aware of the difficulties we face. He allows them to happen to teach us perseverance and confidence. He always has a plan and it is always good. The death and resurrection of his Son Jesus Christ has freed us from the fear of death and the world's judgment of our imperfection. We can live in this world with our eye on eternity in the presence of our Lord. Colossians 3:1-4 encourages us to set our hearts and minds on things above not on earthly things. Jesus Christ, the Lord and Savior of our life sits at the right hand of God and will one day return for us. Pull out that highlighter and make these verses stand out in your Bible. Keep your heart on the right path. Keep your eyes on Jesus.

Dear God thank you for the wonderful promises found in your Holy World. Thank you for the truth of your words. Life can be hard. Help me to keep my eyes on you and my thoughts on things above that wait for me. I know my future is with you and you have prepared a place for me. Forgive me when I fail you. Give me a strong desire to live according to your instruction and your promises. Thank you for your love for me. Amen.

211

Facing the Consequences
Galatians 6:7-10

We all make bad choices and mistakes in life. And sooner or later we have to face the consequences. Sometimes the consequences affect something that can easily be resolved and forgiven but sometimes the consequence greatly affects our life and it takes time to correct it, even years. I try to stress with my children and the youth that I work with that certain choices we make can greatly impact life. Going too far with a friend of the opposite sex can bring on parenthood too soon and change a life forever. One DUI or bad check can impact whether or not we get a job. Relationships can be damaged or destroyed because of a passionate moment or action taken in anger. It is true that we reap what we sow. We must live with the choices we make. Let's not forget though that this rule can positively impact our life as well. Wise choices can affect the direction of life as well. These verses encourage us to never grow weary of doing the right thing. Opportunity comes our way each day and we face hourly choices. The important thing is that we are prepared for each day. We must be in God's Holy Word on a daily basis and have regular communication with him especially listening for his direction. While in school it was not easy to pass a test without studying. How do we expect to pass life's test when we are unprepared? These daily tests could easily alter our life. Hebrews 4:16 tells us that we can approach the throne of grace with confidence so that we may receive mercy and find grace when we need help. We are not in this alone. God is there to offer guidance and direction. It is so important to seek him in every decision and choice we make. We must walk and talk with God daily to have an active and participatory relationship with him as we face each day.

Dear God thank you for your love and mercy. Help me to keep my eyes on you daily and take the choices I make seriously and reverently. My desire is to please you and follow you in everything I do. Forgive me when I think I can handle choices alone. I know you have a plan for me and your plan is good. You always know best. I praise you and adore you for the God that you are. You are my God and my King. Forgive me when I fail you. Amen.

212

Joy Restored
Job 8:21

There has been a point in each of our lives that we thought joy would never come again. We thought we would never get through such circumstances and would never have joy again. Life can change direction quickly and bring hurt. In this verse, Bildad tells Job that God will yet fill your mouth with laughter and your lips with shouts of joy. He encouraged Job that his joy would be restored. Flip over in your Bible to Job 42:10-17 and see how his laughter and joy did return. The Lord blessed the latter part of Job's life more than the first and Job was a very prosperous man to start with.

Job lived 140 years. In Psalm 16:11 David speaks of his trust in God. He says, you have made known to me the path of life; you will fill me with joy in your presence, with eternal pleasure at your right hand. David refers to God as his provider and protector. We draw strength from our relationship with God. The closer we are the more strength we receive. Strength gives us perseverance and hope. We keep our eyes on God and his provision and the joy will be restored. God uses difficult situations to grow and strengthen us. He hurts when we hurt and he is joyful with us when we are restored. Psalm 92:4 says we find gladness and sing for joy at the works of God's hands. Every morning brings new beginnings. Look for the joy in each moment.

Dear God thank you for the joy and gladness that comes from knowing you. You send joy when I think it will never come. Forgive me when I hesitate to trust you in all things. Help me to find the joy that each day brings. I will praise you with a joyful noise. Thank you for your love for me. Amen.

213

Seeking God's Will

Matthew 26:36-44

Sometimes it is hard finding the right words to pray. I have to be careful not to advise God on how to fix my problem or concern. I catch myself in my prayer saying please do this or please do that or please don't do this or that. I have learned to tell God the desire of my heart but to pray for his will not my own. When Jesus knew that the purpose of his coming would soon be fulfilled, he prayed that God's will be done. Jesus set the example for us. Verse 39 says that Jesus fell with his face to the ground. He was sharing his heart with his Father. We can do the same. 1 John 5:14-15 says that we can approach God in confidence. If we ask anything according to his will, he hears us. Knowing that he hears us, whatever we ask we will have. There aren't many things more important than our prayer life. Sure we can pray in the car and as we go about the day but a serious focused daily time of prayer is important. Life is hard. We must take time to seek God's will for our life and for those we love and care about. We must teach our children this truth. Pray and seek God's will for your life every day.

Dear God you are the Almighty God yet you allow me to approach your throne of grace with confidence. Thank you for the blessings in my life. I long to seek you and live your plan for me and will for my life. I pray my heart will be committed to a regular time spent with you. Thank you for sending Jesus to set the example for us. Thank you for the price he paid for me. I love you Lord. Amen.

214

The Death Of Moses

Deuteronomy 33:27 - 34:12

My morning devotion led me to Deuteronomy 33:27 which is part of Moses' blessing on the Israelites before his death. I kept reading and read the twelve verses in chapter 34 of Moses death. Moses was 120 years old when he died. God showed him the promised land but would not allow him to cross over into it. God buried Moses and his grave is unknown to this day. God and Moses had a special relationship. The passage refers to Moses as 'the servant of the Lord'. It also says the Lord knew Moses face to face. My study notes say that until Jesus came no one was superior to Moses. Hebrews 3:1-5 says that Jesus was found worthy of greater honor than Moses. The passage speaks of Moses as a servant in God's house and Jesus is the Son over God's house. Moses has a place of honor in God's sight.

God also knows each of us individually and has a purpose for each of us. God is our refuge and holds us with everlasting arms. We are special in his sight. I remember singing a song as a child that Jesus loves all the children; they are precious in his sight. Through the death and resurrection of Jesus Christ we do not have to fear death. Naturally none of us look forward to dying but we have nothing to fear. Jesus eliminated the sting of death. Even though we often fail in life, Jesus died and arose so that we can rise again. When he is Lord and Savior of our life, death immediately takes us into his presence. There is nothing to fear as Moses had nothing to fear. God took care of him personally and he will do the same for us.

Dear God thank you for the story of Moses. We can learn great lessons of perseverance from him. None of us are perfect but we know that we are precious to you. Thank you for your everlasting arms that hold me and your unconditional love. Give me a heart that longs to serve you in obedience to your teachings. Forgive me when I fail you. You are my God and my King. Amen.

215

Remarkable Respect
Daniel 6:19-23

Most of us are familiar with the story of Daniel in the lions den. Recently, a point in the story was brought to my attention. King Darius was not only Daniel's government authority; he was also Daniel's employer. Daniel had remarkable respect for him. So remarkable that after experiencing a night in the lions den, ordered by the king, the first words out of Daniel's mouth when he was released was, O king, live forever. He showed no resentment towards the king's actions. He showed full respect. While I respect authority, I'm not sure I could have done as Daniel did. Working in state government for many years I have had good supervisors and others were not so good. I have been blessed that many of my supervisors were Christians. There have been many state and federal rules that I have been required to follow that I had to work at developing respect, especially when I was working with my staff. I always thought it was important that managers exhibit respect of authority as an example to their own staff. Everyone, even the president of this country has authority to adhere to. We all have authority over us. God is the ultimate authority. The first commandment in Exodus 20:12 instructs us that we must have no other god before God. Daniel greatly respected authority but did not let it interfere with God's instructions.

God expects us to respect authority. We are to respect the position of authority. 1 Peter 2:18 says to slaves (employees), submit yourself to your masters (employer, supervisor, boss) with all respect not only to those who are good and considerate but also to those who are harsh. This is our responsibility as a godly employee.

Dear God thank you for my job. I pray for those who need employment. Help me to remember Daniel when I struggle with something my boss says or does. Help me to recognize that management positions are not easy and require my respect. I pray now that my boss has a relationship with you and knows you as Lord and Savior. I pray that my example will be positive and influencing to my boss and others that I work with daily. Thank you for your love for me. Amen.

216

Retirement

Numbers 8:20-26

It is my understanding that the only place in the Bible that retirement is mentioned is in reference to the Levites retiring at the age of 50. It is clear that at age 50 they were to retire from their regular service and work no longer. After the Levite had reached the mandatory retirement age he was still free to help the younger Levites but was no longer to do the difficult work he had done prior. Some may argue that this means we must retire at age 50. I am not here to argue that point. I personally retired after 28 years of service, served a brief period as an hourly consultant and was soon recruited to return to my previous area of service. I saw the opportunity as a blessing from the Lord and I strive to serve well in my position until my time ends. I personally think a couple things are important here. First, we seek God's guidance for his plan for our life. I ask him where do I serve (work) and when do I stop. Our desire should be to live within God's plan for each of us individually. I find nothing in God's Word, including this passage in Numbers, which instructs me to retire at a certain age. Some of us are physically able to work longer than others. God has different plans for each of us. Secondly, we follow the same rule for serving in our church or position of God's calling. I try to slap my own wrist when I catch myself saying, 'I've already served my time in the nursery or VBS and it's time for someone else to step up.' Again, we seek God's guidance in where he wants to use us and he will give us what we need to fulfill that position. We also have a position to serve in our homes and community. Look at Titus 2:1-5. Living a good and teaching example is required of us regardless of age or position.

I see another concern regarding retirement that I want to mention. While we do need to be practical in preparing for our older years, we can't focus on the future years and miss the years we are living in. I knew a guy that insisted that he and his family live in a tiny house and insisted on driving an old car so he could save half of his earnings for retirement. I think there is something wrong with this picture. We should never squander our earnings but we need to live daily trusting in God and not miss using his blessings because of worry for the future. We are not promised a tomorrow and must live as best we can today. I would rather do what I can for my family today, seeing their enjoyment and helping them meet their needs, rather than leaving it for them when I die. Again, take it to the Lord and seek his advice and guidance. He wants to bless us and he wants us to enjoy life according to his plan.

Dear God thank you for providing for me and for offering advice and guidance when I seek you. Help me to trust you and seek your plan for me in all things. Staying on the path with you will ensure success for me. When I try to go alone and make my own decisions I will fail. Forgive me when I stray from you. I love you and my desire is to live a life that pleases you. Help me to make decisions according to your desire for me. Amen.

217

God Speaks
Psalm 46

Psalm 46 was written for the musical procession of praise as the people went to the temple for worship. What a marvelous sound of praise from the singers, dancers and tambourines. I was reading through this and when I came to verse 10 I realized it was God speaking. My study notes refer to his voice breaking through as he speaks to the people, Be still and know that I am God. I will be exalted. And the people responded, The Lord Almighty is with us. God is to be exalted. He is to be glorified, praised and honored.

The girls in my Sunday School recently asked why doesn't God reveal himself to us today as he did in Bible times. I believe God does reveal himself to us; maybe not in a physical presence as he did there but he still speaks and is with us. This week has been a difficult one for me. I have felt God's presence so clearly and so present. At night when I am tired and restless from the day, I write in my prayer journal and I feel like he is right there beside me, listening. God is with me. God is with us when we allow him to be. He reveals himself when we are aware of him. Sometimes we miss him due to the noise in our life. Sometimes we miss him because we are too busy trying on our own. We have nothing to fear. Stop now and repeat verses 10-11 out loud. He longs to be exalted and he longs to reveal himself. Be still, close your eyes and absorb his presence. Be still and know that he is God. Exalt him. He is with us.

Dear Almighty God who is with us, thank you for your presence. I cannot do this alone. I need you. I seek you in all things. You are the only one I can trust completely. You are the only one who assures me of unconditional love and hope. Forgive me when I fail you. I desire to live a life that pleases you. I love you. I adore you. You are my provider and my King. You are my friend. Amen.

218

The Lord's Blessing
Numbers 6:24-26

These verses are familiar words of blessing. They have been written to music and often sung at the close of worship services or recited by the minister or priest. I have heard them repeated when visiting the sick or shut in. The Lord gave these words to Moses for blessing the Israelites. These are God's words of blessing. Proverbs 31:9 says to defend the rights of the poor and needy. We are blessed when we know Jesus Christ as Lord and Savior. We should share this blessing with others. There are many in need around us. In my job I work every day with people who have to decide whether to spend their small fixed income on food or medicine or the electric bill. There are those in the armed forces who risk their lives every day to maintain our freedom. They need our blessing. We often get caught up in our own busy lives and forget about those who need our blessing. One way we can offer our blessing is to pray for them. When someone crosses our path who is struggling, we should take the time to stop right then and there and pray for them. I shared a concern with a friend recently and she came to me the next day to tell me that she had prayed for me and apologized for not praying with me when we were together earlier. It is such a rich blessing to know someone is praying for me. It is such a rich blessing to know that God loves me and cares about every moment of my every day. Let's be encouraged to stop and thank God for his blessing. Let's ask God for an opportunity to share these words of blessing with someone today. We will be abundantly blessed by sharing God's blessing with someone else.

Dear God in heaven thank you for your words of blessing. Give me opportunity today to share these words of blessing with someone who needs to experience your love. I am so richly blessed and I thank you. The best blessing of all was the sacrifice of your Son so that I will have eternal life. I pray that the desire of my heart will be to study your Holy Word every day so that I can gain wisdom and knowledge to share with those around me. Help me to commit to spending time with you every day. I love you and thank you for your love for me. Amen.

219

Are You Washed In the Blood?
1 John 1:5-10

Today in Sunday worship we sang the old hymn "Are You Washed in the Blood'?. Are you washed in the blood? Is your soul cleansed by the blood of Jesus Christ the sacrificed lamb? Our sin is forgiven and washed away by the love of Jesus Christ. This passage says that the blood of Jesus purifies and cleanses us from all sin. We sing these words easily but do we really believe this? Are we committed to this truth? My Mom wrote in her Bible that she desired a new and profound reverence for the matchless revelation of the living and true God. Today's devotion is short in words but big in truth. Jesus died for me willing to sacrifice his own blood so that I am no longer condemned by my sin but washed clean and forgiven. Am I really committed to this truth and willing to live my life for him and not for myself? Let's be encouraged to focus on this today and if necessary recommit our heart to serving and obeying Jesus Christ in everything we say and do.

Dear God in heaven thank you for my eternal salvation. I do not want to take this truth for granted. I want to commit my heart to serving you in all I do. Forgive me when I fail you. Help me to accept the forgiveness you give and keep striving to do the best I possibly can in following your instruction for my life. I want to please you and serve you. Thank you for my cleansed soul through your blood. Amen.

220

Taken Captive
Colossians 2:8-10

Paul warns in this passage against hollow and deceiving human philosophy. Some religions or individuals may preach heresy about man made regulations taught to obtain salvation. As my preacher teaches on this subject, we need to constantly check our sources of knowledge. Jesus completes us. Jesus is all we need. No act or tradition gives us salvation including baptism, church attendance and the Lord's Supper or communion. There are many false teachings that can mislead us. Outward acts can only symbolize what is in our heart. The act doesn't provide salvation. Jesus Christ is the only one who had to perform an outward act in order to provide redemption.

In this world we are always looking for something to help us feel that we have achieved our goal or make us think of ourselves as acceptable. It can be marriage, parenthood, the right job or the right house in the right neighborhood. When we commit to the search for these things rather than allowing Jesus to complete us we are taken captive. We will never find an end to our search. The freedom Jesus Christ provides is lost in our search. Jesus Christ is the only one and only thing that can make us complete. 2 Corinthians 3:17 says where the Spirit of the Lord is there is freedom. Why do we allow our own selfish dreams and desires for accomplishment to take us captive when Jesus Christ offers us freedom in his completeness? Let's search our heart and seek the salvation of the Lord through a relationship with him and stop trying to jump through hoops to achieve completeness and freedom. Be still and know that God is God. All things are made complete through him.

Dear Lord thank you for the freedom you bring through my relationship with you. I want to seek you daily and find my freedom in you and not through my own selfish searches. Thank you for your love for me. I know that you have a plan for me and it is good. I want to find completeness in you. I don't need to look anywhere else. I adore you for you make me complete. Amen.

221

Angels
Hebrews 13:1-3

I collect angels. I have 2 cabinets of them that I have collected over the years. My first was given to me by my aunt. It belonged to my Grandmother and I have been collecting them ever since. Many are gifts from family and friends who knew of my collection. I am very careful about those I choose. I do not want silly angels because I think of them very seriously. The Bible speaks many times about angels. Angels bring good news, they bring warnings and they provide comfort or protection. There are good and bad angels. Dr. Tony Evans, pastor and teacher, created a wonderful series of messages entitled The Good, the Bad and the Ugly teaching about angels. Satan, once known as Lucifer, is the dark angel who was once the angel of light but will soon find his doom. His fall is spoken of in Isaiah 14:12-15 and in Luke 10:18 Jesus says he saw Satan fall like lightening.

Angels are spiritual creatures of service created by God to minister to us personally. Even Satan spoke of their ministry when he tempted Jesus (Matthew 4:5-6). We know little about how they minister and serve but I believe they are all around us everyday guided by God. They work according to God's orders. We have heard many stories of survival and praise was given to angels who brought one to safety. I was once lost on an out of town trip and a stranger came out of nowhere and gave me directions. I know without a doubt that he was an angel. I think angels are one of the things that will be revealed to us as Paul says in 1 Corinthians 13:11-12. We see poorly now like in a bad mirror and do not understand everything in God's Word but we will soon see face to face and will know fully. I believe angels are present in heaven and we will see and know them.

This passage in Hebrews warns us about how we treat strangers because they could be angels. This happened to Abraham and Sarah in Genesis 18. Luckily Abraham treated his visitors well. The Bible says one of the three visitors was actually God himself. While angels are sent to serve us we also have opportunity to be the angel. We have opportunity to treat someone in need as if we were in need, just as the angels do. We never know when we are entertaining an angel. Maybe God sends them our way to see how we react. We are to love and treat each other as brothers (or angels).

Dear God thank you for the presence of angels who are your creation and sent to minister to us. Help me to treat any stranger as if he or she could be an angel. I know that you are always with me and know my every need. My desire is to worship you daily, aware of your presence and live confidently according to your promises. Thank you for your provision and protection. I want to live each day in a way that pleases you. Forgive me when I am selfish and fail you. Thank you for your love for me. Amen.

222

Be Still and Know
Psalm 46

I have laid my concerns at the Throne of God. He is in control. I need for him to be in control. I want him to be in control. Psalm 46:10 rings in my ear throughout the day. Be still and know that I am God. As things progress, I feel like I am on a roller coaster ride that won't end. Anxiousness tries to set in. I stop and gather myself and remind myself,

Be still and know that he is God. Peace will come when I will allow it. It is easy to hold on to the anxiousness and 'what ifs'. Satan tries to cause confusion. I believe that confusion only comes from Satan. Confusion does not come from God. Confusion leads to fear. 2 Timothy 1:7 says God did not give us a spirit of fear but a spirit of power, of love and self - discipline. We have power when we are still and allow God to be in control. I am impatient. I want resolution now. Colossians 3:12 says as God's chosen people, holy and dearly loved, clothe yourself with compassion, kindness, humility, gentleness and patience. So, I try to focus on these things rather than confusion and impatience. I know God has a plan for me; a plan of prosperity and not failure or pain. This I know and trust. My confidence is in him as I am still and know that he is God.

Dear God thank you for your wisdom and peace. My strength comes from you to reject confusion and impatience. I recognize that peace comes when I am still and wait. You know what is best for me. You are God and I am not. Forgive me when I forget these truths. Thank you for your presence in my life. Amen.

223

The Act Of One Man
Romans 5:19

Jesus Christ saved us all by his death and resurrection. The death any man could have done but Jesus' act of resurrection gave us salvation. Jesus knew that his purpose for coming as a man was to bring salvation to man. In Matthew 12:40, he predicted it and he arose as he said he would. He said he would spend 3 days and nights in death as Jonah spent 3 days and nights in the belly of the whale. Jesus was who he claimed to be.

1 Corinthians 6:14 says God raised Jesus in his own power and he will also raise us. We are destined for resurrection and eternal life in the presence of our Lord. As the result of the resurrection, we have nothing to fear in death when we have accepted Jesus as Savior. Jesus says in Revelation 1:18 that we have nothing to fear because he was dead but is now alive for ever and ever. Because he lives, we will live for ever and ever. This reminds me of the song "Because He lives".

Because he lives, I can face tomorrow.
Because he lives, all fear is gone.

Because I know he holds the future and life
is worth living just because he lives.

He lives even though he was dead. Jesus was resurrected by the power of God so that we can live too. What marvelous promises we have in Jesus Christ.

Dear Jesus thank you for your resurrection. What a marvelous Savior you are. Your cruel and sacrificial death was for my sin and now I will live forever because of your act of love. Your one powerful act will save us all. Forgive me when I fail you. Help me to live each day, mindful of your great love for me and your plans for me. Help me to love others around me with the same love and compassion that you have for each of us. Amen.

224

Stability
Psalm 91:1-2

I read a brief article today outlining the benefits of a relationship with God. Stability was one of the benefits that caught my attention. Is your life stable today? My life has really changed from when I first started writing this book of devotions. My marriage is not stable at this time. I am living as a houseguest of a friend and must temporarily call this home. The horse that I thought was so right for me is now for sale. No matter how hard we try, life rarely stays stable. I am so thankful that my relationship with God is strong and stable as ever. In fact, God brings the little stability that I do have in my life of instability. One version that I read of this passage says, He who dwells in the secret place of the Most High shall remain stable and fixed under the shadow of the Almighty. Psalm 91 speaks to the security of those who trust in God. My Bible study notes say that the shelter or secret place refers to the temple where the godly find safety. Stability in life brings a feeling of security. The only way to have stability and security that does not waiver is through a relationship with God. We have the assurance that God is stable. He does not change. He is the light and the truth. If our relationship with him becomes unstable, it is because we have moved away or waivered, not him. Strengthening our relationship with him requires that we make it the priority in our life. We commit to spending time with him, listening to his guidance and doing as he says. The world, our own selfish desires and Satan will try to influence us differently which will cause instability to set in. And sometimes what we consider instability is simply God allowing a change of direction in our life, teaching us perseverance and obedience. Life can change with the wind. You can expect it. We can find daily rest and peace in our God. He is our refuge in whom we trust. We can find protection under the wing of his stable and unchanging love for each of us. Isaiah 26:3 says we will find perfect peace when our mind is steadfast because we trust in God. Trust in the Lord, for the Lord is the rock eternal. Don't these promises make you feel more secure and loved and grateful? As Festus on *Gunsmoke* says, it makes you feel 'soul-some'.

Dear God thank you for your stability. Give me a heart and mind that is committed to studying your Holy Word and seeking your guidance in all I do. I need the security and stability that my relationship with you assures me. I trust in you for you are the rock in my life. You are the light and the truth. I praise your name and lift my hands in thanksgiving. I will remain fixed and stable under the wing of your protection and provision. I love you Lord. Amen.

225

Now I Lay Me Down To Sleep
Psalm 3

Did you have a night time prayer as a child? "Now I lay me down to sleep" was mine. The verses in this Psalm remind me of it. I'd like to think that's where it came from. I normally talk with God when I first lay down to sleep. I discuss my day with him and ponder the next day. Normally I rarely have trouble sleeping. However there are times that I wake up and my imagination starts wandering and the 'what ifs' set in and before I know it, I am tossing and turning and fretful. This Psalm brings peaceful promises and replaces the 'what ifs' with confidence. The Lord is a shield around me. I cry out loud to the Lord and he answers me from his holy place. I lie down and sleep. I will wake again because the Lord sustains me. I will not fear the many worries and concerns that plague me because the Lord sustains me. From the Lord comes deliverance. Deliverance from the tossing and turning and fretful thoughts. A friend of mine lost a teenage daughter in a tragic automobile accident. We were talking one day and she told me that when she wakes up at night and can't sleep from the grief, she starts singing praise songs in her head and sings herself to sleep. She said that at other times she quotes scripture verses. What a great way to resist the negative and restless thoughts that Satan tries to fill our minds with so we cannot rest. God knows our every concern and care and wants us to have peace in our heart and rest at night. He does not sleep and is always available to talk, yes even at 2AM. Next time we can't sleep, let's think on these promises - You are a shield around me, O Lord. I cry to you O God and you answer me from where you are. I lie down and sleep. The Lord sustains me. Deliverance comes from the Lord. Choose which promise helps and let's sleep on it.

Dear God in Heaven, now I lay me down to sleep, I pray the Lord my soul to keep. You are a shield around me O God. Thank you for your protection and your desire for me to find rest, not only in sleep but in confidence of my salvation in you. My deliverance comes from you. You are the sole desire of my heart. Amen.

226

Trust In the Lord
Psalm 20

It is so obvious that so many people in this world are looking for something that is right under their nose. They have no hope when it comes with every sunrise. A friend of mine gave me Psalm 20:7 as I was leaving on a mission trip to Venezuela - Some trust in chariots and some in horses, but we trust in the name of the Lord our God. This particular psalm is written for kings going into battle. The psalmist encourages them to trust in the Lord, not in their own strength. We fight battles every day. Trusting in God's Word provides protection. We must be in God's Word everyday to be prepared for daily battles. Remember singing the old hymn "Only Trust Him"?

Only trust him, only trust him, only trust him now.
He will save you, he will save you, he will save you now.

God answers us when we are in distress. He wants to give us the desire of our heart and make all our plans succeed. These aren't my own words to encourage you, they come from this passage - words of hope and success and protection. Why would we even for a second trust in anything or anyone else? We must make God the priority in our life so that we easily trust him regardless of what comes our way. Praise Him! Shout for joy!

Dear God, I put my trust in you. Your Word tells me that you will save us and answer us from your holy heaven with the saving power of your right hand. Help me to soak in this hope and trust you in all that I do. Help me to share this hope with those around me. Amen.

227

Call To Action
James 4:7-10

I have always found the book of James as simply written instruction for Christian living - A Call to Action. Matthew 13:55 suggests that James was one of the brothers of Jesus. I've learned that he became a prominent leader in the Christian church after a time of unbelief of Jesus' teachings. Chapter four calls us to submission to God, addressing the sinful attitude of pride. In these short verses (7-10) there are several instructions for us with promises.

- Submit to God - Keep our relationship with God a priority rather than thinking first of our own selfish desires.
- Resist the devil and he will flee from you - Keep our focus on the Lord in a constant state of worship. Be very mindful of what we allow into our ears and before our eyes.
- Draw near to God and he will draw near to you - Pray continuously. Spend time everyday in his Holy Word, listening to him and talking to him.
- Wash your hands - Keep our outward appearance clean, reflecting our relationship with God.
- Purify your heart - Keep our heart (thoughts and mind) clean and pure.
- Grieve, mourn and wail for our sins - Repent. Apologize. Have a change of heart and soul. Say you're sorry and mean it.
- Humble yourselves before God and he will lift you up - Be still and know that God is God.

More rules to follow? No. Take that thought captive. Not rules but an assurance of God's presence in our lives and his blessings upon us. God opposes the proud but gives grace to the humble (verse 6). Matthew 23:12 says whoever exalts himself will be humbled and whoever humbles himself will be exalted. Let's take time today to reflect on these things.

Dear God forgive my heart of pride. It is so easy to put myself first and I repent of that. Help me to place my relationship with you before my own thoughts and desires. You died for me and now assure me of your love and grace. Help me build a determination to live according to these instructions so that my life is pleasing to you. Thank you for your constant presence in my life and the many blessings you send my way. Amen.

228

Making a Difference
1 Timothy 6:17-21

Several days ago I mentioned the radio station promoting the Drive Thru Difference. Yesterday morning on my way to work I decided to stop for a biscuit and drink. I hoped someone would pull up behind me so that I could try the Drive Thru Difference and pay for their order. A car did come up. As I came to the window I told the cashier I wanted to pay for mine and the car behind me. She told me the order behind me was 6 biscuits. My 1st thought was, 'Oh my' but my thought immediately changed to, 'This is an opportunity to share Jesus with 6 people rather than 1. Yes!' I told the cashier to tell the car behind me, Jesus loves you. I was thrilled as I drove away knowing the stranger behind me was getting the message that their order was covered and that Jesus loved them. I didn't want to be boastful with pride at work but I did tell a couple folks. Both faces brightened and it seemed that the gesture brightened their day just as it did for those who got the free biscuit. All day I thought about it. It could possibly be that the car behind me had decided to stop and surprise friends at her job with a biscuit and my gesture blessed her gesture by paying for it. It could have been someone who wanted to surprise friends at her job with a biscuit but hesitated because she really could not afford it and look what happened. I do not know how this gesture affected the lady cashier. The more I think about it the more excited I get. I will never know this side of heaven the true story but I do know I highly recommend it as a great way to start your day. Yes, the 6 biscuits cost me $12 which I didn't expect but it was worth the thrill and I consider it well spent money.

Paul tells Timothy that we are to put our hope in God who richly provides us with everything for our enjoyment. My $12 was used for my enjoyment which was passed on to others. This good deed was a treasure for me yesterday and still today. I do not know the magnitude of it as it passed through I don't know how many people. Such a simple thing greatly shares the love of Jesus. I thank God for the opportunity and I believe he smiled on this. Life is hard and yes I have problems but this little act of kindness has thrilled me. Think about this and ask God to show you a way to experience this same thrill.

Dear God thank you for the blessings you give and thank you for the thrill of sharing them. I pray that my act yesterday made a difference in many lives and I pray that even today it is still affecting others. Give me faith and courage to accept any opportunity that you send my way. You are the joy of my life. I adore you. Amen.

229

Clouds
1 Thessalonians 4:16-18

Clouds form when water evaporates from oceans, lakes or ponds and rises up into the atmosphere. There are several different kinds of clouds and an interesting facet for weather enthusiasts. It is very calming and soothing to sit on a porch or on the beach and watch the cloud formations particularly when they are moving. As kids we imagined pictures in the sky made by the clouds. It can be breathtaking to watch from the window of an airplane as it moves up through the clouds, particularly when they are puffy and white. However, it can be rather bumpy when they are dark and thick and I assume full of rain. Some speak of a cloudy day as dreary and depressing while I have heard that others enjoy cloudy days. Different things move us and make us feel the nearness of God. Many times I have gazed into the sky shimmering with beautiful bright clouds and felt the nearness of God. I can imagine him looking down through the clouds. A dark stormy sky flashing with lightening makes me wonder if God is angry. The Bible says that as the children of Israel left Egypt the Lord went before them by day in a pillar of a cloud to guide them on their way (Exodus 13:21).

The Bible speaks several times of our Lord Jesus Christ appearing in the sky and meeting us in the clouds. Revelation 1:7 says, Look, he is coming with the clouds and every eye will see him. It will not matter that day whether the clouds are white or dark. Regardless of the weather forecast for that day, the clouds will be white and puffy, bright and pure for those of us who know Jesus Christ as Lord and Savior. I can assure you they will be dark and threatening for those who do not know him. Life is full of clouds. Some are white and puffy and others are dark and stormy. Let's be sure the dark and threatening clouds are not from sin in our heart that we need to repent and move away from. Sin can hang over us like a cloud. When stormy days come, we must be still and know that God is God (Psalm 46:10) and God is in control. God controls the clouds in the sky and he controls the clouds that form in our lives. Because of his grace I need not be concerned by their presence. I do need to be concerned about the readiness of my heart to meet him in the sky. Am I ready to meet Jesus Christ in the clouds? Am I living today as if Jesus Christ may appear in the clouds today? What do I need to change to be ready? Maybe the clouds can be a good reminder to us as we watch for the return of our Lord.

Dear God thank you for the beautiful world that you have created for us. I look up and feel your nearness. Because of your grace, I need not be concerned by the presence of the dark clouds in life. I do ask that you search my heart and show me what needs to change so that I am prepared to meet you in the clouds. I want to live my life as a pleasing offering to you. Give me courage to listen to your voice and do as you say. Amen.

230

Good News
Matthew 28:1-8

I have a devotion book that belonged to my mother Unto the Hills by Billy Graham. It is one of my favorite books to use in my morning quiet time or just when I have a few quiet moments. According to mother's notes, she got it in December 1988. On many of the days she made notes or wrote the date. This always makes me feel close to her knowing that at a certain time she read the same thing I am reading. I think of her notes or under-lined words as being just for me.

When Mary and Mary went to the tomb they were greeted with good news. Not only good news but great news. News that changed history. News that changes lives. News that provides forgiveness and eternal life for all. No matter who reads this news and no matter when it is read it is always good news. It is life changing news. Usually read at Easter time this passage is good for anytime. This news is for each of us. I cannot even imagine how this recorded event transpired. I imagine the two Marys stumbled all over each other getting out of the doorway of that tomb and back down the path to share what they had seen and heard. Their hearts were racing. They were probably crying and laughing and rejoicing. We should feel the very same way each time we read this passage. This is good news for any day. Our heart should be racing. We should be crying and laughing and rejoicing too. It isn't old news. It is good news. He is risen! Jesus Christ died and arose from the dead for me and for you. Are you excited yet? Jesus has gone ahead just as it says in verse 7. He has gone ahead to prepare a place for us. He is preparing a place for us to spend eternity in his presence. This is the good news that God's Holy Word still brings to us today. The message has not changed with time. It isn't news that doesn't matter anymore. It is good news. It is good news for everyday for everyone and it needs to be shared. Read it today. Share it with someone today. Read it again tomorrow.

Dear God praise you for this marvelous good news. Thank you for the sacrifice of your Son. Thank you for eternal salvation. I pray my heart is grateful. Forgive me when I think on this as routine news. It is good news and it needs to be shared. Give me opportunity to share your wonderful story. Give me a heart for those around me who have not heard the news. Amen.

231

Secret To Happiness
Colossians 3:12-17

I find ten steps to happiness in these verses:

1. Clothe yourself with compassion, kindness, humility, gentleness and patience,
2. Recognize that everyone has faults,
3. Forgive and forget,
4. Bind all of the above with love,
5. Stay at peace with Christ,
6. Be grateful,
7. Let God's Word rule your mind and your heart,

8. Caution others of their wrongs,
9. Keep a song (Christian music helps me) in your heart, and
10. Do everything in the name of Jesus Christ.

As you read through this God may speak to you differently. God's Word is full of advice and instruction for happiness and peace. The world has a different idea. Let's focus on God's truths today.

Dear God I can only achieve this guidance through a relationship with you. I cannot find true happiness without you. Help me to recognize that all I need is you. When I follow you and strive to do everything in your name, I will succeed. Thank you for your many blessings. Thank you for your gracious love for me. I love you Lord. May my soul rejoice in you in all that I do. Amen.

232

Have You Heard?

Isaiah 40:9-31

This is a passage full of promise and hope, especially verses 28-31. Do you not know? Have you not heard? The Lord is the everlasting God, the Creator of the ends of the earth. He will not grow tired or weary and his understanding no one can fathom.

Nothing else we choose as a god can satisfy as these promises satisfy. There is nothing else we need for a life of peace, success and contentment. God is the King of all and he is our friend. The first verses in this passage speak to the power and wonder of God. Verse 1 of this chapter offers tender words of comfort from God for his people. These words are for us today as well.

Just a couple days ago I spoke of the good news; good news that does not change with time. It isn't news that doesn't matter anymore. God's Holy Word is full of promise and hope for everyday for every situation. Nothing is too simple to matter to him and nothing is too complex for him to resolve. Verse 11 tells us he tends his flock like a shepherd. He gathers the lambs in his arms and carries them close to his heart. Picture in your mind the loving shepherd carrying a lamb in his arms close to his heart. You and I are that lamb. God tends to us as a shepherd cares for his sheep. He will risk anything to care for one sheep that strays. He sent his own innocent son to a cruel death so that his flock would have eternal forgiveness and life. Do you not know? Have you not heard? The Lord is the everlasting God. Even a young, strong person can grow tired and stumble and may fall but when we trust in the Lord and put our hope in him, we will soar like an eagle and will not grow weary. Our strength is renewed each day for each situation when we trust in the Lord Jesus. Do you not know? Have you not heard? The Lord is the everlasting God.

Dear God thank you for your promises. I would surely fail miserably without you. Give me a heart of trust and hope. In my relationship with you I can feel the love of a shepherd for his lamb and the strength of an eagle in flight. I can soar to new heights. Give me a desire to study your Holy Word everyday, seeking your promises and guidance of wisdom. I praise your name with thanksgiving. Forgive me when I fail you. Amen.

233

Get Behind Me Satan
Mark 8:31-33

I have heard this saying since I was a child and still use it often, maybe not often enough. Jesus tried to tell the disciples more than once that he would be killed and would rise again after three days. Peter just could not imagine this and complained to Jesus for saying it. My Bible says Peter rebuked Jesus. Maybe Peter thought Jesus was scaring the other disciples. Maybe Peter loved him so, he was thinking, Surely not, but Jesus rebuked him saying, Get behind me Satan. Jesus used similar words when he rebuked Satan for tempting him (Matthew 4:10) when he said, Away from me Satan. Oh how Peter must have cringed. Jesus knew Peter's actions were from an evil source and he stopped it quickly and firmly.

Satan does tempt us every other minute of every day. There are many things that can influence Satan's schemes against us – TV, movies, Internet, books, friends, co-workers, etc. We must be careful of what we allow before our eyes and in our ears. Garbage in garbage out. We must take a stand against improper things that can lead us astray, usually very subtly. We must learn to say, Get behind me Satan or Away from me Satan. 1 Corinthians 10:13 says that we are all commonly tempted. God is faithful in that he will not let us be tempted beyond what we can individually bear and will provide a way out so that we can stand against it. Ephesians 6:11 tells us to put on the full armor of God so that we can stand against the devil's schemes. We can stand against evil schemes. There is no room for, I couldn't help it. Secondly, we do not want to be the evil source as Peter was in this passage. Our opinion or attitude or reckless selections and decisions can be the very thing that negatively influences those around us. We must be careful that we aren't the rebuked one. Influences are so strong today especially with the social media sources growing. So many things are carelessly accepted usually because someone else allows it, and we compare ourselves to them rather than to the teachings in God's Holy Word. The Bible has answers to everything. It is our guide. Jesus loved Peter and his reprimand was out of love. We should love those around us that are not aware of the schemes of Satan. We can rebuke them quickly and firmly in love, as Jesus did.

Dear God thank you for your protection from Satan's schemes. Help me to be in tune to the way out that you send my way. My desire is to study your Holy Word and learn the guidance that you provide for my life. I want to be a light that shines for you and not a distraction or hindrance to others who want to follow you or to those who need to see a Christian example. Help me to compare myself to you and not to others around me. You are the truth and the way. Amen.

234

Identity Theft
Revelation 3:5

Unfortunately identify theft is too common today. My daughter worked in a restaurant a couple years ago and her purse was stolen. Before the thief finished, she had to defend over $3000 spent out of her bank account. At this very moment I am dealing with a $99.75 charge for gas at a station in Florida. I live in South Carolina, did not take a recent trip to Florida and did not give my card to anyone, yet someone somehow made a copy of my card and used it. Thank you Lord, I realized the mysterious charge to my account before any more damage was done. Identity theft steals our identity and our integrity. When this theft occurs, we find ourselves having to defend our integrity and convince banks and stores that we can be trusted. We find ourselves having to defend our identity.

The Bible teaches that when we accept Jesus Christ as our Savior, our name is written in the Book of Life. Jesus Christ teaches that once entered in the Book our name cannot be erased. He will acknowledge us before the Heavenly Father and his angels. In John 10:27-30, Jesus calls us his sheep and says that no one can snatch us from his hand or the hand of the Father. We are his and our identity can not be stolen. We are his and we do not have to defend our identity ever again. Jesus Christ is my Savior and I belong to him. No one can steal that from me. Satan may try to discourage us from claiming that identity but once done even he cannot steal it. He will lie and try to make us feel like we must defend it but he is a liar. Satan is the loser. Yes we must be practical and protect our personal identity while here on earth. I encourage you to monitor your bank accounts online regularly. As far as our identity in Christ, it cannot be stolen by any thief. Our relationship with Jesus Christ is rock solid. Our name is written in the precious Book of Life and can not and will not be deleted or erased. We are his and his forever.

Dear Father thank you for your saving grace. Thank you for the eternal security and confidence that you bring. You are the Lord and Savior of my life and I adore you. The desire of my heart is to focus on things above. To love and trust you for the heavenly home you prepare for me. Protect us from the thieves that try to harm and steal our identity. I pray for the person who has a duplicate of my card. I pray that he or she will somehow come to know your plan of salvation so that grace and forgiveness can be found and the theft will stop. People need you Lord. Give me opportunity to share your love. Amen.

235

Filling the Void

Hebrews 10:23, 35-39

Life brings change. We move from one chapter to the next. Sometimes it is normal happenings like the kids leaving the nest, moving or family/friends moving away. Sometimes it is tragic happenings such as death, relationship break-ups or illness. I am speaking specifically when something happens to create a void or an empty space in our daily life. Moving through a major relationship change I have found myself dealing with a real void in my life. I was wisely cautioned to be mindful and careful of how I fill the void. The void can be filled with positive or negative things. I have chosen to fill the void by writing this volume of devotions, exercise and establishing new healthy relationships with women in similar situations. I have dusted off my keyboard and started to play again. My relationship with my Lord is stronger than ever. It is important to me that I spend time with him daily, usually more than once. My prayer journal allows me to write my desires, fears and praises as I start my day and before turning out the light at night. I listen for his voice. He speaks to me through his Word, circumstances and those around me. It is easy for us to fill the void with negative things and new habits that can and will only lead to new and different problems, such as withdrawing from fellow Christians into loneliness (and even our relationship with God), dwelling on anger and bitterness, excessive drinking, substance abuse or unhealthy relationships. Be encouraged to recognize the void and address it properly. It can be overwhelming and cause restlessness and anxiety – I know, I have been there and still deal with it. As these verses say, hold unswervingly to the hope we have for God has promised to be faithful and he keeps his promise. Be strong. Do not throw away the confidence you have in our Lord. Be encouraged to persevere so that when you have done the will of God you will receive what he has promised. Allow God to help you fill the void. Ask and he will answer. You will find yourself busy with new things to do, different places to go and new relationships to build. Do not let the emptiness shake you. It will if you allow it. Recognize and ignore Satan's lies and discouragement. And if you need to, seek Christian counsel. Never be afraid to ask for help.

Dear God thank you for the confidence and hope that comes from my relationship with you. Give me strength and perseverance to address change, recognize the void and fill it properly. Give me a heart convicted to a daily relationship with you. Help me to trust you in all things. Help me to take captive the anxiousness and fears that enter my mind. Walk with me and talk with me. I love you for you are my friend. Amen.

236

Focus On the Truth
Acts 2:22-39

I friend told me recently about a miserable day she had. She heard parts of a story and became convinced that her child was involved in something illegal. At first she was shocked because her young adult had never been in serious trouble but her head was consumed and overwhelmed with fear. She felt tormented all day. Late in the day she heard the whole story and realized she had falsely accused her child (in her head). She said that she felt exhausted and drained from a day filled with worry and fear. We have all done it. We throw ourselves into a panic or argue in our mind with something that hasn't even happened. Sometimes it lasts a few minutes and sometimes longer. We usually feel silly or disgusted with ourselves when this happens. It does leave us emotionally drained and sometimes physically ill. We can learn from this. The Bible cautions us that Satan is a liar and a deceiver. We are warned to be prepared for his schemes. We must learn to stand firm in our relationship with our Lord and not be easily shaken. God is in control. We must learn that when shattering news or happenings come our way, we must immediately claim God in control, turn our eyes to him and maintain a focus on his truths and his promises rather than giving in to our fears. In this passage, Jesus had returned to heaven and Peter was preaching as hard as he could. He taught of God's plan of salvation for us, his promise of hope and his promise of companionship. He professed that we are never alone and need never to be shaken. I read once that God's Word is full of footlights. There are lights along a stage so that actors know where the edge is. These footlights keep them from stepping too far out and falling. An actor would never ignore the lights and continue past them. The Bible is full of caution and instructions to keep us from falling off the edge or stepping too far off the right path or giving in to fear. We've just got to read them and practice using them.

Dear God forgive me when I take my eyes off you. I repent and turn to you. Help me to be serious about my relationship with you and serious about studying my Bible so that I am prepared for Satan's lies and schemes. I will not be shaken. I will not let fear torment me. You are my hope and my companion. You will never abandon me. Amen.

237

Choose Life
Deuteronomy 30:15-20

Life is full of choices. We make choices throughout every day. I love the Old Testament Books. God is so black and white when he speaks to the Israelites. He is clear and to the point. Obey me and prosper he says, ignore my instruction and fail. When we love the Lord our God, walk in his ways and obey his rules we will live a life of blessing. When we put other gods before him and turn from him, we will bring destruction into our lives. It is our choice. God is not a bully. He does not force himself on us. He tells us like it is. He sets boundaries and stands on them firmly as a good Father does. He explains clearly what will happen in life based on our choices. Naturally we say we choose life but do we really mean it? Do will really consider and realize the consequences of our choices? When things don't go right do we immediately search our heart for something that needs to change? God is a loving Father who loves us unconditionally and is always ready to accept our repentance. He does not promise a life with no problems or struggles but he does promise to never leave. Take time to read the entire chapter of Deuteronomy 30. Mark it I choose life! and date it today. It was written many years ago for a different time and day but it greatly applies to us today, here and now.

Dear God thank you for your promises. You are the perfect Father who never leaves and never makes mistakes. You are my God and I adore you. I want to live according to your instruction. I want to live a life that pleases you. Forgive me when I fail you. Search my heart and show me what needs to change. I choose life. Amen.

238

Victory In Jesus
1 Corinthians 15:57-58

There are days that we feel like we constantly lose. I told my friend the other night that I was tired of fighting and not getting anywhere. It seems that way sometimes, doesn't it? My daughter was a young cheerleader for the Recreational Center. They were precious. Victory, victory, V-i-c-t-o-r-y. We want Victory, they yelled. They didn't understand the game and half the time didn't know if they were winning or loosing but they knew their cheers. We sing Victory in Jesus from the hymnal in church.

Oh victory in Jesus, my Savior forever.
He sought me and bought me with his redeeming blood.

So often we sing songs of worship and don't take the words to heart. When we have Jesus in our heart we should never feel defeated. We get victory through our Lord Jesus Christ. Satan lies and wants us to feel defeated but we are not defeated. Satan is a liar. Following Jesus is a win, win. We are encouraged in this passage to stand firm and let nothing move us.

Yes it is easy to get discouraged. That is why we need to be so careful about who we spend time with, where we spend our time, what we allow before our eyes and what we allow in our ears. It is also important to read God's Holy Word everyday for guidance and encouragement. And it is important to stay in communication with the Heavenly Father, talking words of praise and our heart's desire to him and listening for his voice and response. A relationship will not thrive when you have no desire to learn more about your partner and spend time talking with them every chance you get. So is true for our relationship with God. We must maintain it actively. Otherwise, feelings of defeat will emerge and become overwhelming. God is in control. We can trust him in all things. Take time to read about Jehoshaphat's battle with Moab and Ammon in 2 Chronicles 20. I love the story. Do not be afraid or discouraged because of the enemy, God tells them, The battle is not yours but mine. God fought the battle for them and gave them victory. And he is willing to fight our daily battles for us and give us victory. Victory, victory, V-i-c-t-o-r-y! We have Victory! It is ours to have through Jesus Christ.

Dear Father in Heaven we thank you for the victory you give us. Help me to hand my battles over to you and not try to fight them on my own. Why do I do that? You are the victory. I have victory in you. The story is old but the message is still new. Thank you for your love for me. Amen.

239

Blessed Are the Meek
Matthew 5:5

The dictionary defines meek as gentle, showing patience and humility. This passage teaches, blessed are the meek. Psalm 37:11 says the meek will inherit the land and enjoy great peace. I believe this teaches us to have a meek attitude toward others and also toward God. We are to have an attitude of service, putting the needs of others first. This requires respect and a humble attitude. We are not naturally meek. The Holy Spirit in us can make us meek. The world sees meek as weak but an attitude of meekness brings peace. There is no opportunity for jealousy and pride in a heart of meekness. I believe this attitude also brings a willingness to give rather than wanting to receive. The Bible teaches that God loves a cheerful giver. The world would see these teachings (The Beatitudes, Matthew 5:1-12) as unrealistic and weak; that living this way allows others to walk all over us and take advantage of us. However these are the standards for Christian living taught by Jesus during his time on earth. Zephaniah 3:12 says the meek and the humble trust in the name of the Lord. An attitude of meekness can only come from trust in God. When we have this attitude before God it will reflect in our actions toward others. Others will see Jesus in me when I have an attitude of meekness. So what if they see me as weak? Rejoice and be glad, for great is our reward in heaven!

Dear God help me to have a heart of meekness. Give me courage to ignore the opinion of the world. My desire is to have a heart of meekness toward you and toward those around me. I want others to see Jesus in me. I want to have peace with myself knowing that I am following your desire for me. Give me opportunity today to show patience and humility to someone who needs to know of your love. Amen.

240

Is There Room?
Luke 2:7

I came across this verse in an article and it has stuck with me for several days. It is a verse from the Christmas story but very relative any time. There was no room in the inn for the coming of Jesus Christ. While it was all part of God's plan, there was no room for him. Do we make room for Jesus today in our lives and in our hearts? I remember singing songs as a child and hymns from the hymnal about asking Jesus into my heart and making room for Jesus. I'd like to suggest that we take time today to evaluate just how much room in our life do we allow for Jesus. Is he first? Is he crowded? Does he have enough space to grow? We are all busy and time seems short but sometimes I think my life gets crowded because I don't make enough room for Jesus. Having the right relationship with him doesn't make life perfect but it is easier to deal with the imperfections when I make Jesus a part of my daily routine and focus on him throughout the day. There are some things that take up too much room that when eliminated, there is more room and time for Jesus. Let's ask God to search our heart and show us how to make more room for him so that when he knocks we can welcome him in with plenty of room to spare.

Dear God forgive me when there is no room for you in my life. I can be very selfish with my time and space. My relationship with you will grow stronger when I make more time for you. Show me what needs to be eliminated to clear space for you. Help me to clear out the clutter. Thank you for your love for me. Amen.

241

A Change Of Plans
Romans 8:26-28

This will be brief but certainly not short in truth. We make plans and head ourselves in a direction. Sometimes things run smoothly and sometimes we experience a change of plans and become totally lost and overwhelmed with indecision. Take time to stop and seek God's will in your life. Sometimes the change of plans is his will that holds something for me to learn. Sometimes the change of plans is his way of getting me back on the right track according to his will. At times I struggle with seeking God's will. I am afraid it will be painful and not where I want to go. I have to recognize that when I seek his will, trusting him completely, he will change my heart. When I seek his will he will not drag me off kicking and screaming. But I have to admit that sometimes I am afraid that will happen. I often have to ask him for the strength to seek his will. I hope that this is making sense to you today and is helpful. Don't be discouraged by a change in plans. Seek his will and wait in anticipation for the goodness he will bring according to his plan.

Dear God give me courage every day to seek your will in my life. I cannot rely on my own plans. You are full of wisdom and knowledge. You know what is best for me. Forgive me when I doubt you. Amen.

242

Praise To God and Thank You
Luke 17:11-19

This is a story some of us learned as a child. It is one of those stories that I have known for a long time but recently spoke to me differently. Do we often enough give God the glory for what he does for us and do we say Thank You? I can answer for myself. No. In this story Jesus miraculously changed these ten men's lives. They would have died if he hadn't healed them. Their death would have been alone, separated from family and friends, slow and painful. They were given a huge second chance in life. Only one of them started out on the right foot recognizing the miracle of Jesus, gave him praise and said Thank You. Does Jesus not do that for us over and over? And do we recognize his miracle, give him praise and thank him? Oh how he does this for us throughout each day, in big and little ways. Maybe not so little. We have faith in him and trust him in all things and he blesses us, regardless of whether we deserve it or not. He always deserves the praise because he is the Father of miracles and blessings. We are encouraged to spend time with God everyday in prayer and Bible study. Praising him and thanking him should be a part of this time. Sometimes we focus on what we need and desire rather than praising him and thanking him. I'd like to suggest that we thank him before we even ask. He is our provider. He deserves the praise and all the honor and glory for each minute of our day. He is our friend. He knows our needs and wants to comfort us. Let's make a daily habit of throwing ourselves at the feet of God, praising him, even in a loud voice, thanking him for what he does.

Dear God forgive me when I forget to say thank you. Forgive me when I focus on myself and do not give you the praise and glory that you richly deserve. You love me and forgive me unconditionally and I give you the praise and honor for the miracles you perform in my life everyday. Help me to recognize your miracles and not take them for granted. I love you and thank you for the things you do for me. Amen.

243

Days Of Our Lives
Psalm 40

As you read through this Psalm can you relate it to the days of your life? I sure can. Thank God for his patience with me. David wrote this as a prayer for the troubles and distress in his life. He acknowledges that some come from his sin. He also acknowledges that God sets his feet on a rock and gives him a firm place to stand. I hear anxiousness in David's voice yet he persistently recognizes God as his Savior and cries out to him - exactly what we need to do today. This psalm is full of the ups and downs of life as we ride this roller coaster we can't seem to get off of some days. Yet God can put a new song in our mouth every morning and a hymn of praise in our heart. David lived long ago but we are all the same. Let's take a few minutes to study these verses and mark those that are specific to our needs today. Praise God and ask him to hear us as we cry out to him.

Dear God you are my help and deliverer. O my God, do not delay. Forgive me of my sin and take control of my day. Help me to trust you in all things and ignore the enemies in my life. You are my Rock. Set my feet on firm ground and give me victory over my distress. Give me a heart of thankfulness and rejoicing. Amen.

244

Substance Abuse
1 Kings 18:21

In this passage Elijah warns the people that they cannot serve two gods. They must choose. They serve God or they serve another. Individuals professing to be a Christian and struggling with substance abuse are torn between two gods. They want to serve God yet they cannot turn loose of the addictive drug which they serve. They often will not choose. Their friends and family suffer as the abuser declines and eventually looses everything. While I am not here to defend them, I do recognize that the addiction is extremely strong and hard to fight but it can be done. Through a proper relationship with God and Christian counseling the fight can be won and the addiction can be controlled. I recently read an article about substance abuse that ended in a prayer for the abuser. It really hit home for me. It went something like this,

Father, give me a compassionate heart toward those who seek ways to escape that are dangerous and deadly.

The substance abuser is trying to escape from something. Their human side tells them to seek alternative ways to escape rather than seeking God's strength and protection. Some describe it as a sickness. I am not sure about that. Maybe because I am personally involved with a substance abuser but that seems like an excuse to me. Forgive me if you disagree. I do know that our Lord is the Father of miracles. He heals and sustains and forgives. There are wonderful Christian counselors that can provide direction and guidance. The abuser can overcome and live a successful life with a renewed relationship with God. My desire is to forgive and avoid anger for the person in my life who has this problem. While I believe we have to be practical in making decisions regarding such relationships, we must pray for them. We must pray for them consistently with commitment. If you deal with a loved one who has this problem or if you are the one who has the problem, I encourage you to recommit to your relationship with our Lord making sure you are right with him and seek Christian counseling. The abuser and those involved with the abuser need assistance and guidance in dealing with this horrible problem. I pray this has helped someone today or you know of someone to share it with. It is a long, difficult road that I travel. Trusting God and recognizing his control will bring the peace and strength needed to follow the right path.

Dear God I do pray for a heart of compassion for the substance abuser. We are all sinners and fall short. You are the Father of love and forgiveness. Help me to see the abuser through your eyes and recognize the addiction as sin that can be forgiven. Lead me to those who can help me. Thank you for your love. Amen.

245

The Peace God Brings
Isaiah 41:10, 13

It has been one of those days. The kind of day when you feel like you are coming out of your skin because you are so anxious and restless. Decisions are pending that greatly impact the future and God has said to be still and wait. I feel as anxious as a cat in a room full of rocking chairs as Festus once said on *Gunsmoke*. It is so difficult sometimes to be still and wait. But yes, we can do it. We can do it through the strength of God. These two verses are so encouraging and bring peace when I focus on them and set the anxiousness and fear aside. Relief and strength can be mine. God tells us he is with us and we have nothing to fear. He is our strength. He holds us up and keeps us going. He brings peace like nothing else can. A peace that remains with us. The Book of Isaiah is full of encouragement. Isaiah 46:4 reminds us that God made us and sustains us even to our old age. He sustains and he rescues. I see nothing to indicate that the peace that God offers will end. God is always available to us 24/7. This promise reminds me of the song that says God is too wise to be mistaken and too good to be unkind.

How do you relax? What calms you? The Holy Word of God filled with his promises can bring the peace that sustains. Jesus often tells us to cast our cares on him to allow him to carry our burdens. We just have to hand them to him and recognize him as being in control. Psalm 125:1-2 tells us that those who trust in the Lord are like a mountain that cannot be shaken. As the mountains surround the city of Jerusalem, so the Lord sustains his people both now and forever more. Let's mark that verse in our Bible. What a marvelous promise! Yes it is hard sometimes. We are weak and focus on ourselves. It is hard for me today. But I will keep on trusting God, knowing that he is faithful and keeps his promises to those who trust him. He knows my heart and the desire of my heart. Let's allow the peace of God to come in and overrule the anxiousness and fear. I am like a mountain and will not be shaken.

Dear God thank you for the peace you bring. Help me to focus on you and your promises. Help me to be strong and ignore the lies and fear that Satan brings. You are the Victor and he is the liar. You are the God of Wisdom and you know what is best for me. I will tell you the desires of my heart for you are my friend. I will accept your will for my life because I know it is perfect. Thank you for your sustaining love and power. Amen.

246

The Unmerciful
Matthew 18:21-35

This passage is labeled, The Parable of the Unmerciful Servant. Our first thought may be of a master being unmerciful but in this story it was not the master but the servant that had no mercy even though he received mercy himself. We want forgiveness but sometimes are hesitant to forgive. The truth behind this parable is that God the Father, our Master, forgives us willingly and completely and we are to forgive each other just as willingly and completely. Hebrews 8:12 says God forgives and remembers no more. He forgives us and forgets what he forgives us for. Some often started their apology with, 'If I did anything to.....' and tend to point out the other person's part in the incident. I tried to convince someone that to completely forgive from the heart, he must take full responsibility and it doesn't matter what role the other person played in it. To offer complete forgiveness from the heart, the words must be simple, 'I forgive you for what I did' and remember the offense no more. The teaching in this passage can be summed up in one word - Forgive. Easy? Yes, when we seek God's guidance and help. Our earnest desire must be to forgive as God forgives. Colossians 3:13 teaches us to accept each other and forgive whatever grievances we have against each other. Forgive as the Lord forgave you, it says. We all have our faults. Others have offended me but I know I have offended others as well. Forgive as the Lord forgave and continues to forgive. God has no three strikes and you're out rule. He forgives and we are to do as he does. In closing, take a look at verse 34 of this passage and how the master treated the unmerciful servant. Verse 35 says this is how God will treat us unless we forgive others from the heart.

Dear God, give me a forgiving heart. I cannot do this alone. I need your help. Search my heart for any unforgiveness and help me to take care of it today. Give me courage to face any unforgiveness in my heart. I want to have a heart of mercy. I want to forgive as you have forgiven me many times and I know, more to come. Thank you for your patience with me and how you love me. Amen.

247

Why?

Proverbs 3:5

We often ask why. Why? is probably one of the most frustrating habits of a two year old child. Every response is why and then why to the response. We do the same thing when talking to God, especially when experiencing difficulty.

Saturday I took a long walk with a friend. We passed several runners and I noticed that they were carrying on conversation as they ran. I commented that I didn't see how they talked, ran and breathed at the same time. My military background friend told me it actually helped because it forced you to take many small breaths which actually helped you breathe better. She explained that this is one of the reasons drill sergeants teach trainees cadence. It forced them to breathe better as they ran and called the cadence. I wonder how often trainees realize that when they first begin the training. Run ten miles and shout? No, way! This reminded me that so often God requires things of us for our own good and we don't realize it when we experience it, in fact we think we are being tortured or punished for some reason. In our misery, we ask, Why? As time passes we look back and can see the whole picture. God sees the whole picture way before we do. This verse reminds us that we don't need to understand what we are experiencing; we just need to trust God. In Isaiah 55:8, God says that we do not think like he thinks nor do we do things the way he does. I think it is acceptable to ask God why and talk to him honestly through the difficulty. He desires for us to lay our worries and fears at his feet. He wants to replace our misery and confusion with trust and confidence. God wants us to trust that while we may not understand at the time, he understands and knows exactly what he is doing. What a wonderful promise.

Dear God sometimes I don't understand. Feelings of confusion and worry overwhelm me. Your Holy Word gives promise of your love and mighty wisdom. Help me to overcome negative feelings of anxiousness with my trust in you. You are the solid rock in my life that never changes and is always there for me. I know that you have wonderful plans for me. The battle is yours to fight not mine. I will be still and trust in you with all my heart. I will not be shaken. Thank you for how you love me. Amen.

248

I Need Thee Every Hour

1 Peter 5:6

If you have been reading through this collection of devotions you have heard me say that this has been a difficult year for me. While I still experience this storm in my life, I stand here today and say in confidence that God is with me and has been with me every step of the way. I have not understood everything but I know God is with me and he does have a plan for me. I want to share with you one of the things that has been life saving to me – my Prayer Journal. It is my life line to God. It has connected me to God in ways that I never dreamed. Many days I find myself in the midst of confusion and worry. Nothing, not anything helps like picking up my journal and talking to God. Talking to him honestly, telling him openly of my fear(s). I hold nothing back, not even the anger and asking why. Writing helps me to focus and limits the distractions in my mind. Peace comes immediately. Sometimes I get answers but it is peace that comes first. Peace and confidence that God is with me and has not and will not forget me. Peace and confidence that he cares about the little things that won't even matter tomorrow and the big things that will affect me years from now. While I have a good Christian counselor, she recognizes that my counseling sessions with God help me more than she can. It isn't really answers that I seek. I seek help to get me through the next hour and it works. One of the first cross stitch patterns that I worked said, Take care of the minutes and the hours will take care of themselves. These words have stuck with me over the years and are so true in my relationship with Jesus Christ. The peace and confidence that God sends helps me more than the answers will. The battle is not mine, it is God's. Be still and know that I am God, he says in Psalm 46:10. God helps me get through the minutes and the hours. I recognize the peace God sends and my relationship with him helps me to recognize the confusion that Satan sends. Satan is a liar and a loser. Jesus Christ brings victory and confidence over the confusion and fear. I will admit to you that I am not very good at maintaining the peace that God sends. I return to my life line daily and sometimes (most of the time) more than once daily. But that is okay. There is no limit to my life line. God knows my weakness. He is there whenever I seek him no matter how many times I need him throughout the day. He teaches me everyday how to depend on him for support and confidence. I have no desire to get to a point of confidence that I do not need him anymore or as often. I remember singing an old hymn, I Need Thee Every Hour. Consider this today and find a way to connect your life line.

Dear God thank you for the peace and confidence that you send me. You recognize my weakness and send me hope and confidence every time I ask. Thank you for how you lift me up and care for me. When I call you are never too busy for me. Your help gets me through the minutes and hours of each day. You are my Lord and Savior. You are my lifeline. I love you. I adore you. Amen.

249

The Will Of the Father

1 Thessalonians 5:15-18

A couple days ago, someone said something that made me angry and I responded in my anger. I felt convicted throughout the day. I knew without a doubt, I was to apologize for speaking in anger and did so the next morning. I was probably justified in my anger, yet I knew that the will of my Heavenly Father was for me to respond differently from the way of the world. These short verses express the will of our Father. God's will for us is to never repay wrong for wrong and to treat everyone with kindness. His will is for us to remain joyous and thankful regardless of our situation, staying in continuous conversation with him. The ultimate sacrifice has been paid for our sinful nature therefore our joy and thankfulness remains constant and does not depend on our circumstances. This is the will of our Father. Life can be hard. Our days are often like a train that misses each station stop. Regardless of my circumstances, God loves me and sacrificed his only Son for me. My life here on earth is only a whisper in the wind, only a few minutes of eternity. I was created to worship my God and spend eternity in his presence. God's will for me is joy, thankfulness, loving those around me and continual conversation with him. Nothing is bad enough to darken these truths. I can do all things in the strength and companionship of my Lord and Savior.

Dear God thank you for your will for me. Thank you for your love for me. Give me a heart committed to living joyously and thankfully regardless of my circumstances. You are my hope and my strength. My relationship with you is the rock that holds me to solid ground. I love you and adore you. Amen.

250

Lesson In Provision
Exodus 16

The Israelites had much to learn on their journey to the promised land. This was one of their earlier lessons. There are lessons for us in this.

The Israelites were in need of food. Well, not exactly in need, the Bible doesn't say they were out of food; it seems that they craved food that they were used to having. Isn't that just like us all? Rescued from misery and slavery and already complaining 45 days later – complaining for something they wanted not necessarily needed. Granted, they would eventually run out of the supplies they brought with them but couldn't they see that God was watching over them and caring for them? They could see the glory of the Lord appearing in the clouds (verse 10). They had just seen God roll back the waters of the Red Sea and they were worried about the kind of food they had to eat. God did provide bread from heaven, manna. He established rules for gathering it along with consequences for greed and disobedience. They were to gather manna for six days and be prepared to rest on the Sabbath. The Israelites were grumblers and I must admit I am too. God provided for the Israelites and he provides for us. It takes a committed heart to find joy and contentment in all circumstances. I see God work miraculously in my life yet I still grumble and fret when things don't go my way. I worry about the simple pleasures of life forgetting to be thankful that my basic needs are always met; in fact I have more than I need. Let's take time to reflect on this story and search our hearts for grumbling and inappropriate discontentment. Let's ask God to show us where we are greedy and disobedient in managing what he gives us.

Dear God thank you for the lessons your Holy Word teaches us. Search my heart and show me greed or disobedience. Forgive my ungratefulness. Help me to see your glory regardless of my circumstances. Help me to see the manna that flows from heaven to meet my needs. Thank you for how you graciously provide for me and my family. Amen.

251

God Is With Me

Joshua 1:1-9

These are verses I often go to when I am afraid. The verses remind me that God is with me. Difficulties in life bring fear, mainly fear of the unknown. Fear of bad decisions. Fear of consequences of mistakes made in the past. We sometimes feel terrified and trapped, unable to move into the next moment. Our faith in God is the only peace that is always available to us. A peace that helps me take a breath and move into the next moment and on from there. I can only try to imagine how a soldier in battle feels when he or she takes that first step out of the trench and into the line of fire. How terrifying it must be. But it doesn't always take that kind of battle to make us feel terrified and shaken. David often says in his psalms, I will not be shaken. I need to take the same stand. I will not let my fears shake me. God tells us not to be terrified or discouraged. He knows exactly how I feel. He uses the very words that describe what I feel. The Lord my God is with me wherever I go. He knows me and he knows what frightens me. He doesn't promise to be with me in only certain circumstances. He promises to be with me wherever I go. What a marvelous promise.

Dear God thank you for your promises. I will not let my fears shake me for I know you are with me. Give me a heart committed to obeying your Holy Word. Your Word urges courage and promises success when I am obedient. My desire is to trust you in everything. I want my faith to increase everyday through the experiences you allow that build my strength and courage that will come from you. I love you Lord. Amen.

252

Is It My fault?

Proverbs 3:30

I came across this simple verse the other day in an article about how we never blame ourselves for anything. It is always someone else's fault. I had to stop and think, how often I say, It isn't my fault, but when I stop and think about it maybe it is often my fault. Rather than saying It isn't my fault, maybe we should ask ourselves, Is it my fault? We all make bad choices. We all make bad decisions but we all don't readily admit it. I had to deal with an employee who is late most every day, anywhere from 15 minutes to an hour. The employee submitted the reasons for each day's tardiness. The list went from the dog getting out to trains, traffic, a sick child, and it went on and on. Not once did I hear, I got up late, I wasn't prepared for the day or I left the house too late. Need I say more?

Yes, things happen to us that truly do not come from our own actions. I am only suggesting that we step back and take a look. What problem am I dealing with today that comes from a bad choice of mine and what can I do today to resolve it? Is there someone I need to go to and apologize? Are there habits that may bring moments of enjoyment but cause problems for me? Do I have medical problems because I don't take care of myself? Do I not have peace and success because I am living a life of disobedience to God's Holy Word? Does my day go better when I start with time with my Lord? This proverb says do not accuse someone else or anything else for no reason. We laughed at my young son who would rarely admit to doing wrong. His answer for everything was, It was in an accident. Thank goodness he has grown up now and doesn't use that line anymore. However, even as adults we often refuse to accept the blame. Let's take a few moments with God and ask for conviction by asking, Is it my fault?

Dear God in Heaven, Is it my fault? Please help me search my heart for areas in my life where I can make better choices and decisions. Help me to see where I can change habits that will improve my life. I know strength and courage will come from you. Thank you for loving me as I am. I know I can trust you to help me live according to your commandments and promises. Your Holy Word says success comes from obedience and that is my heart's desire. Help me to be still and quiet and listen to you. Amen.

253

My Birthday
Jeremiah 29:11-14

I am fifty six years old today. As I woke this morning, I felt a little blue. My life is in a rather upheaval state and for the first time in a long time I woke up alone on my birthday. After a few sips of coffee and starting my morning Bible reading, I get a text from a dear girl friend and before long, a couple entries on my Facebook wall wishing me a happy birthday. My spirits began to lift. After reading from my devotional, I turned to this passage in Jeremiah. God has plans for me, plans to prosper, plans to give me hope and a future. When I call to him, he listens to me. I can find him and he will bring me out of captivity. As I wrote in my prayer journal, Dear God, thank you for caring for me and for being my friend, thank you for my friends and family.... the thought came to me, I have more than I am missing. Life does take some uncomfortable turns that seem to hold us captive; captive to thoughts of loneliness and feelings of being misplaced. God loves me and cares for me. My friends love me and wish me well and my children and siblings remember this is a special day. I have more than I am missing because of my relationship with my Lord. God has a plan for me and it is good. I also turned to another favorite passage, Lamentations 3:22-26 which reminded me that because of the Lord's great love I am not consumed, for his compassions never fail, they are new every morning. Great is God's faithfulness. I say to myself, the Lord is my portion; therefore I will wait for him. My spirits continued to spiral. At work we celebrated with red velvet cupcakes from my assistant, a few gifts, several cards and birthday greetings throughout the day. My friends and family made my day special. My Lord encouraged me and comforted me when I needed him. I end my birthday writing these thoughts for you hoping that this will encourage you to seek God for comfort and encouragement when you feel down. He is available and always ready to send hope and comfort and confidence. I do not know what this year will bring but I know God has a plan and it will be good. I have nothing to fear for he is with me.

Dear Heavenly Father, help me to trust you when I don't understand. You are my refuge and I seek you. Thank you for the hope, comfort and confidence you bring. Thank you for my friends and family who love me. I began my day with tears of sadness and end my day with tears of praise because of you. Great is your faithfulness, O God my Father. Happy Birthday to me. Amen.

254

Quiet Moment
Psalm 84:1-2

Today I had a special visit with my Mother. She is 93 years old and is in a facility for Alzheimer patients. She normally sleeps a lot but today she was awake and rather bright eyed yet expressionless. The nurse had rolled her hair and she was sitting quietly in her room. I arrived at lunch time on Saturday as I often do to feed her. It is unusual to visit in her room. Usually she is out in the area with the other patients or at one of the large dining tables where the TV is usually on and lots of voices and other noise. Today it was just the two of us in her room. I can't remember when I felt so close to her as I fed her and talked with her. She has little expression, rarely speaks coherently; just jabbers and is extremely hard of hearing. When I finished feeding her, I scooted my chair up close, facing her and held her hands. As I told her that I loved her and missed her, I was hoping she could feel what I was saying from my face and touch. I told her I knew Daddy was waiting for her in heaven and was probably smiling down on us. It was a very sad moment yet precious. I regret not loving her better and hopefully our quiet moments together reached her in the Alzheimer world that she lives in. I felt the presence of God with us. I left and sat in my car for a few moments and cried. I don't recall if I was happy or sad but I do know that I will cherish those quiet moments.

Quiet moments in today's world are rare. Quiet moments with my Lord are very important in our relationship and so are quiet moments with those we love. I know that my Mother's days here on earth are few and she will soon meet our Lord and the other members of her family that have gone on before her. We also know that death can come like a thief in the night and does not only take the elderly. We should take time for quiet moments and cherish them. Take time today, away from the noise with someone you love.

Dear God thank you for special moments that you give us. Thank you for my Mother. It is hard to understand why you keep her here to live in her Alzheimer world but I know you are kind and good and you are wise. Thank you for quiet moments together when you speak to me in a special way. Thank you for your love for us. Amen.

255

Prayer Of Confession
Psalm 51

Psalm 51 is David's humble prayer for forgiveness and cleansing after committing adultery with Bathsheba. God wants a broken spirit and a repentant heart. In Zachariah 8:17, God says that he hates sin. He doesn't want any kind of bargaining or promises but recognition of our sin and a humble request for forgiveness. Let's read through this passage out loud as a prayer to God.

We teach our children to 'say you're sorry'. We need to be sure our motive is right and we are turning from our sin. We need to be sincere about our confession and repent with a desire to change so that we don't repeat the behavior again. Our choice of lifestyle should reflect our desire to live for our Lord. While we still must face the consequences of our sin, he blots it out and remembers it no more. I heard someone say one time that the only thing God can't do is remember forgiven sin. He wipes it out and forgets it.

Dear Lord, accept this prayer of confession. Create in me a pure heart and renew a steadfast spirit within me. Grant me a willing spirit. Help me to be serious about my sin and turn from it. Keep me mindful that when I sin it is against you. Give me a strong desire to be in your Holy Word and in your presence everyday so that I will keep a faithful walk with you. Amen.

256

Choose For Yourselves
Joshua 24:14-18

I remember Joshua for these words - Choose you this day who you will serve but as for me and my house we will serve the Lord. Joshua is challenging the Israelites to place their loyalty with God, to fear and serve him with all faithfulness. He cautioned them of serving other gods before God. Joshua publicly makes his commitment hoping to encourage others to do the same. The people answered, we too will serve the Lord because he is our God.

Loyalty is very important. It is important that we are loyal and it is important to us that others are loyal. But then loyalty can be misplaced. Loyalty is a choice. Loyalty to God is our choice. Loyalty to other gods is also our choice. I once heard a former drug addict's testimony. He said that cocaine was his god and he served it well. He rejoices now that he has turned his loyalty to Jesus Christ and serves him with all that is in him. God waits patiently for our choice. 2 Peter 3:9 says that he is patient, not wanting anyone to perish but everyone to come to repentance. God desires our loyalty, our decision to serve him, setting an example for our house to serve him as well. We may need to join Joshua in publicly making our commitment so to encourage others to do the same.

Dear Father in Heaven, help me to search my heart for misplaced loyalty. Forgive me when I give other things priority in my life. I choose this day to serve you. I humbly give my loyalty to you from this day forward. Convict my heart when I reduce the seriousness of this matter between us. O God it is so easy sometimes to give in to the ways of this world. Speak to me clearly if I need to publicly make this commitment to anyone. Give me opportunity to encourage others. My desire is to serve you with a heart of loyalty. Amen.

257

Everywhere I Go I See You
2 Corinthians 4:18

Where do you see God? I saw a video today of the song by Michael W. Smith "Everywhere I Go I See You" and it has stuck with me all day. We see God everywhere we go. We have never actually seen him in a physical presence but we know he is here. We have never seen the wind but we know it is real. We see God daily in marvelous wonders of this earth – in a sunrise, in a sunset, in a newborn's cry, in the magnificent mountains. Yet this verse reminds us that what we see here is temporary and does not compare to eternity.

We don't have to look far to find him. We don't have to try very hard to hear him. Do we go to sleep with him on our mind and think of him when we first awake? Hebrews 11:1 says our faith is being sure of what we hope for and certain of what we do not see. I don't want to get to a point where God has to get my attention. We must keep our eyes on him. Someone dear to me called me tonight and tearfully told me of a broken relationship. I encouraged her to draw near to God and look for the marvelous wonders she could see as his plans for her unfold. I encourage you, as I did her to look for God throughout your day. He is near and longs for us to see him.

Dear God, everywhere I go I see you. Praise your Holy Name. Help us to draw to you and look for you in the good times and the hard times. Help me to remember that what I see here is temporary. Help me to live daily in your presence knowing that you will come for me one day to leave this temporary place and live with you in eternity in your mighty kingdom. Amen.

258

First Love
Revelation 2:2-5

When we first love something or someone it is an exciting and overwhelming feeling that lingers. We can't get enough of it, can't say enough about it and want to be close to it, experiencing its closeness every possible minute. However as times moves on we can become complacent and take it for granted. We stop putting effort into keeping the fire burning and glowing. In this passage, Jesus is referring to the church's love for him which I think includes their commitment to living a lifestyle reflecting his message. He says to them, You have forsaken your first love. In other words, you have forsaken me. There is a song by Stuart Townend "My First Love" that describes this perfectly. He speaks to remembering his first love for Christ as a blazing fire and a rushing river and doesn't ever want to lose it.

Let's stop and think, first of all, where has my relationship with Jesus Christ fallen short? What did I do when I first came to love Jesus that I do not do now? What repentance is needed in my heart? To have a relationship with Jesus we must talk to him regularly, seek him regularly and study his Holy Word to increase our knowledge of him. We must spend time with him. We must be willing to be honest with him and listen when he responds. The fire in our relationship with Jesus cannot continue to burn if it is smothered by other things that we put before him. Take a few minutes to think about that.

We also need to consider what other relationships have suffered from complacency. Who did we once love with excitement that we now take for granted? Who do we no longer appreciate? Family? Friends? This is all a part of a conscious relationship with Jesus Christ. We can't love Jesus as he wants us to without having the same love for others. 1 John 4:19-21 commands us that if we love God we must also love our brother. What is love if it is not seen and shared?

Dear Father in Heaven, forgive me for allowing my fire for you to smolder. Your love for me never changes. You love me no matter what I do or say or neglect to do. Thank you for your gracious love for me. I want my love for you to remain strong. Give me strength and encouragement to keep my relationship with you as strong as a first love. Convict my heart when I allow other things to become more important. Forgive me when I forsake you. Amen.

259

Remember
1 Chronicles 16:11-12

I think I do fairly well in taking my concerns to the Lord yet I catch myself sometimes. I will have a concern, talk with others about it and mull it over in my mind. Then think, I need to pray about it. I sometimes get it in reverse order. This is a lovely passage. It is part of a psalm of thanks written by David. Look to the Lord and his strength. Seek his face always. Remember the wonders he has done, his miracles and the judgments he has voiced. I look back over the pages of my prayer journal and see days that I was overwhelmed and at a lost of what to do. Now it seems so minor and unimportant. Once we lay our concerns at Jesus' feet the fear subsides. The major thing for me is God's timing. He rarely moves when I want him to. He is so wise and knows just when to respond. He teaches me patience over and over. When I see how things work out I am grateful that it didn't go according to my plan but to God's.

Unfortunately we must be reminded to pray and we must be reminded to remember what God has already done. How easily we forget and try to handle things on our own. He longs for us to bring our burdens to him and forget them. Look to the Lord. Our strength is his in us. Seek him in everything. Remember the wonders and miracles that he has done. Remember to pray....first.

Dear God thank you for the wonders that you have done in my life and the miracles I see. My strength comes from you. Help me to remember to seek you in all things. I am as a silly ignorant sheep that has no idea what is best for me. Help me to keep my relationship with you strong and the priority of my life so I will remember you in every moment and every thought. I love you and adore you. Amen.

260

Selfless Or Selfish?

1 Corinthians 13:5

Love is not rude and is not self seeking. Love is selfless. Love is not easily angered or provoked. Love is not selfish. Let's think for a minute, what usually provokes me? I am provoked when someone does not agree with me or someone steps in front of me or a decision is make that is not of my opinion or choice. Can we agree that we are usually provoked or angered when we don't get our way? Can we agree that we are usually provoked or angered because we are selfish? John 3:30 says Christ must become greater and I must become less. If I could change something about myself I would want to love others according to 1 Corinthians 13. I wish that I could live everyday and love everyone selflessly. Additionally, love keeps no record of wrong doing. Hebrews 8:12 says God forgives sin and forgets it. Once forgiven, he keeps no record of our sin. It can be easy for me to forgive but it is harder to forget. We must be able to love selflessly in order to forgive and forget. To love as God loves us and to love according to scripture, we must put aside our selfishness and live selflessly.

Dear God thank you for your selfless love for me. Thank you for forgetting my sins when you forgive. The desire of my heart is to live and love selflessly as you love me. It can be so very hard sometimes Lord. I always want my way and I always want to be first. But I know that I must allow you to become greater and I must become less. That is the only way I can love as you teach me to love and forgive as you teach me to forgive. Thank you for your Holy Word that guides me in the true and perfect way. Amen.

261

Do Not Be Afraid
Exodus 14:13-14

I often go to the Book of Exodus for encouragement. I love these stories. The Israelites were scared to death. The Egyptians are coming for them in full force. Moses tries to calm them saying, Do not fear. Stand firm and you will see the deliverance the Lord brings today. The Egyptians you see today you will never see again. The Lord will fight for you. You only need to be still.

What a marvelous miraculous story. The story is old and it is true but it isn't just a story. The event happened to glorify God and is written for us so that we may glorify God. It applies to us today. It applies to every fear we have. Our own *egyptians* are often after us, coming for us in full force, scaring us to death. We have nothing to fear. We stand firm and see the deliverance that the Lord brings. The fears that we see today we will never see again. The Lord will fight for us. We only need to be still. We have victory over fear and obstacles through our Lord and Savior. Our fears and obstacles are defeated and washed away just as these soldiers and their mighty weapons and chariots were washed away like toys.

Dear God you are my victor over fear. I stand still to see the deliverance that you will bring. I will not fear. I trust you to remove completely any obstacle that tries to stand in my way. My strength comes from you alone. Thank you for the marvelous stories in your Holy Word. Give me a desire to study them every day. Amen.

262

Need Answers?
Jeremiah 33:2-3

Hardly a day goes by that I don't need an answer. There is always a question, what to do, what to say, how to, etc. Some are simple but pressing, some are frustrating and some tend to shake me. No matter the question, God is faithful to answer. God urges me to call to him. He assures me he will answer. He has great things to tell me that I do not know. He invites me to ask and assures me he will respond. When I look at the Concordance in my Bible under the word call, there are numerous verses that encourage me to call on God. Verses 1-14 in this passage are a wonderful promise of restoration. Take time to read them. God is omniscient which means that he knows everything. He knows what we need before we even ask. It is important that we ask to acknowledge that he knows all the answers and to give him the glory for always knowing how to respond. I heard a comment recently that maybe we are too quick to 'google' rather than ask God. I thought that pretty silly at first but then I can think of times that I searched for something on my own that I could have discussed with God. Jeremiah 10:12 says God made the earth by his power, founded the world by his wisdom and stretched out the heavens by his understanding. God has answers for us today. We only need to ask the question.

Dear Father in Heaven, you are the God of wisdom and understanding and I praise you. I call on you because you urge me to. Forgive me when I seek answers elsewhere. I know that you love me unconditionally and wait in anticipation for me to seek you. Thank you for your faithfulness. No matter the question, you are faithful to answer me. I love you and adore you. Amen.

263

No Longer Downcast
1 Samuel 1:10-18

I have started a study of 1 Samuel. Today I read chapter 1. These verses touched me and encouraged me today. Hannah was troubled because she could not have a child. She prayed to God. The Bible says she then went her way and ate something and her face was no longer downcast. We have troubles and we take them to the Lord. Do we come away no longer downcast? Hannah was able to lay her burden with the Lord and leave her feelings of discouragement. She believed and she trusted that God would answer her prayer. She found peace. We know that she did conceive and gave birth to a son. She named him Samuel, saying 'Because I asked the Lord for him.' But she found peace before her prayer was answered and so can we. It is easy to get discouraged. Sometimes it seems like we go from one problem to the next. Psalm 28:7 says the Lord is my strength and my shield; my hearts trusts in him and I am helped. My heart leaps for joy. I believe this is what Hannah felt after she prayed. Her heart leaped for joy and she went about her meal, no longer downcast. My heart should leap for joy when I am able to take my troubles to the Lord and leave my downcast feelings with him. It is hard to let it go but peace comes when we do.

Dear God thank you for the peace you bring to my heart. You are my strength and my shield. My heart leaps for joy when I trust you. I thank you and praise you for your grace and mercy. Where would I be without you? How would I deal with life without you? Thank you for my salvation and your unconditional love for me. Amen.

264

Judge and Avenger
Romans 14:10

It is easy to judge others. It is normal to want to get back at someone in revenge. The Bible is very clear on this. In Matthew 7:1 Jesus cautions us not to judge others for we will be judged in the same way by the same measure. Ouch! Romans 12:19 instructs us that revenge belongs to the Lord. In fact we are told to feed our enemy when hungry and give them something to drink when thirsty treating them with kindness and care. Ephesians 4:26 gives us a way out of our anger by advising us not to let the sun go down on our anger. We should resolve our anger before the end of the day. God is the ultimate judge and avenger. Sin is committed against God and it is his to deal with. Anger and thoughts of revenge are heavy burdens to carry and can consume us. God wants to take these burdens from us. He is the highest authority. We can overcome evil thoughts with good and not allow then to overcome us. We can take our hurt to God and lay it at his feet. When we do this asking for peace in our heart, he will respond welcoming our honesty and our desire to do as he asks in these passages. We can't do it alone but through Jesus Christ. As the psalmist says in Psalm 138:7, though I walk in the midst of trouble you preserve my life with your right hand and save me. Be encouraged today to speak to God about any unresolved anger or thoughts of revenge in your heart. Let it go and allow him to bring peace and healing to your heart.

Dear God thank you for being the ultimate authority. You are a wise and compassionate judge and avenger. Cleanse my heart of ill feelings toward anyone. Search my heart and show me anything that is not right and true. Heal me and bring peace when I am troubled. Give me strength to live as an example of forgiveness to those around me. Thank you for the truths that you teach for my own good. Amen.

265

Why Be Faithful?
2 Corinthians 5:1-21

Our pastor spoke on this passage today and it touched my heart. Why must we be faithful? Why do I believe that I must be faithful? There are a couple reasons in this passage. First, we are faithful because of a healthy fear of God. Verse 10 says that we are responsible for our actions while in our body and are accountable to God. God gave us his Holy Word to instruct us and teach us and expects us to follow him. We have a choice but there are also consequences. Secondly, we are faithful because Jesus Christ died for us. Verse 14 says our love for Christ compels us to live for him and not for ourselves because of his sacrifice of his life for our sin. Thirdly, we are faithful because we are a new creation living in Christ with a responsibility of being an ambassador for him. What is in it for us? (we selfishly may ask) There is an eternal house in heaven waiting for us (verse 1). God always gives blessing in response to obedience. Our ultimate goal is living in eternity in God's presence. That's why we are faithful.

Dear Lord, strengthen my spiritual vision. Help me to see the heavenly purpose you have for us. I want to be faithful willingly. This life is temporary. I want you to be pleased when you come for me. Forgive me when I fail. Search my heart and show me my sin. Help me to live by faith and not by sight or feeling. I love you Lord and I want to trust you more. Amen.

266

Confess To Each Other
James 5:16

James instructs us in this verse to confess our sins to each other and pray for each other so that we can be healed. It is helpful and relieving to have someone to talk to. To be honest and confess a sin to someone we can trust and then pray together begins healing. If you do not have such a person I suggest that you find someone. We can hold each other accountable and help with healing. The last part of this verse warms my heart. The prayer of a righteous man is powerful and effective. The prayer of an honest, true and authentic person is powerful and effective. Sometimes honesty is hard but honesty always brings peace and relief. Holding on to sin without confession brings pain and stress. I need someone that I can share with honestly and reveal my true feelings, fears and mistakes. Jesus Christ longs to hear our confession. He rejoices when two come together for confession, prayer and fellowship. Romans 3:23 says all of us sin and fall short. Never listen to Satan's lies that you are the only one who has sin to confess. There are no perfect people or perfect families. Each of us has sin in our life and a need for confession. Find someone to trust and build a relationship as described in this verse. We need each other. Turn to Romans 4:7-8. We are blessed when we confess and our transgressions are forgiven. The Lord forgives and will never count our sin against us again.

Dear God thank you for the fellowship of Christian friends. Help me to understand that confession is good. Thank you for your forgiveness and mercy. I confess my sins and ask for healing and restoration. You are my God and King. Amen.

267

Sparking a Smile
1 Thessalonians 5:14

I have been telling you about the Drive Thru Difference. Today is Friday. One of the first thoughts that came to my mind early this morning was the Drive Thru Difference. I believe that God puts things on our mind and expects an active response. I decided that I would have a BK croissant for breakfast and encourage the car behind me. As I drove to the window, the clerk was very solemn, not really unfriendly; just rather somber. As I paid there still was no one behind me. As the clerk gathered my money a car drove up. As she handed my change to me I told her I wanted to pay for the car behind me. Her face lit up and the biggest smile came across her face. She told me the order was $1.51 and I told her to take it out of my change. As she got the money from the register I could still see her smile. She got me excited. As I drove off I told her to tell the man behind me that Jesus loves him and to have a great day. She said she would and just beamed. What an experience. It really touched me that she seemed to get the blessing. I hardly even thought about the man in the car behind me I was so excited about the lift my gesture seemed to give her. This is the third time for me and it has been an experience each time. This verse came to my mind. Encourage the timid and be patient with everyone. We never know when the slightest $1.51 gesture can change someone's attitude and whole demeanor. I can only imagine the smile the man behind me got from her. It works. God can multiply the simplest thought or gesture and bless a multitude by our obedience to his bidding whispered in our ear in the early morning. Verse 21 in this chapter says hold on to the good. I have held on to this all day and I believe the other two that were at BK this morning are doing the same.

Dear God thank you for your instruction that brings blessing from obedience. I pray for this lady and the man behind me. I pray encouragement is still with them and they will pass it on to others. I don't know them and I don't know their circumstances but you are God and you do. Thank you for bringing us together and crossing paths. Thank you for your love for us. In all circumstances we give thanks and praise. Amen.

268

Testing Our Work
1 Corinthians 3:10-15

Our works cannot qualify us for salvation. Only our repentance, faith and acceptance of Jesus Christ as Lord and Savior assure us a place in heaven. There will be a judgment day when our works while here on earth will be measured. I believe our works cannot win us salvation however God will judge our works and use them to determine our reward and our place in heaven. We must be careful how we build. Gold, silver and costly stones represent honest and durable work based on sound doctrine and living that will withstand the test of fire. Wood, hay and straw represent weak, worthless works that will not withstand the test of fire. If our works do not pass the test we still gain eternity but we will escape the fire of hell with smoke in our hair. Our works show the truth of our faith. This passage causes me to stop and search my heart for what needs to be changed. If I profess Jesus Christ as my Savior, are my works soundly and consistently reflecting my faith and beliefs based on the teaching and instruction of my Lord? Go back to Matthew 7:26-27. Everyone who hears the Word of God and does not put it to practice is like a foolish man who built his house on the sand and it crashed when the wind and rain came. The Day of Judgment will come and we will be held accountable for our life here in earth. We will be held accountable for how we practiced what we heard. 1 Thessalonians 4:13-18 clearly tells of the coming of the Lord. No one knows when the day will be, it could be today or tomorrow or next year. Are we ready? What do we need to repent of and where do we need to start building works made of gold, silver and costly stones? What works of wood, hay and straw need to be torn down and rebuilt? Let's be encouraged today to take a serious look at how we spend our time preparing for the coming of our Lord and for the test of our works. 2 Corinthians 5:10 says that we will all appear before the judgment seat of God to receive what is due us for the things we did while here on earth, whether good or bad. Today is a great place to start. Tomorrow may be too late.

Dear God forgive me where I have failed you. Search my heart and help me today to see where I need to change my building blocks from wood, hay and straw to gold, silver and costly stones. Give me courage to tear down any foundation of sand and rebuild on the rock of my trust in you. Help me to encourage those around me. I want to be ready when you appear in the sky. Amen.

269

Who Do You Honor?
1 Samuel 2:29-32

Eli and his two sons were priests in the house of the Lord. The sons were evil, stealing meat from the sacrifices of the people, participated in prostitution and maybe even rape. Eli knew of their sin but could do nothing with them. They were out of control. Eli rebuked them (verse 25) cautioning them of sinning against God. His rebuke was too late. God spoke to Samuel (3:11-14) of his anger against Eli and his sons. The Lord said to Samuel, I am about to do something in Israel that will make the ears of everyone who hears of it tingle. Yes, God was quite angry.

A prophet accused Eli of honoring his sons more than God. Who do we honor? How often do we overlook our own sin but also the sin of those around us, even our family? Eli's inappropriate parenting skills led to God's refusal to accept a sacrifice or offering in atonement for their sin. Eli's sons had persisted in their evil ways for so long that the Lord's judgment against them was determined. You can read of their death in 4:12-18. An unfortunate story. I find this passage calling to our hearts for a time of searching and conviction. There are several instances of dishonor to God in these couple chapters. The Israelites dishonored the ark of the covenant by treating it as an object to bring them victory and it was stolen. Let's take a few minutes to read through this passage (chapters 1-4) and search our hearts for any dishonor that we need to get rid of. As we read, let's allow God to speak. Hear his voice and respond, Speak for your servant is listening.

Dear God I believe you are speaking today through this passage. Search me and show me any dishonor in my heart. Speak for your servant is listening. Forgive me of the ways that I dishonor you. I want my life to honor you in all I do. Convict my heart and show me what I need to change in my life. Give me courage to be honest and face what you reveal to me. Thank you for your mercy and forgiveness. Amen.

270

Can We Handle the Truth?
Romans 2:1-4

God will judge us all one day. This passage is not about salvation but judgment. We often pass our judgment on those around us. We are warned here that when we judge others we are setting ourselves up for judgment. God's judgment is based on the truth, reality, how it really is. God is graciously patient and shows kindness but that doesn't mean when judgment comes he will not be harsh. He will be fair according to the truth. We cannot misconstrue his kindness as a lack of intent to judge us because we are his. We will be held accountable and it will be based on the truth. God knows the truth in our heart, the truth that we hide from others and wear behind our mask. That truth is how he will decide our reward. We need to get serious about this. There is no escape. We may escape judgment and punishment of our actions according to our judicial process. The guilty and the innocent often escape by the skin of their teeth because of a technicality or gracious judge. There are no avenues of escape open to man in regard to divine and absolute judgment. We often study the Bible and become complacent in our testimony and assurance of salvation. It can't stop there. I came across an interesting verse as I was studying this passage in one of my Mother's old Bible study books – Revelation 10:9-10. We may stick to the verses in the Bible that make us feel good and are sweet as honey, which is God's intent, however as we read of judgment and truth that sweet taste may turn bitter because we are uncomfortable with the truth and the reality of God's plan. God's graciousness and goodness should bring us to our knees, asking him to show us the truth and give us courage to face the truth in our hearts, ready to repent. I saw a church sign recently that read, Stand firm by bending your knee.

Dear God, help me to take this seriously and make needed changes. You are gracious and you are loving but you are my God and King and you are the ultimate judge of us all. I want my actions and the thoughts of my heart to please you. Rid me of my sinful nature and bring me to my knees. Forgive me when I judge others. Forgive me when I forget that I am a sinner too. You are my strength and my courage. You are my comfort and my loving Father. Thank you for how you love me and bless me. Amen.

271

My Refuge
Psalm 9:9-10

God is good all the time. All the time God is good. Even a good day can end in rain. Yesterday didn't start out as a bad day but it ended for me with a troubled and confused heart. A couple things were said during the day that weighed heavily on my heart and then a conversation with someone raised an issue that I thought had been resolved. By the time evening came I was confused and in tears and weary. I wondered, do I call a friend to talk, do I call my counselor, do I go play my keyboard, do I read, do I find a movie to watch? What do I do to rid my heart of these troubling thoughts? I prayed, cried and went to bed. I decided not to set my alarm but to sleep until I woke and take it from there. As I rose this morning after a good night's sleep, I decided to take a few personal hours from work and spend time with the Lord. I have been in my Bible study books and this developing book of devotions for about three hours now and I have found my refuge. Jesus Christ is my refuge. The problems and concerns are still here but I am strengthened. Through my faith in God I have regained peace and courage. Faith is being sure of what we hope for and certain of what we do not see (Hebrews 11:1).

Do you need refreshment and refuge today? You may not be able to take a morning off like this but God can take only a few minutes to give restoration. Find time to rest in him. It may mean giving up something else but I assure you it is worth it. God longs for us to experience the joy from seeking him. The Lord is my refuge and a stronghold in times of trouble. Stronghold is not a word that I use very often in conversation but it is the definition of my Lord's presence in my life. I trust in him and he has never forsaken me when I seek him.

Dear God you are my refuge and the stronghold of my life. You bring peace and confidence to my troubled heart. You bring rest to ease my troubled soul. My help comes from you, the maker of heaven and earth. Thank you for how you love me. Help me to face this day with strength that comes only from you. Thank you for my friends and counselor but you are the constant in my life. Spending time with you renews and refreshes me. I want to know you more. Amen.

272

Finding Quiet
Isaiah 32:17

Peace comes from doing what is right. Peace brings us quiet and confidence forever. Isaiah 30:15 says our strength comes from quiet and trust. How often do we take opportunity to sit outside in the quiet of a morning? There is something about the quiet that is different from other times of the day. Oh, there is noise, dogs barking, the hammering of an early roofer near by, cars passing but there is still a special quietness. This morning I took a few brief moments outside on my porch with my coffee. I wondered how differently my days would go if I started them with a few minutes of peace and quiet. I didn't pray, I tried not to think I just looked at the glory of a new morning and listened to the peaceful sounds. We miss out on so much because we are so busy. You may say, okay you tell me to have a time of Bible study and prayer and now you're asking me for a few more minutes outside. Yes, I am. I am suggesting that for you and for me. Times like these may be more valuable than anything we do. Times like these will bring us quiet and confidence for the day. We are willing to make time for things that busy us and stress us, why not give up a few of those moments? I think it is worth a try. I recently had a doctor appointment and had to wait several minutes in the exam room. The doctor rushed in apologizing profusely. I actually had enjoyed the few minutes flipping through a magazine and assured him I was quite fine enjoying the quiet. Think on Psalm 23:2. He makes me lie down in green pastures, he leads me beside quiet, still waters. He restores my soul. Animals lying in green pastures are content and secure. When you look on quiet, still waters, immediate refreshment and peace come over us. We've talked about a few quiet moments outside to start our day. It seems that peace, confidence, truth, refreshment, contentment, security, quiet and strength can come from these few moments. Your choice.

Dear God give us strength to take time for quiet. Yes, I ask for strength for this is hard for us. We find ourselves too busy for the things that we really need. Forgive us when we are too weak and busy to see the truth. Thank you for the peace and contentment my relationship with you provides. You are my rock and my stronghold. Lead me beside the quiet waters and restore my soul. My hope is in you all day long. Amen.

273

Thirsting For Righteousness
Matthew 5:6

This passage is referred to as The Beatitudes or The Sermon on the Mount preached by Jesus. There are nine declarations for blessedness or happiness. Today I came across verse six and it grabbed me. In my Sunday School class of high school girls we have been talking about righteousness. A righteous person is one who does what is right. This verse refers to someone thirsting for righteous – someone thirsting to do what is right. It says, those who thirst to do what is right will be filled. Have you been so thirsty you quickly drank a bottle of water and then felt filled up and full? What a marvelous teaching. What a marvelous truth. When we thirst for doing what is right we will be filled. I am familiar with this verse but don't recall it hitting me as it did today. Do I thirst for doing what is right? Do I realize the benefit of thirsting for doing what is right? Am I seriously convicted to do what is right? Verse 10 says blessed are those who are persecuted for doing the right thing, their reward is the kingdom of heaven. Doing the right thing is not always the most popular thing to do in this world we live in. Remember that the reward is not of this world. The reward is our inheritance of the kingdom of heaven.

In Genesis 4:7, God warned Cain about not doing what was right, sin was crouching at the door. Sin desires to consume us and we must learn to master it. We must learn to master doing what is right. We must thirst for it. We must thirst for righteousness. God offers many instructions and advisements but he always attaches a reward for our obedience. The choice is ours and the consequence is ours as well, blessing or failure. When we thirst for righteousness we will be filled with blessing.

Dear God thank you for your wonderful promises. Thank you for how you desire to bless obedience and a desire to do what is right. When I thirst for doing what is right you promise that I will be filled. If persecuted you have a heavenly reward waiting for me. What marvelous promises. Give me courage and confidence to do what is right and to thirst for righteousness. Forgive me when I hesitate. Thank you for giving me new opportunity to serve you every day. Amen.

274

Self Condemnation
1 John 3:19-20

Our mind is often a battle filed. We condemn ourselves in our thoughts. We know the truth yet we tend to listen to negative thoughts that plague us. Romans 8:1 tells us the truth. There is no condemnation for those who are in Christ Jesus. Revelations 12:10 recognizes Satan as the accuser who condemns us day and night. Satan is a liar and is doomed. Negative thoughts can bring us to a halt, making us ineffective. Proverbs 4:20-27 is a heart warming passage that gives us reassurance of the truth. We must guard our hearts from the evil and abuse of negative condemning thoughts. There are things we can do to combat this. First, daily time with

God in his Holy Word, talking to him and listening to his voice establishes a stronghold against condemnation. Secondly, we can monitor what we allow before our eyes and into our ears. Inappropriate viewing and hearing can allow subtle opportunity for Satan to get his foot into the door of our mind. What we allow into our minds will sooner or later determine our actions. Thirdly, regular fellowship with other Christians is a must. We all have problems and struggles and need encouragement. We all need Christian companionship. These things help us to maintain our focus and prevent swerving from the right or the left. We must pay attention. In closing, I refer you to Philippians 4:8-9. Maintaining characteristics of virtue in our lives will produce a wholesome thought pattern that will result in less self condemnation and abuse. Whatever you have learned or heard or seen from the instruction of Jesus Christ, put into practice and the God of peace will be with you.

Dear God there is no condemnation for those who are in Christ Jesus. Help me to recognize self condemnation and hold these thoughts captive so that they do not grow to harm me. You are the truth and the way. Help me to maintain my focus on your truths. Help me to keep my thoughts on things that are admirable. My desire is to make time for the things that will build me up and not stress me out. Thank you for your grace and mercy and your love for me. Amen.

275

We Want What We Want
1 Samuel 12:12-25

God had led the Israelites out of Egypt's bondage and continued to care for them. The people decided they wanted a king like the other territories had. God was offended because he was all the king they needed. He also knew their hearts better than they did. There was already potential and outside influence to worship other gods and this brought additional temptation for divided loyalty. But God gave them what they wanted, warning them of the consequences of any disloyalty.

Do you see yourself here? I sure do. Many times I think I know what I want. It is just what I need to make me happy, besides others have it. I often put things before my dedication to my Lord. There are things that I want to do that interfere with my time with God or my time serving him. I am sure that he chuckles at some of my desires. I am also sure that he allows some of my desires to happen knowing that it isn't right for me but will bring opportunity for me to learn from a mistake. My desires are often for something other than God himself and his plan for me which is truly all I need. Turning to desires of our own which are useless and powerless may bring needed discipline. I like Samuel's response to them in verses 14 and 15. He knew God was giving them what they wanted and cautioned them that as long as they continued to fear the Lord, serve him, obey him and do not rebel against him they would be okay. But if they were disloyal or let this new king affect their relationship with the Lord God as their true king, they would be in trouble. In other words, God is giving you what you want but he is watching and you best behave. Let's be sure today that first of all, there is no division in our loyalty. Let's be sure our relationship with Jesus Christ is our first priority and fulfilling his desire for us is what drives us. There may be another(s) god in our life that we serve. Our loyalty to Jesus Christ, our true King must be solid and true. Are we living as Samuel suggests in verse 14? Do we lack in fear of the Lord? Do we serve and obey him well? Is there any rebellion in me? Let's spend some time in prayer and ask God to search our hearts for any disloyalty.

Dear God thank you for loving me and wanting me to be happy just as a good father does. But I know there are times that I go out on my own and want what I want without first seeking your desire for me. I want my heart to be right with you. I do not want any misplaced loyalty in me. Help me to fear you and serve you and obey you as I should. Search my heart and show me any changes I need to make. Give me courage to follow your desire for me. I love you. You are my King and I want to serve you well. Forgive me when I put other gods before you. Amen.

276

The Day Of the Lord
Malachi 4:1-6

When I read this passage this week, it first of all tickled me to think of the joy of a calf frolicking in a pasture. Calves and any baby animal or young child have a certain innocence that gives them energy to frolic and play all day long. The day of the Lord's return is imminent. It will be a time of horror for the non-believer but Jesus Christ, the sun of righteousness will rise like the sun for the believer. This short passage of verses gives the joy and peace of the fulfillment of God's promise to return for us but also the horror that will come for others. Reading through this causes me to be still. Still with confidence in my faith and trust in Jesus Christ but also anxiousness for those who have a day of true regret coming. It makes me hurt for those who I know that do not know Jesus as Lord and Savior. I know what is coming but do they recognize where they are heading? There is a stretch of Interstate in our area that often backs up in the morning traffic as cars are exiting to go into downtown. You come over a slight hill and then immediately see that backup. I have been in a four car pileup in the area myself and always approach it now cautiously. One morning as I was approaching the hill, a car came past me traveling at a speed that I knew was too fast for the upcoming problem traffic area. As I topped the hill I saw him approach the backed up traffic. He could not slow down enough to prevent running into the back of a car that had already slowed. I saw it coming and saw it happen. I remember saying out loud, Slow Down, Look out! I thought about this as I read this passage. 1 Thessalonians 5:2 says the day of the Lord will come like a thief in the night. He will come unannounced as we are going about doing as we do. Just like that car heading to town apparently in a hurry was totally caught off guard by the traffic and was brought to a screeching halt, hopefully escaping injury. On the day of the Lord there will be no escape from injury for those who do not know Jesus Christ as Lord. Life as we know it today will come to a screeching halt. God is not a bully. He is our Heavenly Father. He allows us to make our own choice but also clearly reveals the consequences of the wrong choice. I hope you are ready. You know if you are not. Don't pass over today without slowing down and preparing for the day of the Lord. We have been warned. We know the consequences. Encourage others (1 Thessalonians 4:16-18). Let's be prepared for the day of the Lord.

Dear Lord, reveal to me what I need to hear from this passage. How can I be better prepared for the day of your return? What do I need to do in anticipation? Help me to be still and quiet and hear your voice. Knowing you as Lord and Savior of my life, I long for the day of your return. I long to begin living eternity in your presence. Thank you for your forgiveness when I fail and thank you for your love for me. Amen.

277

The Voice Of Truth
Psalm 86

Satan is the father of lies. He fills our head with thoughts that cause anxiousness, fear and confusion. The voice of Jesus Christ is the voice of truth. We often have to get still and quiet and listen because there is so much noise in our head. Through prayer and determination we can control our thoughts and take captive those that are negative and untrue. We take them captive so that they are restrained and cannot go any further and eventually die out.

My husband and I joined our church together several years ago as a couple. Unfortunately, I go without him now. I started feeling like I was an outcast, like everyone was seeing me as a couple-minus-one. Thoughts of leaving and finding another church started to consume me. I was convinced that I no longer belonged and decided that God was leading me away from my church home and friends. I allowed negative thoughts to convince me that I stuck out like a sore thumb; everyone was looking at me and talking about me. As I prayed about it I started to realize that I was listening to a voice of lies. As I took a serious look, no one was treating me differently; I was the one that was telling myself that I was different. Well I am different now. My life is taking a different direction. Different didn't mean that I no longer belonged. Not a person had said anything to make me feel this way, in fact I received nothing but caring encouragement and invitations to meals, movies and coffee. I was allowing thoughts of anxiousness, fear and confusion to mislead me. Through prayer and time with God I soon regained control of my thoughts and turned up the volume of the voice of truth. I tuned out the noisy lies. This isn't to say that God may truly lead me down a different path but he will not do it in a way that makes me feel inadequate and out of place. This way of thinking is never from God. My strength and contentment comes from the Lord. Staying in tune with the truth allows Jesus Christ to take the discouragement and depression out of our lives. Optimism and joy come from a relationship with Jesus Christ. Don't allow your mind to become a battlefield.

Dear God thank you for your voice of truth. Give me strength and determination to control my thoughts and cast out the lies that come to mind. I will call to you and you will answer me. Bring joy and lift my soul for I am needy. Thank you for your love for me. I will listen and hear your promises of peace. Amen.

278

Confidence
1 John 5:14-15

I know someone who went to work today and was terminated without a moment's notice due to budget cuts. She was thanked for her service, told to gather her personal items and leave. Thankfully she did receive two weeks pay. She had worked for 12 years, received exceptional employee ratings and got along well with everyone. As I listened to her story I felt devastated for her. She was confident and at peace. Her confidence came from her belief in the Son of God. Her peace came from knowing her life was in God's hand. She reminded me of Jeremiah 17:7-8 that says blessed is he who trusts in the Lord, whose confidence is in God. I couldn't have been happier for her. She will be fine. She lives as a tree planted by the water and will not fear or worry in a year of drought and continues to bear fruit. I will be better for hearing her story.

We who follow Jesus Christ have the belief to live each day but do we truly place our confidence in our Lord? I am not sure I could handle a day like hers in the same way she did yet we are the same. God doesn't give her more confidence than he gives me. She seeks more confidence from God more than I do. Hours after hearing her story I still marvel at it and I want what she has. She is the one without a job but I want what she has. Life can change without a moment's notice. Let's learn from this example and be ready to face anything tomorrow.

Dear God, you are my light and my salvation, whom and what should I fear? You are the strength of my life, of whom and what should I be afraid? Thank you for this lady who showed me the value of living in confidence every day. I pray marvelous blessing on her for the confidence she has in you and for sharing it with me today. There are no promises for tomorrow. Help me to grow my relationship with you so that I fear nothing. Give me the confidence that I need to face anything. I love you Lord. Forgive me when I doubt you. Amen.

279

You Can't Hide
Romans 2:1-16

I have been riding with a friend who is boarding a horse for someone. We take them to riding trails early on Saturday morning. As she hitches the trailer to her truck the two horses always go out to the far side of the pasture and stand behind a tree in the far corner. They stand and watch as we get things loaded. Every time, we have to walk out and get them. They stand still as we walk up and put on their halter and come willingly. Once we get them to the trailer, they are fine and we have a great ride but they seem to always give a try at hiding behind the tree as if we can't see them, putting off the inevitable. As I write this I smile envisioning Jess and Fred standing behind that tree as if we can't see them. Before I even start I'm sure you already have my point. Do we sometimes think we can hide from God? Is there anywhere we can hide to avoid conviction and repentance? Not any more than those two horses can hide behind that tree. I remember as a child, my teacher would often have us return test papers with our parent's signature. One time I tried to copy my mother's signature and turned it in to the teacher. She probably knew it immediately and called my mother. Boy did I get it when I got home. What was I thinking? Did I really think I could get away with it? Let's be certain that sin will catch up with us. The truth will find us either on this side or on the other side of judgment day. We can run but we can't hide. Don't let shame keep you from God's mercy and grace. Don't listen to Satan's lies that God will punish us unfairly rather than being a shelter of love and forgiveness. Psalm 32:7 says the Lord God is our hiding place and will protect us from trouble, surrounding us with songs of deliverance. Come out from behind that tree. Lay your sin before the Father and seek forgiveness and grace.

Dear God thank you for sheltering me from trouble. Help me not to allow my shame to keep me from you. My sin separates me from you and hinders my relationship with you. I need you and I need your forgiveness. Search my heart and show me what I need to lay at your feet for forgiveness. Thank you for your grace and mercy. Amen.

280

Embracing Each Others Quirks
Luke 6:27-36

We all have our own way of doing certain things. Sometimes these ways irritate others or they think we are weird or even rude. I heard a radio announcer talking about this on a recent morning show and she suggested that we embrace each others quirks. What is your quirk? And don't say you don't have one. I only like buying either white paper towels or with a border print – I don't like print across the towel. I always must have lots of ice in my cold drinks. I can only read in quiet. I don't like people to start a side conversation during a meeting or service. I don't like to hear someone talk disrespectfully to the boss. I don't like it when someone in a group turns to another person, whispers to them and then laughs out loud. Admit it, we all have our ways. And we all think our way of doing things is best. While we are all different individually we are all the same. We are all sinners (Romans 3:23) and we are all taught to love each other. That isn't easy for us to accept. Every day someone does something to irritate us or cause us to pass judgment. You know who I am talking about - that person, co-worker or family member who we dread seeing cross our path because we dislike something about them. That person who insists on doing things differently that causes me to cringe. That's the one. That's the one I need to embrace. That's the one I need to pray for. That's who I need to ask God to give me grace and mercy for. I have my own oddities. I have my own quirks. I do things that irritate others. Not everyone likes me as a person. That is okay! We all have our individual ways and likes/dislikes but we must strive to love each other as a child of God just as God loves each of us. We must embrace the quirks of others.

Dear God give me patience with others. Help me to accept my own individualities and the differences in those around me. You created each of us and you love us all. We don't have to vie for your attention. Help me to embrace the quirks of others. Forgive me when I pass judgment. There is no difference for we all have sinned. There is no difference for you forgive freely. Thank you for your love for us. Amen.

Jesus' Desire For Us
John 17:20-26

These verses are a portion of the prayer Jesus prayed before his arrest and death. He prayed for himself, he prayed for his disciples and he prayed for you and me. Take a few minutes to read through these beautiful verses. Jesus is praying for the believers and for those who will come to believe from the spreading of the gospel. He prayed for unity among believers with a confidence that the gospel would spread and there would be new believers. I find this passage full of love for me as he includes me in his relationship with God the Father. I was watching an old western this Sunday afternoon and the movie was about a friendship between a white man and an Indian even though their people were at war. Several times during the movie when the two of them would meet, the Indian would say, 'it warms my heart to see you…'. While I recognize God's supremacy, I also feel included. It warms my heart. I feel Jesus' longing and urging me to join him and allow his love for me to live within me, like a warming in my heart that nothing else can bring. In our world, kings and supreme authority are set above and apart from their kingdom with lines drawn that are not to be crossed. Jesus includes us and embraces us as a part of him and his mission. He draws no lines. We can approach the throne of the high priest with confidence to receive mercy and grace (Hebrews 4:14-16). He has made known to us the path of life, as the psalmist writes in Psalm 16:11. Sometimes we feel rejected and may not be where we want to be in our circumstances but Jesus is always there ready to embrace us, inviting us to live in him. We are never alone or rejected when Jesus is our Lord and Savior. We can live in unity with him and God the Father. Jesus' desire is that the love of God that is in him dwells in us and that he himself is in us.

Dear God thank you for your wonderful plan for me. I cannot fathom the love that you have for me, such a sinner, but I know it is true. May the desire of my heart be to accept your love for me and to share it with others so that they will know you. Thank you for the sacrifice of your Son for me and that he prayed for me before he died for me. You are an awesome God and I praise your name. Amen.

282

God Prepares For Me

1 Corinthians 2

As I have said before, I travel a good bit in my job. Yesterday I had the first time privilege of driving alone to downtown Atlanta to attend a meeting. As I got into the city my prayers became more constant however I remained surprisingly calm even when I located the 75 story hotel but could not find the entrance. I drove around the block, dodging one way streets for the second time. Atleast I knew I was close; it was just a matter of finding the entrance. As I was slowly driving along, the truck ahead of me started his flashers and back up lights to try to back into a driveway. As I came to a stop, out stepped a city policeman to bring me to a halt. Aha, my answered prayer. I motioned for him to step toward me and as the truck did his thing, the policeman directed me to the entrance of my hotel. Seems like a little thing but it was huge to me at the time. God prepared the way for me. I love it when God shows me he cares for me and prepares the way for me. I love it when he shows me that the little things in my life are important to him. Jesus tells us in John 14:1-4 to trust him in all things. He was leaving his time on earth and comforted the disciples that he was going away to prepare a place for us. We have nothing to fear. Whether you're lost in traffic in an unfamiliar place or facing major issues in your life God cares for you and prepares a way for you. No eye has seen, no ear has heard, no mind has conceived what God has prepared for those who love him. Trust him today in all things. Give him your fears and he will answer. I saw an insurance ad that read; Take the scary out of life. You can do that by trusting in God in all things.

Dear God thank you for your wonderful promises. You are a loving Father and I praise your name. Thank you for being interested in even the little concerns and fears in my life. Thank you for preparing a way for me. Forgive me when I hesitate to trust you. Open my heart to what you desire to reveal to me through the Holy Spirit. Calm my fears and anxiousness so that I can hear and trust you. You are so precious to me. Amen.

Jesus Is All We Need
Matthew 6:7-8

We think we know what we need. Relationships sometimes let us down. Sometimes they are repairable and sometimes they are not. We often think that because we do not have a spouse or sibling or mother or father we are not whole. We feel alone, unworthy and maybe even abandoned. I think especially when without a spouse or special friend of the opposite sex we find ourselves searching for someone, anyone to fill the void. We panic at the thought of growing old alone and feel left out in the world. If you feel this way today I challenge you to seek Jesus Christ as your special friend and recognize that he is all we need. I suggest that we acknowledge Jesus Christ as the only one we need before we even consider searching for someone. I suggest that we lay at his feet our loneliness and unworthiness, giving him first place allowing him to first fill that void with his love. Then seek his guidance but only after finding full confidence, worthiness and satisfaction in our place in the world. All things are from him and of him. We are never alone. This is where Christian fellowship with other believers is so important. Between work, church, friends and family my days are full yet I have no partner in my life at this time. And you know what? That is OK. I am by myself only when I choose to be. Yes, life often takes disappointing turns but my relationship with my Lord makes me whole. It isn't being in a relationship with someone else that makes me whole. Jesus is all we need. My faith and trust in Jesus is what gives me confidence, worthiness and satisfaction. Think about it and seek him today. Tell him about your fears and loneliness. He will show you how to fill the void. Don't look in the wrong places, look up.

Jesus Christ, you are all the world to me, my life, my joy, my all. You are my strength from day to day, without you I would fall. You are all the world to me. I want no better friend. When I am sad, you make me glad. Thank you for your love for me. Forgive me when I think I need someone else to give me confidence and make me feel loved. I place you first in my life. I turn to you first for companionship. You are all I need. Amen.

284

We Are In Good Hands

Romans 8:28-39

Life can be hard. Life can be overwhelming. As I read this passage today the thought comes to me, We are in good hands. As a youngster we sang, He's got the whole world in his hands. These are old familiar words repeated so often that we hardly take them seriously as we say or sing them but they are full of hope and peace and assurance. We know that in all things God works for the good of those who love him. We know without question that in everything, not some things, everything God works for the good of those who love him; not those who are the best Christians or seemingly live the perfect life or have it all but those who love him. Jesus Christ who died and was raised to life intercedes for us. Can you think of anyone else you would rather advocate for you? Not me. We are not just conquerors; we are more than conquerors through Jesus Christ who loves us. Nothing can separate us from Jesus Christ, not death or life or angels or demons or the present or the future or powers or depth or height or anything else in all creation. Go back and read the passage again. These are not my words, these are God's Words. How do we gain this assurance? Love. God works for the good of those who love him. Do you feel better? I do. You should too. There is nothing I can't face; nothing I can't go through. I am not alone. The battles are not mine yet I am winning. The battles and struggles are for Jesus Christ to win for me. He loves me and he is working out his plan for my life and it is good. All I have to do is to continue to love him and trust him. Whatever our concern is today let's hand it over to Jesus Christ. Let's not doubt for a minute that he is in control and works for the good of us who love him. We are in good hands.

Dear God thank you for the promises and assurance you bring to my day. I need you today. I need to trust you today. Help me to trust that nothing can separate us. I know that in all things you work for the good of those who love you. I love you Lord. I don't show it sometimes but I love you. I want to trust you with all my heart in all things. Forgive me when I hesitate. Thank you for your plan for me. Amen.

285

Benefits Of My Faith
Philippians 2:1-2

Philippians is made up of letters of encouragement and sometimes reprimands from Paul to the Christians churches. These verses spoke to me recently of the benefits of my faith. Benefits that I enjoy in common with fellow Christians. It speaks of encouragement, unity with Christ, comfort from his love, fellowship with the Spirit, tenderness, compassion, joy and unity with those who have faith as I do. Quite a benefit package, would you say? Nothing or no one, can at any time reduce these benefits. I would be certainly devastated if I lost my insurance benefit package from my employment. But how does that compare to the benefit package from heaven that can never be taken or reduced? No comparison. Yet I probably hold on to the insurance more than I realize the magnificent value of the benefits of my faith in Jesus Christ. From my relationship with him flow all the benefits and fruits of my salvation such as those listed in this passage. Jesus tells us in John 10:28-29 that no one can remove us from the Father's hand. Once we have given our heart and life to the Heavenly Father and place our trust in him, no one can take it away from us or reduce the benefits and fruits of it. We may step away and change the relationship by our selfish desires and actions, but Jesus Christ will never step away from us or allow anyone else to reduce our benefits. Let's not take our benefits for granted.

Dear God thank you for the benefits that flow from my relationship with you. You are a loving, gracious Father. Forgive me when I take your love and blessings for granted. Forgive me when I think success and provision come from me. Benefits of this world cannot compare to the benefits of my relationship with you. All that I have comes from you. My desire is to live a life pleasing to you. I long to live in eternity with you in the place you prepare for me. Thank you for my Christians friends. Help me not to take them for granted either. Help me to love others unconditionally as you love me. Amen.

286

Just For Today
Philippians 4:11-20

My work has taken me to Denver, Colorado. Yesterday I spent the day getting here, from airport shuttle to Charlotte, flight from Charlotte to Atlanta (yes, flying back over my house) and then from Atlanta to Denver. It was one of those days that I stayed stressed. The shuttle was late, the airport check in and security lines were very long and slow getting me to my gate just as they were boarding. Late into Atlanta which made me one of the last to board on the flight to Denver which meant at 1:00 I still hadn't had breakfast or lunch. My seat was at the very back of the plane which made me last for the beverage and peanuts. Fortunately I had thought to bring a trail mix bar. As I relaxed in my room last night, I thanked God for getting me here safely and on time. He sent back to me the thought, then why did you spend the day stressed? Why did I? Each difficulty worked itself out and just in time. God sends me just what I need for the day and in perfect timing. Yes, I was later than I like to be but not too late. Yes I was hungry but not that hungry. I had a great dinner after checking in and went to bed perfectly satisfied. As I look back, I am so frustrated with myself for spending even a moment in worry and frustration. When will I learn to chill?

Paul had it so right. He knew how to be content whatever the circumstances. He depended on his God to protect and provide for him. I have a feeling he would have handled yesterday very differently. He probably would have taken advantage of the opportunity to mix with others (in line), waiting patiently and in expectation of just how God would get him to Denver and just in time. I think that is the kind of person he was. Oh I'm sure he had moments but not as many as I have. I think he would have thought, so what if I have to stand in line after line, I have ample opportunity to set an example and maybe change the day for a stranger. And so what if I miss the flight, I'll catch the next one. God knows which flight he wants me on. And so what if I miss lunch, I probably don't know what hungry really is and will greatly appreciate my dinner. Regretfully I missed all this because I was the one frustrated and worried, stomping my foot muttering, Oh brother, this is making me wait and late. Lesson learned. My days left on this trip will be different. I will strive to have an attitude of confidence and peace, no matter what, for I will be content whatever the circumstances. I can do everything through God who strengthens me. I have just what I need for today, amply supplied. My God will meet all my needs according to his glorious riches in Christ Jesus.

Dear God thank you for the lessons that you teach me each day and the guidance you provide in your Holy Word. Forgive me for being so needy and impatient. You provide all that I need. Help me to be strong and faithful in being content whatever the circumstances. Help me to faithfully trust you, every minute of the day. I love you and want to live a life that pleases you. Thank you for how well you bless me. Amen.

287

Exhausted
1 Kings 19:1-8

Elijah was exhausted. He was running in fear of his life and was exhausted. He prayed to God, I have had enough Lord, take my life. Have you ever prayed this prayer? Have you ever asked God to please just take you on to heaven? I have. There were several painful months of my life that I often prayed that as I went to bed at night and I was as sincere as I could be. I was not contemplating suicide but I honestly felt like I could not handle life anymore and pleaded with God to go ahead and take me to heaven. My relationship with God was tender and I wanted to be with him. I know how Elijah felt. God has carried me through those troubled times just like he did Elijah. God had different plans for both of us and for you as well. God sent angels to encourage and care for Elijah. He did the same for me. He sent me comfort, wisdom and peace. He sent me Christian friends and a wonderful counselor to strengthen me. He helped me make decisions to get me where I am today. I was reminded that when we ask for help it is on the way. Even when we don't see the answers we are to keep our head up because we walk by faith not by sight (2 Corinthians 5:7). Elijah was also physically tired and run down. Sometimes we don't get the rest we need which hinders our ability to handle the bumps and harsh turns in life. Jesus said in Matthew 11:28 to come to him for rest. He offers to carry our burdens. As I look back, I am not proud of the requests I made of God but I was exhausted and sincere at the time. It is not wrong to long to be with Jesus. We know that he prepares a place for us to live with him in eternity and I look forward to starting eternity with him. But for today he tells me to give my burdens to him and let him carry them.

He knows the number of my days here on earth and I try not to make such requests anymore. My faith and trust are much stronger since those days. God has taught me patience and given me hope. He also tells me to rest properly (Exodus 20:8-11). Jesus often rested and took quiet time alone to pray. We should too. Elijah recovered and finished the tasks God had for him to do and hopefully I am doing just as well. When exhaustion comes, turn to God for strength and support. Ask him for guidance and help. He is waiting to be our strength and refuge.

Dear God, you are my refuge and strength, an ever present help in trouble (Psalm 46:1). Thank you. Give me courage to seek you when troubles come and stand firm in my faith and trust. Forgive me when I hesitate to trust you and give in to the exhaustion. Help me to rest properly. I want to love you more. Amen.

288

Pat and Penny
2 Samuel 22:21-37

I have a friend that I met a couple years ago that has a wagon and mule team, Pat (Patricia) and Penny, that he uses for wagon rides. He goes to events, nursing homes, churches, etc. and gives wagon rides usually free of charge. He even has a special wagon that a wheel chair can roll into. He has friends who also have a wagon and mule team. They take overnight trips for several days, enjoying the ride and fellowship. He is 73 years old and fun to be with, full of stories. He has taught me to drive the team and I help him from time to time. A few days ago we spent most of the day giving rides for a school charity event.

Everyone loves Pat and Penny. They want to pet them and ask questions about them. Pat and Penny are usually expressionless, taking anything and everything in stride. No matter if there are crying babies, rowdy teens or rambunctious groups, the mules do as we say even learning the path after only a couple rounds. A mule is the offspring of a male donkey and a female horse. The mule is more patient and sure-footed than horses and they are considered less obstinate, faster, and more intelligent than donkeys. You know I am partial to mules because Festus on *Gunsmoke* always rode a mule named Ruth. I don't see mules as emotional and needy as horses; not as high maintenance as they can be like us.

Our relationship with Jesus Christ is always the same no matter the load, no matter the emotion, no matter the need. Jesus Christ is the same yesterday and today and forever (Hebrews 13:8). This passage in 2 Samuel is David's song of praise when the Lord delivered him from danger. He sang these words to the Lord. It says to me, no matter if I am good or bad the Lord cares for me and protects me. He guides me and rewards me according to my ways and the desires of my heart. God is good all the time. I need him in every aspect of my life all the time. It is God that gives me strength and directs my path. This encourages me to stay close to him, to maintain my relationship with him, never turning from him. I must always make time for him. Time for praise, thanksgiving, repentance and learning more about him. Time and relationship with him as consistent as Pat and Penny pull the wagon never questioning the circumstance or the load.

Dear God thank you for your never changing consistency in my life. Thank you for your never failing love for me. My desire is to please you. I want you to smile on my ways. Give me strength to never question my circumstances but to trust you every day no matter what comes my way. I love you and praise your name. Forgive me when I fail you. Amen.

289

The Coming Of the Son Of Man
Matthew 24:27-35

I recently saw a video of a church service and the preacher was preaching to the fact that Jesus Christ could return at any moment. Suddenly there was a loud clap of thunder and flash of light and most of the congregation disappeared. Those left were in shock, disbelief and devastated. Then this verse (27) appeared on the screen. I have to admit that I do not recall reading this verse before or atleast it did not draw my attention like this did.

This is not the only reference in the Bible to Jesus Christ's return. Each time I read one of these passages I am encouraged to live each day as if it is the day Jesus will appear. I am thankful for the salvation I received through his mercy and grace. This means I will not be here for the aftermath of his return. Chapter 25 of Matthew speaks to parables that remind us to be prepared and keep watch because we do not know the day or the hour of the beginning of the end of the world as we know it. These words of warning should cause us to search our heart for unrepented sin and bring change to the life we live in preparation for the return of Jesus Christ. I am traveling this week and as I sit in a hotel room and write this, it is possible that I will never make it home again because this foretold truth could come to pass before I check out. It could happen before I go to bed in a couple hours or before I get up in the morning. Just like packing my bags in preparation for this trip several days before I left, we must prepare for his coming. We must keep watch and be prepared. We must take advantage of each opportunity to share this truth with anyone who crosses our path. We must get ready.

Dear God show me any preparation I need to make before your return. Search my heart for sin that I need to eliminate from my life. Thank you for your words of warning and thank you for your saving grace. Who do I need to speak to? Who do I need to warn? What do I need to do to get ready? Speak to my heart today. Amen.

290

Wisdom From Heaven
James 3:17-18

My mind is sometimes a battlefield. A battlefield between the wisdom from heaven and the lies from Satan. There are times that a problem arises and I nearly panic. I feel overwhelmed by fear and what ifs. This passage reminds us that wisdom that comes from heaven is pure, peace loving, considerate, submissive, full of mercy and goodness, impartial and sincere. The wisdom from heaven is first of all pure and then peaceful. The lies of Satan bring anxiousness and fear. When God speaks to me he can be persistent but his voice is full of grace and patience. Satan puts my stomach and throat in knots and the muscles in my body tense up. He causes the panic and fear. We can tell the difference. We can stop where we are, voice our fear and confusion to God and he will show us his voice. When we seek him, he finds us (Jeremiah 29:13). Don't allow the panic and fear to consume you. Stop where you are and pray. Today, hundreds of miles away from home I realized something that I could not control from here. Nothing major but it did cause me concern. Satan immediately tried to fill me with fear and consume me with panic. I had to stop and pray and ask God to calm me. I turned to him to seek wisdom from heaven. He sent his peace and in a short time things worked out well. We choose which voice we listen to and react to. No matter the outcome, the peace and trust comes. The wisdom from heaven comes when we seek him and listen for his voice. What is on your mind today? What troubles you? Stop and pray.

Dear God your wisdom from heaven is pure and peaceful, full of mercy and sincere. Help me to listen for your voice and seek your wisdom. Close my heart and mind to the lies of Satan. When I seek you, you will find me. Thank you for your wonderful promises. Your way is perfect and your word is flawless. You are a shield for all who take refuge in you (2 Samuel 22:31). Give me courage to stop and pray when I need your wisdom. Amen.

291

Your Will, Not Mine
John 14:12-14

Praise be to the Lord to God our Savior who daily bears our burdens (Psalm 68:19). We often question just why things happen as they do. Why does a relationship that I once thought would thrive til old age, come to an end leaving me devastated? People are sometimes dishonest and let us down. People get sick and die. Unthinkable crimes are committed. We often ask, why? I read a story about a young nursing student who struggled with personal emotional feelings for her patients. She was afraid that her strong feelings for her patients would prevent her from being a good nurse. She decided to handle her problem by praying for her patients and handing them over to God. She prayed, He belongs to you, not me. I give him into your mighty, healing hands. Your will, not mine, be done. She decided she would do as she could as a nurse and leave the rest to God's tender mercy. Jesus tells us to have faith. But sometimes it takes more courage and faith to hand our troubles to God to handle than it does to try to handle them ourselves. We often wait until we are exhausted with worry and fear before we take things to God. And then we look back and ask, what took me so long? When will we learn to take our troubles to God daily in prayer and thanksgiving rather than spend a moment in worry and fear? Jesus taught that we are not to worry, for tomorrow will worry about itself; each day has enough trouble of its own (Matthew 6:34. Go back and read 6:25-34). God patiently waits for us to ask for his help and commit to his will and not our own. This young nursing student was trying to carry the burden of care and concern for her many patients and recognized quickly that it was an impossible task to handle on her own. She found freedom to do her job when she turned the hard part over to God. Let's be encouraged to start our day with God and commit our day to him, to his will not our own.

Dear God, praise be to you my Lord and Savior who daily bears my burdens. You my God are a God who saves. I praise your name with a heart of thankfulness and adoration. The desire of my heart is to obey you and not carry worry and fear within me. I lay my burdens at your feet and commit myself to faith and trust in you in all things in my life, big and small. Forgive me when I hesitate to trust you. Amen.

292

Forces Among Us
Daniel 10 - 11:1

In this passage Daniel is waiting for a response from God. He anguished but persisted for three weeks. A vision of a man finally came and told him that since the first day that he set his mind to gain understanding and to humble himself before God, his words were heard. The passage speaks of a demonic influence for 21 days overcome by Michael the archangel who protects the people of God. Peace and strength and confidence came to Daniel through a vision from God messaging his response. I find this passage full of hope and confidence for me. I am not a scholar and do not understand this completely but the passage says that there are evil forces among us that are real and strong. But God provides protection when we humble ourselves before him and are persistent in our prayers. I like to think of the passage in verses 15-19 as God's warmth and love coming to touch this believer (just like us) who knew from where to seek and find guidance and support. We all have concerns and troubles that often overcome and consume us. Daniel experiences this but he persisted and received a response. We must never give up hope and confidence that our Lord will hear and respond to our requests. Romans 8:26-27 gives us additional support assuring us that the Holy Spirit is within us for strength and will intercede for us when we cannot find the right words to pray. We simply must humble ourselves before God and ask from our heart. Our hearts may be heavy today. Let's bow before our God and lay at his feet our troubles. He is the Almighty God who can overcome any force among us. He waits in anticipation for our cry.

Dear God in heaven, I ask you to forgive my sins and hear my prayer. Your Word says the Holy Spirit will intercede for me when I cannot find the words. There are forces among us that I do not understand but I know you are truth and strength. I lay my requests at your feet and wait in peaceful anticipation and confidence for your will. I release this concern to your will. Bring me peace and comfort. I praise you Lord for I know you hear me and care for me. You are my God and my strength. I trust you with all my heart in all things. Thank you for your mercy and blessings. Amen.

293

Ezekiel's Call
Ezekiel 2:9 - 3:3

Ezekiel and his fellow Israelites were living in captivity in Babylon. God called Ezekiel to warn his people of harsh judgment coming from God. He was called to preach of their only hope which was turning to God for salvation and redemption. In this passage Ezekiel is speaking. He tells of God revealing a scroll full of written words of mourning and woe, even on both sides. God has lots to say about the harsh judgment that was coming. God tells him to eat the scroll and Ezekiel did. In fact he says simply, So I opened my mouth and did. Sometimes God asks us to do unusual things. I think sometimes it is his plan and sometimes it is to see if we will do as he asks. God has often told me to give a gift sometimes monetary to someone, sometimes in secret and sometimes in person. He has waked me at night and started talking to me or told me to get up and read something in my Bible. He often tells me to write a note of encouragement to someone just out of the blue. He has told me to start a warm conversation with a total stranger. He told me to join in a mission trip to Venezuela which was way out of my comfort zone but I will never forget it. None of this may seem as strange as eating a scroll but my point is that we should be waiting and listening for God to speak and respond as Ezekiel did without hesitation. Verse 3:3 says that the scroll tasted as sweet as honey. God told him to eat the scroll so he did and it tasted like honey - sweet reward for obedience. Each time God has asked me to do something, a sweet taste of peace and assurance always follows my obedience. In Psalm 119:103, the psalmist writes that the words of God are sweet to taste, sweeter than honey. Another thought that comes to me here is that we should be anxious to consume God's Word. We should be eager to daily read his Word and spend time with him. We should be eager to respond to God's call. We crave the taste of sweets. Do we crave the sweet taste of God's Word? Are we eager to gobble it up and want more? Do we have the same desire to follow God's calling? In verse 3:10, God tells Ezekiel, listen carefully and take to heart all the words I speak to you. Let's take time today to listen. Find a place to shut out the noise and listen to what God is calling us to do today.

Dear God, the desire of my heart is to listen carefully and take to heart all the words you speak to me. I want to listen to your call and respond without hesitation. I want to experience the sweet taste of obedience. I want to crave and consume your words. Thank you for your love for me and the salvation you offer even though I am rebellious and selfish. Forgive me when I fail you. Amen.

294

God Hates Unrighteousness
Romans 1:18 - 2:11

I for one, am so tired and disgusted with the sexual overtone and acceptable promiscuity in not only TV shows, but the commercials too. What is sexy about fast food? I heard a guy on a commercial for a salad offered by a fast food restaurant say '...I took her home with me last night and she was crazy!' Marketing techniques for fast food, shampoo, cars, etc., use sexual overtones regularly. It's everywhere you turn. And don't think they wouldn't be using it, if it wasn't increasing sales and accepted by the viewer (that's you and me). And we wonder why teen pregnancies are on the rise and our young girls think that love is sex. Additionally, ads constantly insinuate that the man of the house is whimpy and stupid. No wonder many of our young families lack male leadership. I find it very difficult these days to find acceptable TV. The commercials are nauseating. Lingerie commercials border porn. When are we going to wake up and stand up? Do we boycott the products? Do we contact management? Do we contact our legislative representatives? Do we do nothing, turn our heads and accept it? Do we turn off our TV? I'd like to suggest that we seriously pray about this. We need to humble ourselves and pray and then do as the Lord guides us to do. Judgment is coming. Accountability is imminent. God will give to each person according to what he has done. Forgive me for standing on my critical soapbox but this has been burning inside of me today.

History testifies to the fact that one person can make a difference. Sometimes one person can change the world for the worse, while another can make it better. Ultimately, man has the desire and power to change the course of the world by his or her actions. That desire can be very, very contagious. Jesus Christ transformed the lives of millions by his miracles and wisdom. It is evident that one person can make a difference. It can be done and it is being done everyday. The question is will you make a difference? Will you allow God to use you to make a difference?

Dear God forgive our unrighteousness. Forgive me when I laugh at an inappropriate or even cruel joke. Forgive me when I turn my head or accept sexual overtone or promiscuity. Strength to make a difference will come from you. Guide me, lead me and give me courage to do your will. Speak to me and tell me the desires of your heart. I am not ashamed of you and I have no excuse. Touch my heart and speak to me today. Amen.

295

Power Of Prayer
Romans 12:12

Today on the radio I heard a wonderful story. A lady called in giving witness to the power of prayer. She said that her daughter had a bird that got out of its cage and flew out the door. The daughter was devastated. That night she prayed at bedtime for God to please return her bird to her. She insisted the next day on putting up posters in the neighborhood and in the local pet store. The mother was very reluctant in encouraging her daughter and feared she would never see the bird again. Still the young girl prayed for its return. A few days later the pet store called and said someone had located the bird. Apparently it had flown into the yard of a lady who somehow got it into an old birdcage. The lady took it to the pet store where the family had put up a poster. The young girl and her bird were reunited. A bird folks!! Finding that bird was next to impossible. Believe what you want but God answered the prayer of the young girl. There is no other explanation and I do not want another explanation. God cared about her loss and sent the bird to just the right place and sent the lady to just the right store. God answers prayer and God cares about our discouragements, big and small. He is a magnificent and powerful God yet cares about the prayer of a young girl for her bird. What concern do you have today? Take it to the Lord in prayer. He is waiting to show his mercy and power. Be joyful in hope, patient in affliction and faithful in prayer.

Dear God thank you for your loving care. You are our God and King yet you care about the little things in life. Give me courage to stay joyful in hope, patient through troubles and faithful in prayer as your Holy Word tells me. My certainty in you is a cause for joy. Your love never fails. Thank you for this wonderful story that encouraged me today. I pray this young girl and her family will continue to trust you in all things. Amen.

296

The Gift Of Peace

Luke 2:14

Do you recall a gift you received and it became the most cherished of your belongings? Do you recall a gadget that you picked up that you now could not get through a task without? So often we do not understand the magnitude or appreciate the existence of something when we first receive it. Do we realize just how marvelous the gift of peace Jesus brought when he came to earth? Peace with God is received by faith in Christ Jesus. We don't realize the magnitude of this gift. Where would I be without it? How would I get through the day without it? Jesus Christ came as a baby in the quiet of the night and gave his life to ensure his gift of peace. It is a gift because it is free and unconditional. It isn't something we must compete for or meet certain criteria to obtain. He offers it to us and we accept it. Zachariah prophesied the coming of our Lord proclaiming that he would guide our feet into the path of peace (Luke 1:79).

We all need peace. We need confidence and hope to live each day. Peace comes from our faith in Jesus Christ. Peace comes when we seek him and trust him in everything. Do you need peace today? I do. Let's take time to search for peace in God's Holy Word. Ask God to show you the words you need for encouragement today. Take time to absorb it and hold on to it.

Dear God I need peace and confidence that comes from you. Only my faith in you can give the peace that I need. Show me words of encouragement that give me just what I need. You are the Father of hope and peace and comfort. Thank you for my salvation in you. Amen.

297

Clueless
Mark 9:30-32

We usually call someone clueless when they are totally uninformed about what is going on. They don't seem to have a clue or any idea of what is actually occurring. Jesus warned his disciples of his coming death and told them of the resurrection but they just didn't seem to get it. They were clueless regarding this teaching of Jesus. It says they were afraid to ask him about it. No one likes to ask a stupid question. But we all know there is no stupid question. How often has this been said hesitantly and then the so called stupid question was the very one we have in mind and are glad that it was asked. Jesus was patient with them and kept teaching and kept warning. After Jesus' resurrection and return to God the Father, the Holy Spirit was sent to help them understand (Acts 1:8). Accepting Jesus Christ into our heart and into our life brings upon us the Holy Spirit to guide us and help us understand. We should never be clueless regarding our relationship with Jesus Christ. He speaks to us in individual ways to guide and teach us. We have to be willing to listen and do what we need to be informed. Daily time in God's Holy Word and communicating (talking and asking and listening) with our Lord helps to keep us in tune to him. There is no stupid question to ask of him. Jesus Christ wants us to ask and seek guidance from him. He desires to be in control and in the leadership position of our life. Don't be like the disciples were here. They did not understand what he meant and were afraid to ask him about it. One day we will have the opportunity to sit at his feet and ask him. Don't wait until then. Seek him in all things. Don't remain clueless.

Dear God thank you for your patience with me and your truthful and perfect guidance. Give me a heart committed to studying your Holy Word every day. Walk with me and talk with me. Help me to be quiet and listen. I trust you in all things. You are the sole desire of my heart. Thank you for your Son who lived to die for me. I pray I never take your sacrifice for granted. Amen.

298

My Last Nerve
Psalm 62:1-8

Sometimes our days are so full and busy that we find ourselves unsteady and our very last nerve is almost shot. Do you find yourself having to go sit in a bathroom stall to gather yourself or maybe take a walk around the block? This passage in Psalms speaks to finding rest in God and insists, My soul finds rest in God alone, the psalmist writes. I will not be shaken.

God is all we need to find rest even in the most stressful day. Maybe we need to tape to our computers or our refrigerator at home, I will not be shaken. God wants us to find rest in him. He does not want us to feel shaken. I can think of no time that I feel closer to God than when I stop and say, Lord help me; and he sends down that marvelous peace and confidence that warms and softens my heart like a warm marshmallow. It is such a good feeling to seek God and know that he has found me. Sometimes we feel such distress and anxiousness. We cry out to God for peace and he will send it. I often notice a complete change in my attitude and 'mood' during the day when I resist the shakiness and ask God for help. Sometimes I just don't understand why I feel like I do but I find peace when I seek him. Trust in God at all times. Pour out your heart to God for he is our refuge. When we need to, let's say it out loud, I will not be shaken. I will not be shaken.

Dear God, my soul finds rest in you alone. I will not be shaken. You are my rock and my salvation and my fortress. I will never be shaken. Thank you for the peace that you bring to my heart. I cannot get through the day without you. I lift my hands in thanksgiving and praise. Amen.

299

Try, Try Again
Hebrews 10:23

Today I helped out at a horse show. My assignment was to greet folks coming in, collect any information that didn't come in with the registration, hand out rider packets and show them where to park. From where I was up on the hill, I could see the entire show happenings in the three arenas. I always particularly enjoy watching the jump arena. Twice today, I saw riders experiencing difficulty in getting the horse to jump. Each time, the horse would stop just at the jump. Once a rider went flying to the ground. She jumped right up and climbed right back on her horse. In both cases, the riders circled around, sometimes 3 or 4 times until the horse went over the jump. Many of us would want to just walk away and I imagine that did cross their minds but the rule is you finish the routine you start, no matter how many times it takes. Both riders held on and finished their routine to applause from the crowd. They were able to coax and guide their horse to get them to follow their lead.

This same thing is so true for our relationship with God. So many times we struggle to get over an obstacle or come to a screeching halt and go flying. Sometimes we get confused and move around in circles. Maybe we should use the same rule as these horse riders. We keep trying even if we get thrown completely. We get back on and keep circling around until we finish to applause from Jesus Christ. Hebrews 2:1 says that we must pay more careful attention to what we have heard so that we do not drift away. Sometimes we need a little coaxing and special handling when trying to follow God's lead. He is willing to work with us as many times as it takes. He loves us unconditionally and desires for us to finish each task we start to his applause. Hebrews 10:23 encourages us to hold unswervingly to the hope we profess, for God who promised is faithful. In Christ there is a promise of hope without doubt or hesitation. He who promised is faithful.

Dear God thank you for your faithfulness. I know you must get dizzy from the circles I make. Thank you for loving me unconditionally and being patient with me every day. Forgive me when I allow obstacles to bring doubt. Forgive me when I want to give up. Give me courage to trust you in all circumstances. Thank you for your forgiveness and your love for me. Amen.

300

The Measure Of Giving
Luke 6:37-38

I recently came across these verses and they really struck me as never before. Jesus is talking about giving. Picture someone filling a container of flour or wheat for someone else. These verses say to pour it in, press it down, shake it and fill it to running over. Imagine filling the container with flour or wheat. You're shaking it and packing it down to see just how much will fit in there. In other words, give all that the container will possibly hold and let it run over. That's how Jesus tells us to give. When we give focusing on how much we can give, we are not focusing on what we are losing or what will be left for us. When we give in this manner the blessing we receive will be running over as well. Jesus warns that we will be measured by the measure we use. The blessings we receive will be measured based on our measure of giving. In Acts 20:35, Paul refers to Jesus saying, It is more blessed to give than to receive.

In this world of needy people we face many opportunities to give in addition to our regular tithe and offering. When we donate clothing do we give what is stained or torn? Do we hold on to good clothing just in case we can wear it again even though it is a couple sizes too small or large? When we give food donations do we search our cabinets for outdated goods or do we buy something we would not eat because it is the cheapest? Do we use a wicked excuse such as, 'well this is better than what they have now'? The next opportunity we have to give, let's keep in mind that container of flour poured in, pressed down, shaken and filled to running over. I believe it is more blessed to give than to receive. I believe when we give with the heart Jesus desires for us to have, we will give generously (and then some) and will be blessed enormously in return.

Dear God, I pray that my giving will be poured in, pressed down, shaken and filled to running over. Give me a generous heart. Knowing you as my Lord and Savior is all the blessing I need. Help me to place little value on my material possessions and to have a generous heart for those in need. Give me an opportunity to fulfill your instruction and may I respond with the heart that you desire. Amen.

301

The Limelight
Joshua 1:6-9

What do you think of the celebrities in the Hollywood limelight? Do you envy them? Do you think they are the lucky ones? Do our youth desire to be just like them? Let's hope not. I don't say that in a judgmental way. I say it because most of those folks would change lives with us in a minute. Their lives are far from what we see on that red carpet, flashing cameras, smiles and waves. No one is exempt from problems and hard times. Money, glamorous careers and fame is not what success in life is about.

In this passage, Moses has died and God has established Joshua as the leader of the children of Israel. God gives instruction to be careful to obey his words. When we are cautioned to be careful it is because there are consequences when we aren't. We are told to meditate on God's Word day and night so that we will be careful to do everything written in it. Then we will be prosperous and successful. Success does not come easily or automatically. Success comes from obedience. Following these words gives us strength and courage to face the world. God knows the temptations we will face. He knows that our human side desires the glamour and success of the limelight. God gives us instruction for a successful life. Our inheritance is blessings from him and eternal life in his presence. So the next time you are temped to wish you were in the glamorous limelight of the celebrities, thank God for what you have and for his eternal promises and say a prayer for the celebrities.

Dear God thank you for where you have placed me in life. Thank you for being the Lord and Savior of my life. Forgive me when I am envious of others. Help me to recognize the goodness and blessings that you send my way. Give me courage and strength to face each day. Thank you for your love for me. Amen.

302

Why Are We Sad?
John 14

What makes us sad? There are lots of things that may cause us concern but what really makes us sad? What really hurts? Just today at lunch a friend was talking about having to give herself a shot. I could never do that, another said. Someone mentioned, Well it's better than the alternative of dying. Everyone agreed but I spoke up that I didn't think the alternative was so bad. Everyone looked at me like I was suicidal. But think about it. I know Jesus Christ as my Lord and Savior and I look forward to being with him. The alternative for me and you I hope is eternal life with him; no pain, no worry and no sadness. He is preparing a place for me. His peace is real and everlasting. While we do have to make the best of what we have here on earth, including giving ourselves a shot if we have to, the sadness and pain is only short lived. The source of our happiness and peace is our relationship with a real God who is with us every day of our time on earth. This passage of scripture is Jesus trying to prepare the disciples for what was coming and he felt their sadness. Do not let your heart be troubled, he said. Trust in God. Trust in me, he said. He abides with those who trust in him. That should take away our sadness.

Lord, help me to trust in you and not be troubled or sad. Help me to focus my mind on the place you are preparing for me. You are coming back for me and will take me to be with you so I will be where you are. I know the way to the place where I am going. You are the way and the truth and the life. There is no room for sadness when I think on these things. Amen.

303

Live Out Loud
Matthew 18:21-35

We can't control the way others act but we can control how we respond to them. In my job I often have to deal with personnel issues addressing folk's inappropriate behavior. There have been times when a person responded in a loud and aggressive manner. That happened to me today. An individual who had been counseled more than once, sent an abusive email directed toward me and a few others to a large group of employees, submitted a letter of resignation and left. When I saw the email I burned with anger and dreaded the thought that many staff was reading it as I did. I knew I had to quickly let it go, to set a good example not only because of my management position but because of my Christian beliefs. Proverbs 30:33 is an interesting verse which says as churning the milk produces butter and twisting the nose produces blood, so stirring up anger produces strife. It is best for us to squelch anger before it grows and consumes us. It can be contagious and affect anyone who comes in contact with it.

Peter asked Jesus how many times we were to forgive. Jesus' answer was pretty much, As many as it takes. We must be willing to forgive to be forgiven. God is willing to forgive us many times each day and we must be willing to do the same. The Bible says several times that our God is slow to anger. I personally appreciate that fact. We are to follow the example that is set for us. Ephesians 4:32 says to be kind and compassionate to each other, forgiving each other, just as in Christ, God forgives us. As we ask God for forgiveness in our daily prayers we must search our own heart for any situation needing our forgiveness. Is there someone that you hesitate to approach because you know you have not been willing to forgive? We are uncomfortable being around someone that we need to forgive. Unforgiveness in our heart affects our relationship with God. We can't come to him completely with unforgiveness in us. Let's search our heart for anything that we need to forgive. The first few words come with difficulty but once it is done we are free from the heavy burden and restraining chains of sin. Let's choose to forgive.

Dear God, help me to be forgiving. Forgive me when I do not forgive. Show me where forgiveness is needed. Keep me from harboring anger and resentment toward someone who has offended me. Help me to follow the truths of your Word and to set an example of forgiveness for those around me to see. I praise you and know that blessings will come from my obedience. My heart longs to please you. Amen.

304

Letting Peace Rule
Colossians 3:15-17

This passage tells us to let the peace of Christ rule in our hearts. According to my dictionary, rule is defined as exercise authority; be in control or command; to maintain at a specific rate or level. We are to allow the peace of God to exercise authority and control our heart. It further tells us to let the word of Christ dwell in us richly. The dictionary defines dwell as to live as a resident; to fasten one's attention. Rich means having great worth or magnificent. The word of God should take up residence in us with great value and worth. I pick these verses apart because sometimes I need to be hit over the head with how magnificently God wants to be a part of my life. Jesus Christ alone gives this attitude of peace that replaces a negative heart, doubt and fear. This peace must rule in all our relationships and circumstances. It must take up residence in us so that the human characteristics can't fit in. In the final verse of the passage, we are told to do everything, whether spoken word or deed, to do it in the name of Christ.

Colossians 2:10 says we are complete in Christ. My Mom noted here in her Bible that complete means full. She wrote, when a person is full he has no room for anything more; when you have Christ, you have it all.

Paul speaks to this as putting off the sinful nature. When we allow the peace of Christ to rule in our hearts and let the word of Christ dwell in us richly, we can better defend ourselves from the sinful natures that tempt us and try to lure us. We can better work through the relationships in our lives and deal with daily living. And our relationship with our Lord will certainly benefit when we strive to follow this teaching. As we ponder this, let's focus on the strong words used here to instruct us: rule, dwell and richly.

Dear God thank you for the instruction you give to enrich our lives and our relationship with you. Help me to strive to have the desire to allow your peace and your word to take command of my heart and my life. Forgive me when I allow the sinful nature to turn my focus from you. I need you and I want my life to be complete in you. Forgive me when I fail you. I want to love you more. Amen.

305

The Lion Collection
Daniel 6:1-28

Several years ago I was promoted to the position of Division Director. While I knew most of the folks in the area, I decided to schedule a retreat for us to spend the day out of the office to do some team building activities and planning for the coming year. I somehow came up with the idea to have a time of Show-n-tell. While the staff was surprised at the planned activity, they seemed to be excited about it as they prepared.

Today's church bulletin reminded me of one of these presentations. The bulletin showed a large picture of a lion with the verse Daniel 6:23. It reminded me of Regina's Show-n-tell. I knew that Regina had a couple drawings of lions in her office but did not realize that she collected lions. She brought books, cards, statues, jewelry and paintings of lions that she had collected for several years. She talked briefly about each item and told us that her interest in lions came from the Bible story of Daniel in the lions den. She then pulled out a Bible and read Daniel 6 out loud. Her voice was graceful and full of a spirit of praise. There was not a dry eye in the room as we all heard the story like it was brand new. Little did we know that within 5 years Regina would succumb to lung cancer and leave us. At the time of her death many of us gathered to speak of her and remember her and we recalled that day as we grieved for her. She was a very lovely, lively person with a beautiful laugh and we all miss her to this day.

God has a plan and has a reason for every single thing that happens in our lives. When Regina started her collection with the very first lion out of her love for that story, she never dreamed how she would be able to use it to touch about 35 lives. I am sure I am not the only one that remembers that Show-n-tell when we hear a reference to Daniel and the lion's den. Daniel was taken out of the lion's den uninjured because he trusted in His God. We too can survive the terrors and fears in life, uninjured, when we trust in our God. I believe God used the courage of Daniel to prepare Regina for her time of illness. That courage and protection from death with eternal life is available to us all. Go back and read verses 26 and 27 in praise to God.

Dear God, you are the living God. You endure forever. Your kingdom will not be destroyed and your dominion will never end. You rescue and you save. You perform signs and wonders in the heavens and on earth. You rescued Daniel from the power of the lions. You rescue me from the powers that lurk around me and forgive me when I fail. Thank you, Lord. You are my God and I love you. Amen.

306

The Voice Of Jesus
John 10:27-30

Psalm 23 appropriately refers to our Lord as our shepherd. This passage in John speaks to the same relationship between us and Jesus Christ. When we accept his call we are granted eternal life and nothing or no one can take that away from us. We are eternally in his flock. We are completely secure in his hand. A shepherd calls his sheep by a certain sound or voice. The sheep of his flock know his call and respond to it. Even if the sheep get mingled with another flock, the shepherd can identify his own and they will respond to him. This should be true for us and our Lord. We must know his voice, listen for it and cling to it for protection and direction. Jesus Christ knows his sheep and longs to shepherd us. In Deuteronomy

30:20, God told his people to love him, listen for his voice and hold fast to him. For the Lord is your life, he says.

No matter what we must deal with today our Shepherd longs to care for us. He longs to lead us, guide us and restore us. Close your eyes and picture a shepherd quietly watching over his grazing flock in a pasture of green grass. A predator cowers behind the rocks. The shepherd fearlessly eyes it and destroys it before the flock can be harmed. Look into the eyes of that shepherd and see his love and mercy for you. You do not want for anything and have no fear as long as you are near him and can hear the sound of his voice. No one is stronger or greater than your shepherd.

Dear Lord, you are my shepherd and I want for nothing. Thank you for being my shepherd. Thank you for your love for me and the protection you bring. Help me to draw close to you and stay ever aware of your voice and guidance. I pray I will not stray and will stay in fellowship with others of your flock. I long for the day that I will be in your presence and spend eternity with you. Amen.

307

I Surrender All
Matthew 10:37-39

This morning in worship service we sang the song "I Surrender All". As I sang, All to Jesus I surrender, the words caught in my throat and I was immediately convicted. Do I give my all to Jesus? Judson W. Van de Venter, born in 1855 wrote these words as he recalled the day that he had surrendered his life to Christ and dedicated himself completely to Christian service. This old hymn was first published in 1896. I grew up on hymns like this. The words cut right to the heart of God's message and often move me to tears. This is conviction and this is a good thing.

I will ever love and trust him, in his presence daily live.
I surrender all. I surrender all. All to thee
my blessed Savior, I surrender all.

Jesus spoke the words in Matthew saying, the cost of following him is complete surrender of everything. He repeats this warning in Luke 14:33. Jesus gives this as a warning because he knows it is not easy. We must surrender everything to him and seek strength in him completely. We often think we know what we're doing and take off on our own only to return realizing we must surrender to him. Yes, we must surrender all to Jesus. We are only able to do this in a constant relationship with our Lord and a continuous attitude of praise. We acknowledge him in all we do and seek his presence throughout our day. Let's stop now and ask God to search our heart and our lives and to show us what we need to surrender.

Dear God I want to surrender my all to you. I want to trust you completely and never doubt or fear. I will ever love and trust you and in your presence daily live. I surrender all. Search my heart and show me what I need to surrender. Give me confidence and strength to do as you say. You are my strength for I am weak. Thank you for your love for me. Amen.

308

God Quiets Us
Zephaniah 3:17

Zephaniah is a small book that we probably don't read from very often. While it is written by the prophet Zephaniah warning the people of God's coming judgment, I find that this verse gave me quite a lift today. It tells me encouraging things.

- God is with me
- He is mighty
- He delights in me
- He quiets me with his love
- He rejoices with me
- He sings over me

Just when I need him these words remind me of his love for me. As I sat and read over this verse a few times I felt such warmth in my heart. It brings me to tears. (This is a verse that needs to go on my computer at work.) God does bring discipline and judgment but he is the most loving Father there can be. In this great big world full of people full of problems, most of them bigger than mine, God delights in me. How many people do you know delight in you? How marvelous. He calms me and quiets me when anxiousness arises. I am anxious only because I do not ask for him to calm me. I have learned to speak to him when it comes and he always brings comfort and calm. He rejoices with me. He rejoices with me when gladness comes but also when I feel his presence in times of trouble. Rejoicing because I know he delights in me and sings over me. Listen, God sings over us. Wrap yourself around these promises and praise him! This gets me excited and I hope it does the same for you.

Dear God, quiet me now as I seek your presence. There are no words to express the joy this brings me but I thank you. Thank you for your love for me. Forgive me for I take your love for granted. I often forget how much you care for me and want to be my Heavenly Father. I allow loneliness and anxiousness to take over when I know all I have to do is ask for comfort from you. I praise you and rejoice in your wonderful promises. You are mighty and I adore you. Amen.

309

We Need Each Other
Ecclesiastes 3:9-12

None of us like feeling alone. None of us want to feel like we have no one to go to for help or companionship. Even misery loves company. This scripture encourages us to seek relationships and ask for help when we need it. It cautions us about the result of trying to accomplish things alone. Some of us take pride in our work and feel totally and unnecessarily exhausted at the end of the day. First of all we must recognize our need for Jesus Christ. Then we need each other.

Much of Ecclesiastes is written as a reference to how meaningless life can be unless it is centered on God. I do no think it is an accident that this book follows Psalm and Proverbs. Without God, nothing satisfies. He has an order in mind as he goes about fulfilling his purpose for us. He created us with our individual limitations which we must acknowledge and accept in order to enjoy life as God gives it. It is wrong to place unrealistic expectations on ourselves. We often set ourselves to fail. God does not want us to fail and he does not want us to go about life alone. According to his Word two is better than one (I do not refer to marriage here). Be willing to ask for help and be willing to give help when asked. Do not try to go it alone. This is not God's plan for you.

Dear God help me to recognize when I need help. Give me an eagerness to help others when asked. Help me to focus on you and your plans for me. I want to live my life within your will for me. Show me how I can help someone today. Amen.

310

Paul's Charge Regarding Money
1Timothy 6:17-19

The two books of Timothy are full of instructions and charges from Paul regarding Christian living. Some people think that rich people cannot be good Christians. That is not true. It is true that it will be easy for those who are wealthy to allow their money to hinder their relationship with God by putting their wealth as their first priority in life. We don't have to be wealthy to do that.

This passage tells those who are rich with money not to be arrogant, putting their hope in their monetary wealth. Hope in monetary wealth is uncertain. Paul encourages the rich to put their hope in God who generously provides for the enjoyment of life. He provides what is needed and then some. The rich are encouraged to do many good deeds since they are wealthy and to be generous. This is how the rich can be assured to have treasures in eternity. In this I see a great responsibility for those who are blessed with wealth.

In Matthew 19:23, Jesus explains that it is difficult for a rich man to enter the Kingdom of Heaven. He says it is easier for a camel to go through the eye of a needle. Only with God's help is this achievable. The rich man must be willing to give it all up should the Lord ask it of him. He must be willing to generously share his wealth because it is a possession of God not his own.

I'd like to suggest that this is good for all of us to live by. As Christians we are wealthy. Our salvation is worth more than any amount of money. Some of us are blessed with money more than others but we all should put our hope and trust in God for what we need. We all should be willing to generously do good deeds. We all have something to give. If God has a mission for us he will provide what we need to give. We only need to act in trust and obedience. Today is a good day to search our heart and ask God to show us any attitude regarding money that we need to change.

Dear God thank you for how you have provided for me and my family. Forgive me when I focus on the balance in my account rather than focusing on you. I put my hope and trust in you with a desire in my heart to be obedient to your calling. Help me to be a cheerful giver and realize that I only give back what you have given me. My possessions do not belong to me. They are yours and only leased to me to take care of. Help me to seek your instruction on being a good steward of what you have placed in my hands. Thank you for your love for me. Amen.

311

Trust
Luke 1:37-38

Mary trusted God. The angel brought her incredible news. According to this she never flinched. She accepted God's will and moved on. I'm sure there were moments when she was afraid and confused but she started out with trust.

I think of her response often. I know God has a plan for me. I know he wants me to prosper. He doesn't want me to face harm. I try to seek his will but sometimes I hesitate to trust. Sometimes I wonder what others will think or I may have a plan of my own. Life is like a book of many chapters. Each chapter deals with the different experiences in my life. Some have been easy and some have been difficult. Some have been short lived and some seemed to last forever. One thing I have learned is to draw to God and seek his will when a chapter seems to be closing and a new chapter starts. By now you would think we would know the drill. But trust comes easily sometimes and other times it takes a while for me to realize that trusting God is the only way to deal with the different chapters of my life. When I run to him and allow him to take on the challenges that come my way it is amazing where he takes me. I can always look back and say, Oh now I see. Be encouraged to trust God in all things. No matter how incredible the news or challenging the new chapter of life seems, trust God. He has all the answers. He wants to lead and direct every step of our way. Just answer, May it be to me as you have said.

Dear God, forgive me when I hesitate to trust you. I pray that your will for my life will be accomplished. May it be to me as you have said. Forgive me when I stand in your way. Forgive me when I don't readily trust you. Thank you for your love for me. Thank you for your plans for me. Amen.

312

Sing To the Lord
Psalm 33:1-4

I read about a North Carolina man going the extra mile when it comes to helping those in need by working with the Salvation Army to collect donations. He isn't the typical bell ringer. He sings loud and proud across the grocery store parking lot. I read that if you were passing by his station you would never know by his jolly demeanor that he once hit rock bottom. He was addicted to drugs like crack cocaine, marijuana, and alcohol. This man is homeless but instead of trying to collect money for his own needs he is manning the Salvation Army kettle to help others. His gift of singing inspires many to give. When interviewed by a reporter, he said: I died three times. I can't just ring the bell. I have to let the gospel ring. I've tried singing other things. It doesn't work. It sounds awful. I have to sing gospel. God has done so much for me. I have to do my part. God told me I still have work to do.

Sometimes we don't feel like singing. Because of our situation at the time we hardly smile much less sing. We are to sing joyfully to the Lord. It is fitting for us to praise him. We have lots to sing about. The Word of the Lord is right and true. That's reason enough isn't it? Well there is more. God is faithful in all he does for us. So whether I am ringing the bell for the Salvation Army, whether things are good or not I will sing to the Lord. I will praise him for his goodness and what he does for me. When I have troubles he is there to bring peace and confidence. He is always with me. He loves me. Sing to the Lord. Sing joyfully to the Lord.

Dear God, thank you for your greatness and your mercy. I sing to you because you are my God and my King. I love You Lord and I lift my voice to worship you. You know this man in this story that sings for you and I thank you for his testimony. Please bless him as he blesses others. Help me to learn from it and to be grateful for what you do for me. Especially the gift of salvation you gave through the death of your innocent son. Amen.

313

Behind the Scenes
Job 38-39

As I read this passage it makes me think of the behind the scenes tasks that many of us do at work, home, church and in our community. We all have experienced Mom or Dad going away temporarily and discover the little things they do for us and when left undone, we are quite dismayed and helpless. How about at work when we need a new ink pen and none are in the storage cabinet? How about arriving at church and the heat is not on or there is no toilet paper in the restroom? When this happens someone is really missed.

In this passage, God is speaking to Job and his friends. He reminds them of all he does. I can't even begin to list them all but he refers to the things we take for granted, like creating the dew, knowing when the mountain goat gives birth, growing the horse a mane and causing the changing of the seasons. On my job we create a Position Description for each employee that generally lists the individual's duties and the last entry is always, Other duties as assigned. This includes the little non-routine things that we are asked to do but we seldom recognize that when these tasks are not done it greatly affects the operations of the office.

What if one day the seasons didn't change? What if the dew completely stopped? Would we notice? I think we would. God is with us every minute of every day taking care of us when we don't even realize it. Doing things for us that we never think about like the things listed in these two chapters and this doesn't nearly cover all he is doing. Let's not take God for granted. Let's thank him every day for what he does for us to provide for us and take care of us. The Bible says he knows the number of hairs on our head. He cares about us even to the details that may not seem to matter. It matters to him because he loves us more than we can imagine and cares for us in an unfathomable way.

Dear God the words thank you are not nearly enough. Forgive me for taking you for granted. Thank you for the everyday things you do for me. Thank you for loving me and caring about every detail of my day. You are an awesome God. I praise your name with a grateful heart. Amen.

314

Give Thanks
1 Thessalonians 5:16-18

This passage is made up of very short words but a huge message. Be joyful always. Always means at every time, at any time, in any event. First message here is to be joyful regardless of the day or the situation. Joy comes from the heart and is not affected by how we feel at the time. Secondly, pray continually. We are to be in a constant state of prayer, talking to God throughout the day not just in our quiet time or at church. Thirdly, give thanks in all circumstances. All means every, only, each and every one, any whatsoever. There is no room for exception with the words always and all. And finally, this is God's will for us through Jesus Christ.

God wants us to be joyful at all times, talking to him continuously and thankful in all situations. This is what he wants for us. This is why he sent his Son, Jesus Christ. I recognize that this is easier said than done. Someone reading these words right now is saying, I can't. You just don't know what I'm going through. Listen. God knows exactly what we're going through. He knows what we feel without our even saying it. God has a plan for us to prosper. He does not want us in pain or frustration. This year has been full of disturbing, painful family issues for me. A couple months ago I was thinking, How will we get through the holidays?. Now I realize that in these thoughts, I was doubting what God could do. I was not allowing him to be in control. I took my eyes off of him and lost sight of my joy and thankfulness and confidence in him. Just like the story of Peter walking on the water toward Jesus (Matthew 14:25-31). When Peter took his eyes off of Jesus and focused on the wind he started to sink. Jesus asked, Why do you doubt? My problems are still here but we are working through them with God as my focus. My eyes are now on him, not the storm and wind. Christmas is almost here and I will celebrate Jesus' birth regardless of my current feelings. God has reminded me to be joyful and thankful in all circumstances. He is in control. He is working and will finish what he has started. I can't get caught up in the worries when my faith is in him. I take all my concerns to him. When my focus remains on him I can be joyful always, pray continually, thankful in all circumstances and praise him for his will for me. Just like the hymn we love "Turn Your Eyes Upon Jesus".

> Turn Your Eyes Upon Jesus.
> Look full in his wonderful face.
> And the things of earth will grow strangely
> dim, in the light of his glory and grace.

Let's give thanks for this wonderful promise.

Dear God help me to keep my eyes on you and to be thankful and joyful in all circumstances. Help me to be continually in conversation with you. I trust you in all things. May the things of earth grow strangely dim, in the light of your glory and grace. Amen.

315

Delight In Weakness

2 Corinthians 12:7-10

In preparation for the Thanksgiving holiday our worship leader asked if anyone had a testimony to share. A lady spoke to her thankfulness for how God was healing her. She added that she was thankful for the sickness because it had made her closer to God than she had ever been. She had learned to trust him more. This scripture passage is just what she was talking about. Paul speaks to some type of ailment that he was living with. He had asked God to remove it but later realized that it was there to strengthen his relationship with God. Our weakness is a grand opportunity for God to show his power. We can delight in our problems, difficulties and sickness because God's grace and strength is perfect in our weakness. Paul said he would boast of his weakness so that God's power would rest on him. He knew God would show up just when he needed him.

1Timothy 6:6 says godliness with contentment is great gain. We can find peace, contentment and strength in times of trouble. Paul and my friend shared their testimony of how God was blessing them in their time of trouble and through their affliction. Even if God doesn't remove it, his blessing and grace is provided to us in abundance. We experience weakness so that he can bless us. Instead of asking, Why me?, let's ask, What will God show me in this? James 1:12 says blessed is the man who perseveres under trial because when he has stood the test he will receive the crown of life that God has promised to those who love him.

Dear God many times we move away from you when we are sick or discouraged. It is hard to look for your power when we are weak. But I believe your promise and I ask you to help me seek you in the good times and in the bad. Help me to trust your grace as sufficient in my weakness. Help me to look for your strength when I am weak. Thank you for your love for me. Amen.

316

Responding To Misfortune
Ruth 2:8-13

We are living in a difficult economy. Some businesses are suffering more than others. I ran into a guy recently who had a top management position in state government for many years but had unfortunately lost his job in budget cuts. He was now working as a stockman in a department store. He admitted that it had thrown him for awhile but God had provided his needs and he was actually enjoying his job. He admitted that he did not miss the many difficult decisions he stressed through in his former position. He even said, 'I think this is God's plan for me.' I walked off feeling so impressed with him. Ephesians 6:7 says to work with enthusiasm as if working for the Lord rather than people. This man was following this to a tee.

Please take time to read the story of Ruth. It is a short four chapters and full of selfless devotion and kindness. Ruth was a woman of determination and dedication. Her life went from marriage into a loving family, loss of her husband in death, following her mother-in-law to a life of poverty and uncertainty and into another marriage to a loving God fearing man, finding her place in the record of the genealogy of Jesus Christ (Matthew 1:5). Ruth accepted her circumstances that placed her in a humbling position more than once. It seems that my friend experienced the same and they both responded in a positive way without giving in to a loss of hope.

How do we accept a change in circumstances facing misfortune? Do we continue on with enthusiasm? Sometimes when our circumstances change we feel like we are taking steps backward in achieving our goals in life. Maybe we are single again. Maybe we aren't as healthy as before. Maybe we are unemployed or in a job with less pay and a few steps down the ladder. Maybe we have lost someone dear to us. Maybe we aren't driving as nice a car or now rent instead of own. This isn't easy for anyone. It wasn't easy for my friend or for Ruth. Our best option here is to take it to the Lord. Seek his advice and his peace. God has something to teach us in every obstacle that comes our way. He has not forgotten us or placed us to the side. God's grace is sufficient. Turn to 2 Corinthians 12:9-10. Mark and highlight it. God is always ready for us to lean on him, finding peace and confidence that only he can bring.

Dear God forgive me when I doubt you and allow fear and frustration to control me. You are sufficient for me. I need nothing else. I seek you daily and find peace through my relationship with you. Help me to be content in my circumstances and trust you completely. What can I learn from you today? Amen.

317

Be Ye Kind
Titus 3:1-11

Ephesians 4:32 is probably one of the first Bible verses I learned as a child, Be ye kind. The book of Titus is written by Paul to Titus one of his helpers. I started to say one of his followers but he was a follower of Jesus not Paul. The book of Titus summarizes the characteristics that should be reflected in the life of a follower of Jesus. This particular passage is entitled in my Bible, Doing What is Good. In verse 5, we are reminded that our salvation does not come from acts, even acts of kindness but through God's mercy; the same mercy that we should show others. As we allow God to work in us kindness will flow naturally from us daily to those around us.

There is a Foundation of Acts of Kindness www.actsofkindness.org . This private foundation encourages the practice of kindness in all sectors of society. They practice that when kindness is expressed healthy connections are nourished and people are inspired to pass kindness on. This is so true in our daily lives. When someone holds a door for me I am always prone to hold it for the person behind me. This simple act almost always produces a smile and a Thank You. Kindness is contagious. No act of kindness is wasted even if we don't get the response we want. God's love and mercy is contagious as well. Unfortunately our world does not always give God the response that he wants. God's magnificent act of kindness, sacrificing his own son's life for our sin, makes us heirs of eternal life that we will spend in his presence. God's act of kindness should cause me to devote myself to doing what is good. I am moved by the final words in verse 8, these things are excellent and profitable for everyone. If only our world could live by this. Show kindness to someone today. Ask God for a special opportunity. Get ready. He won't let you down.

Dear God above, help me to share your love and kindness to those around me. Help me to be the one who initiates it. You love me without me asking you to and you are kind to me when I don't deserve it. Thank you for your love for me. Send me opportunity to show kindness today. Give me an opportunity to serve someone eagerly today. Amen.

318

Retreat
Luke 11:9-10

For the first time in my life I am on a retreat alone. I am dealing with a serious matter in my life and have felt quite overwhelmed in the past couple weeks. I decided to take advantage of a long weekend and get away alone. I am not completely alone because my Lord is with me. Just getting here I am some restless but I truly believe the Lord has something to say and I am here to listen.

This passage has come to mind. This is a difficult time for me but I know that my Lord is in control. While he has given me a couple steps to take I am in a waiting period now. I do not know what my future holds in a certain relationship but I know that God's plan for us is to prosper and to grow. This passage is encouraging to me now because I am here knocking on the door seeking him. I want to make the right decisions and the only way I can is to seek him. My faith in God assures me that he will open the door and I will find my answers. Maybe not all the answers this weekend but I know the peace and confidence will come. I will find him as he promises.

I told a friend my plan to go away and she sent me a very encouraging message. She encouraged me not to allow Satan to put uncertainty and fear in me. She said, sometimes we can get caught up in worrying about what the future may hold instead of relying on our Father, day by day, moment by moment. She encouraged me to rely on God's promises, his grace and love moment by moment. To think of all the things he has already brought me through and know that he will continue to be faithful. She said, I hope you feel God's arms around you this weekend as you spend time alone with him. She ended with, Know that you are loved. Wow! He was speaking before I even got here.

Dear God I ask and I seek and I knock. Help me to feel your presence. Help me to find physical rest too. I need you so much. You know exactly the situation. I know you care. I know you weep when I weep. You know my fears and you know the desires of my heart. Please bring me peace and confidence from my faith in you. Give me the courage to follow as you lead and to wait when you tell me to wait. Thank you for the many ways you bless me and take care of me. I pray this same prayer for the others involved in this situation. I love you Lord. Amen.

319

He Knows Us
Revelation 3:14-22

Am I comfortable knowing that God knows my heart and my mind? We can hide our thoughts, secrets and opinions from those around us but we cannot hide them from our Lord. He knows our thoughts and deeds. He knows us through and through. According to this passage we are either for him or not. There is no sitting on the fence. When we give ourselves to God halfheartedly he spits us out. Picture it. Recall tasting something so bad that you spit it out. Not a pretty picture.

God sees us as we really are. We must search our heart daily and ask God to reveal any impurity that we need to spit out. We desire to follow him. We want those who love us to be proud of us. We want our Lord to be pleased and proud of us. He wants us to know him and enter into a relationship with him. He desires our company and we should desire his. But God doesn't want us half way. He wants us completely and wholeheartedly. He wants us hot and on fire for him with a desire that never cools. Let's take time now to talk with our Lord honestly and be sure we are right with him. When we ask for a check up he is ready and waiting. We must be ready to repent and reaffirm our commitment to him.

Dear God forgive me for a half hearted commitment. You gave yourself completely for me and my desire is to give my life to you. I want to completely trust you in all things. Forgive me of my sins and allow me to recommit myself to you. Oh Lord, I don't want you to spit me out. I want you to be pleased with me. I want to know you more. I want to love you better. Amen.

320

How Do We Love?
Ephesians 4:25 - 5:2

As I was reading this passage this morning intending to stop with 4:32, my eyes dropped down to 5:1. Forgive each other, just as in Christ, God forgives me. Be imitators of God. It immediately came to my mind that this is how I am to love. I am to love as God loves me. We are to love imitating the love God shows us. He loves me unconditionally no matter what I say or do. He is always available to forgive and love me. Whether I am at peace or my life is a mess God is there for me with wide open loving arms.

We are instructed here to be honest and speak truthfully. Why do we put on a front? Why can't we admit when we are hurt or offended? Why can't we admit it when we have problems and are hurting? Why do we think we must always reply, I am fine, when we aren't? One of the reasons we are instructed to have Christian fellowship is to encourage each other. Sometimes we have opportunity to encourage and sometimes we need encouragement. Don't be afraid to ask for encouragement.

When speaking the truth we are to use words that will encourage and build. Sometimes we use the excuse of truth to speak hurtful and destructive words that can't be forgotten once spoken. We must not let the sun go down and still carry anger in our heart. We are to let it go quickly because Satan will use it to cause pain and destroy relationships which will lead to sin.

How do we love? As God loves.
Why do we love? Because God loves.
How do we forgive? As God forgives.
Why do we forgive? Because God forgives.

I am still on retreat. Day 2. As my Ipod plays the Brooklyn Tabernacle Choir singing "I Adore You" I wonder why God sends me this lesson. Yes it came from my devotion book but God still directs where I go in my Bible each day. We had snow last night. Really, really unusual for South Carolina. As I venture outside I anxiously look forward to a day with my Lord.

Dear Father in Heaven, I adore you. Lamb of God, my Savior, Prince of Peace I adore you. Jesus you mean all the world to me. I adore you Lord. Walk with me today and talk with me. Give me the courage to listen and obey. Forgive me when I fail. Help me to love and forgive as you love and forgive me. The desire of my heart is to imitate you. Amen.

321

Nothing More Precious
Psalm 19:7-10

This morning as I put my diamond ring on my finger my mind went to the fact that the Lord's presence in my life is more precious than diamonds. I have mentioned before that my Mother has Alzheimer disease. One day my brother and I were cleaning out an old dresser of her and Daddy's that we were giving to friends whose house had burned. I was going through one of the drawers and found a bag full of peppermint candy wrappers. My brother and I paused for a moment. When we come across things like this we choose to laugh rather than cry. I was just about to trash the bag when I felt something in it. I pulled out a diamond ring that we immediately knew was my Grandmother's. My mother wore it when we were younger but we hadn't seen it in a while. It is atleast a half carat in a square setting and we knew it right away. It is gorgeous. My brother and sister agreed that since I found it I could keep it. My older sister had my mother's diamond. I did not get a diamond when I married so I was excited to get it. More than that I felt such pride in wearing the diamond I knew my Grandmother had gotten when she became engaged many years before I was even born. It is a cherished blessing from God that came from the sorrow and pain of a horrible disease that has taken over my mother's mind.

These verses bring encouragement that the glory of God is precious and provides total satisfaction in our life. The law of the Lord is perfect. His statutes are trustworthy. The principles of the Lord are right and bring joy. The ordinances if the Lord are pure. All these things are more precious than gold or diamonds and sweeter than honey.

This brings me such comfort and peace. It comes as only my God can give. I am on retreat. My prayer is that all concerned will feel this same peace and confidence that God brings me today. I pray that we will fall on our knees before him and give it all to him down to the dirt under our nails. I pray that we will acknowledge anyone or anything that he places in our path to minister to us. I yield myself to him fully and completely, trusting him with every hurt and every need. We feel like life is a mess and we need answers. God's first desire is for us to yield to him and wait for him to move. He has much to accomplish but we must be ready. If our eyes aren't on him we will miss something important.

Dear God, may the words of my mouth and the thoughts in my heart be pleasing to you. O Lord you are my rock. You are my redeemer. You are my total satisfaction. You are more precious than gold, silver or diamonds. Nothing is better than you. I fall before you and ask you to take my life in your hands and lead me. Lead me to the truth and confidence that comes only from you. Bring restoration. Thank you and Amen.

322

Our Prayer Life
Matthew 21:18-22

From time to time we may need to check our prayer life. Do we pray daily? How can we expect to have a proper relationship with our Lord if we don't talk to him on a regular basis? Sometimes we find ourselves praying only when we need something or are troubled. If we believe that God will hear and answer our prayers it should be a regular part of our day. Hebrews 4:16 says prayer is our opportunity to approach the throne of grace with confidence so that we can receive mercy and find grace to help us in our time of need. Our Lord stands ready to help when we approach him.

There are a few things that will enhance our prayer life. For one, find a prayer partner. It is good to have someone that I can trust with my prayer requests and pray with me on a regular basis. In turn I know her desires and I pray for her. It often takes my mind off of me and I focus on praying for her. It strengthens our relationship with each other and with our Lord when we together experience answered prayer and encouragement. Another is having a prayer journal. Writing my prayers benefits me in several ways. It helps me to focus. My mind doesn't wander as much when I write my prayers. I can go back and read my prayers and rejoice in the answers and continue with those that I still wait for. I can also see where I have been when I read them. Reading through it helps when praying seems hard. I love my prayer journal. I have several in my cedar chest that I hope will be meaningful to my children one day. While we should be in prayer continuously (1 Thessalonians 5:17), we need a place to pray. I have a place in an extra room where I keep my Bible, devotional and journal. I go there daily to pray. Whatever time I need to get up, I set my alarm early to have time for prayer before I start my day. Weekends are not quite as scheduled but I still find the time before starting my day. It becomes habit before you know it. I often feel excited as I awake knowing that I have something to share with the Lord. I encourage you to try these ways to be better at prayer.

Dear Heavenly Father, thank you for prayer. Thank you for the opportunity to come before you and talk to you as my Savior and friend. Forgive me when I fail in praying continuously. Forgive me for taking opportunity for prayer for granted. Help me to be committed to pray to you every morning and as I go about my day. I need to focus on you all day. I love you Lord. Amen.

323

Standing Firm
Exodus 14:13-14

This morning I was sitting at the Battery looking out at the beautiful Charleston Harbor watching a huge barge come in. As it slowly approached the harbor, two tug boats only a fraction of its size came along beside it and took control. It is my understanding that these huge vessels relinquish their power to these small but powerful tug boats and rely on them to get into the harbor without getting stuck or crashing into the shore or pier. The small tugs actually push the huge barge as it slows or neutralizes its powerful engine. It hit me that something so huge must trust something smaller for support to successfully reach the port without insisting on doing it on its own. It is in reverse that we are small yet hesitate to relinquish our feeble strength over to a huge and powerful God.

The Israelites had fled Egypt after witnessing the powerful and miraculous strength of God yet crumbled in fear when the Egyptians took out after them. They were so quick to give up. How powerful Moses' words to them are to me still today. Do not be afraid. Stand firm and you will see the deliverance the Lord will bring today. The Lord will fight for you. You need only to be still. And I guess I shouldn't be accusing of the Israelites because I crumble in fear just as they did and God has done powerful and miraculous things for me as well. O how whiney we are.

After God delivered them from their enemy, Miriam led them in a song. The Lord is my strength and my song (15:2). In your unfailing love you will lead the people you have redeemed (15:13). The Lord will reign forever and ever (15:18). No matter how difficult life can be the Lord will fight for me. I have nothing to fear. His desire for me is to be still and stand firm and let him fight the battles for me. I need to cut my engine and allow God's mighty strength to push me and maneuver me through the harbor no matter how close the obstacles appear and frighten me. The Lord is my strength and my song. He leads me beside quiet waters and restores my soul (Psalm 23:3).

Dear Lord above, thank you for being such a mighty powerful living God. You are my strength and my song. Give me the strength to stand firm and allow you to fight the battles of my life for me. I love you and I trust you with everything. May my daily song be, I have nothing to fear. In your unfailing love you will lead the people you have redeemed. Amen.

324

Unusual Sunday
Psalm 16

I am on retreat. I decided to attend the Sunday morning worship service at a church a couple blocks away. It is a large Baptist church that I recall visiting as a child for Girls Auxiliary (GA) clinics and children's choir festivals. I checked their website to confirm the time. I awoke excited about visiting the church but especially felt led to be in the house of the Lord. As I walked the couple blocks I saw no cars parked out front and no one around. I started feeling very anxious. Being across the street I even walked past it afraid there was no service. Thankfully as I approached the crosswalk I looked back and saw a couple climbing the steps to the front door and I followed. I was welcomed warmly by the usher and a couple sitting in front of me. For some reason I felt very emotional. As the opening song started I could hardly get out the words feeling like my throat was tight and I wanted to cry.

We sang, Bless the Lord, O my soul and all that is within me. Bless His holy name.

I strongly felt the presence of the Lord. After a welcome and prayer we sang again. It was a song I hadn't heard before which really brought me to tears. It was lovely.

In His presence there is comfort, in His presence there is peace.
When we seek the Father's heart, we will find such
bless'd assurance, in the presence of the Lord.

The song really moved me emotionally but as we sang the fire alarm started ringing, the alarm strobe lights started blinking and everyone started pointing to 'smoke' coming from a heater under the window. We finished the song and the Pastor asked everyone to be seated and remain calm. He explained that it was steam we were seeing from an old unit which set off the fire alarm; it had happened before. He warned us that the fire department would arrive shortly, probably with sirens to confirm there was no danger. He explained the service would be different in that we would be watching a video, The American Experiment. The firemen did arrive with sirens and there was slight commotion. The video was from the Truth Project focusing on the question, 'Do you really believe that what you believe is really real?' and Psalm 33:12. While it was a good message I was somewhat disappointed, seeking different words of encouragement from God's Word. I had felt so led to the service and so moved that I thought the message was going to especially inspire me. I still left the church confident that I had been obedient in attending. I felt confident and strong from being in God's presence in warm fellowship with other believers even though they were strangers.

Psalm 16 is a prayer for safe keeping and of trust. Verse 1 says God fills us with joy in his presence. As I look back this evening I imagine the reason God wanted me there was to experience his presence in a house of worship and feel inspired from the words of the songs we sang. I felt God's presence so strongly. He was right there beside me. Over the next few days I may even come up with more to learn from my morning. God always has something for us to learn especially when we are obedient and seek him.

Dear God I thank you for the joy and peace you bring when we seek your presence. Help me to stay close to you and draw from your strength. Help me to seek you more. For the past couple days I have been led to the scripture about approaching your throne to receive mercy and grace. Help me to listen with my heart and follow obediently and confidently. Amen.

325

Keep On Keeping On
Romans 12:11-12

I am on retreat. My sister called me to check on me knowing I am in a difficult time. I told her I was still trying very hard to seek direction from God and was still in a holding pattern. I was getting lots of rest and quiet that I needed. She was encouraging, telling me that sometimes God wants us to be patient and wait. These verses in Romans tells us to never, yes never, be discouraged; to keep on keeping on serving the Lord. It tells us to be joyful in hope, patient in affliction, faithful in prayer. God tells us to be faithful in prayer because sometimes we tend to withdraw within ourselves when we are fearful about something. He tells us to be patient in affliction because patience doesn't come easy when we're hurting or anxious. But why does God say to be joyful in hope? It may be hard to be joyful when we are anxious about something because we fear the outcome. So what is there to be joyful about? I think God wants us to be joyful about our future and the fact that he is in control. We can let go of our fear and burden turning them over to him. Our joy is in our hope of the future. We can joyfully praise God in our hope because God is good all the time. Our hope is in the promises of the return of Jesus Christ and an eternal future with God himself. Our hope is in the fact that God never gives us more than we can bear and walks with us all the way. We have so much hope that we can't help but be joyful.

Dear Lord, my hope is in you all day long. Whatever I face today I face it knowing that you love me and you are in control. My heart is joyful and patient. My faith is in you. I praise you for you are the King of Kings and Lord of Lords. In your presence there is comfort. In your presence there is peace. Thank you for your love. Amen.

326

The Lord's Serenade
Zephaniah 3:17

I love old movies and TV shows especially westerns. Often when a cowboy falls in love with a girl, he will grab a guitar, place himself outside her window usually at night and sing love songs to her. He loves everything about her and puts aside his pride to show her with a song. He keeps up his serenade until she sends him away or comes outside and professes her love to him. He promises to love and protect her as long as he lives and they live happily ever after. What a neat story but only found in storybooks, right? Not necessarily.

There is no greater love than God's love for us. There is no other love as unconditional or satisfying. This verse says that the Lord is mighty to save. There is nothing he isn't capable of handling. The Lord delights in us. He knows us and loves us even when we are not at our best. The Lord quiets us with his love. He knows our fears and when we are in pain and longs to quietly calm us. Are you stressed or afraid? Seek him and his arms will comfort you. The Lord rejoices over us with singing. He serenades us. I think God sings over us not only when we are happy and he rejoices with us but he also sings over us when his plan comes together or we move obediently to his call or we finally get something right. He rejoices over us when we don't realize there is something to rejoice about. He knows each of us so individually that he sees us moment by moment. Verse 16 says, do not fear, do not let your hands hang limp. Clap your hands. Look up and praise God for his love and for his singing. Seek him in all things. Know that he is out there professing his love for us, serenading our heart asking us to live with him happily ever after.

Dear God I need your loving touch today. Sing over me and comfort me with your love. I find rest and confidence in your love for me. There is nothing else that will satisfy me more. I lay my worries at your feet and trust you in everything. Forgive me for my doubt and pity party. Forgive me of my sin. Cleanse my heart and put opportunity in my way today to share my belief with someone else and show them how you are mighty to save. I will tell them that you delight in us, quiet us with your love and sing over us. Amen.

His Compassion For Us
Luke 7:13

My morning devotion focused on the compassion of Jesus and this verse. In this passage Jesus gave a dead son back to his mother (7:15). He had compassion for this widow as she mourned the death of her only son. He said to her, Don't cry. My mother's King James version says, Weep not. As I wrote in my prayer journal the verse printed on the page for today is Jeremiah 31:3 which says, I have loved you with an everlasting love; I have drawn you with loving kindness.

Jesus speaks with compassion. I have spent the last couple days resting and focusing on my relationship with my Lord. While I left my retreat with the same problems that I arrived with, I know Jesus cares for me. I know he has compassion for the fears and concerns that my situation brings. He sees me and he says, Don't cry. Weep not. When we are drained physically and emotionally we can find rest in Jesus. He loves me and you with an everlasting love and draws us to himself with loving kindness. He knows our every fear and need. Jesus has compassion. Isaiah 35:4 says to those with fearful hearts, be strong and do not fear. Your God will come and he will come with vengeance. With divine retribution God will come to save you. Find that verse and mark it. Date it today. We know today to be strong and fearless. Jesus looks upon us saying, Don't cry. Weep not.

Thank you Jesus for the time I was able to spend on retreat with you. Thank you for the provision and opportunity. Thank you for your love for me. Give me courage to cast my cares on you. Give me courage to be strong and fearless. Bring tears of joy to my heart and not of fear and sadness. Give me strength for each day to deal with my situation. Thank you for the many ways you bless me and take care of me. I pray this same prayer for the others involved in this situation. I love you Lord. Amen.

328

Rolling Back the Waters
Exodus 14:10-31

This story lingers on my mind. A couple things draw my attention as I read through it. God knew that the Egyptians would come after the Israelites. He knows everything that will happen before it does. He would gain glory from their sin and interference in his plan. During this incident the presence of the Lord moved from in front of the Israelites to behind them and in between them and the Egyptians to hold them off. He actually turned the Israelites and headed them back toward the sea. What appeared to be confusion was really God's plan to bring glory to himself. The Israelites felt the chaos and the Egyptians saw it and probably laughed. Miraculously and purposefully the Lord held back the waters all night so that the thousands of Israelites could cross on dry land. He brought confusion to the once fearless Egyptians as they drove through the dry sea bottom. God wanted them to see that he brought imminent danger. He caused them to recognize him and fear him. At day break God brought doom to the Egyptians by sending the waters back and saw that no one survived. At day break he brought the Israelites miraculously through the attack of the Egyptians and restored their trust bringing glory to himself. The Lord's victory was complete. The Israelites recognized the power of God and put their trust in him and his servant Moses. They got out their tambourines and danced before God singing, Sing to the lord, for he is highly exalted; the horse and its rider he has hurled into the sea.

We stand before the rushing waters of life and trust God to roll back the waters. We must recognize the fact daily that God knows each situation in our lives and knows the outcome of each day. He has a miraculous and purposeful plan for each of us. Confusion and danger come when we take our eyes off of God and do not recognize him for who he is. We stumble when we misplace our trust. God moves in his own time and has a purpose in everything he does or allows. We focus on the chaos and forget that God is in control and is working out his plan. We try to fight the battle ourselves and only get physically tired and frustrated rather than being still in our faith. We stand before the rushing waters and wait for him to part the waters so that we can move forward according to his purpose. We keep our eyes on him as we cross and reach the other side.

Dear God thank you for parting the rushing waters of my life. You are highly exalted as you hurl the obstacles of this fallen world out of my way. Help me to trust you in all things and never take my eyes off of you. My desire is to seek you and live within your will for me. Forgive me when I hesitate to trust you. Amen.

329

Desperation To Peace
Psalm 40:1-3

I was reading a magazine short story about a single Mom dealing with issues with her child and the school. She had met with the adviser and got little or no resolution. Sitting in her car she cried out to God in desperation. She said that very quickly she felt peace and calm overcome her feelings of desperation. She knew it was God speaking to her and comforting her. On her drive home several ideas came to her mind that eventually brought resolution to her problem. These verses exactly describe this experience. When we turn to God and ask for his help, he lifts us out of the slimy pit of desperation and mud that keeps us from seeing clearly. He picks us up and sets us up on a rock giving us a firm solid place to stand where we can clearly see in all directions and trust his plan. We praise him confidently with a new song of peace and deliverance on our lips. We put our trust in God. We find peace and leave the desperation behind.

I have felt this same peace and some of you probably have too. The only regret we have is waiting so long to cry out to him. We suffer much too long in our desperation. If you haven't experienced this, be encouraged to cry out to God in your desperation and ask for his direction and peace. It will come and it will come quickly, be assured. Answers may not come as quickly but the peace will come. Also comes the confidence and comfort of knowing that the God of all wisdom and compassion hears us and longs to respond. He tenderly calls us to seek him and cry out to him knowing our desperation will turn to peace.

Dear God thank you for turning my desperation to peace. I praise you for you are the God of compassion and understanding. You have all the answers when I have none of my own. You send peace and comfort when I seek you. Forgive me when I delay calling on you, suffering in my misplaced trust. Thank you for caring for me. Amen.

330

911

Psalm 91

In 1968, 911 was established as the national emergency number for the United States. Calling this number provides a caller anywhere in the United States access to police, fire and ambulance services through what is known as a common Public-safety answering point (PSAP). We often hear stories of lives saved, babies delivered, fires put out and criminals apprehended due to the heroic efforts of those who call the dispatchers and the responders. I have had to call 911 once in my life and hope I never have to again but I am glad it was there when I needed it.

Psalm 91:1 is our PSAP. This entire psalm is an awesome testimony to the security of those who trust in Almighty God. It speaks to the assurance of our Lord's protection and our triumph over the threat of disaster. Nothing happens to us that God is not aware of. He dispatches his angels to guard and protect us. I believe angels are among us throughout the day and night sent by God himself to prevent disaster or provide a presence when disaster does strike. We are never alone. We don't need access to a phone to call upon the Lord. He is present in our heart and watches over our every move. Because he loves us he promises to rescue and deliver us. Satan will tempt us with his lies that will only increase the disaster and prolong our pain and fear. When you feel the need for 911 call upon the Lord through Psalm 91:1 and have no fear. The Almighty God is the one who can provide the protection that we need in our lives.

Dear Lord I thank you for your love and protection. When I trust in you and keep my eyes on you, I have nothing to fear. Forgive me when I hesitate to call on you. Forgive me when I give in to fear. Thank you for your undying grace and mercy. Amen.

331

Just What I Needed

Isaiah 40:28-31

Are you aware that in our devotion time God leads us to just the right scripture that we need for that moment? He absolutely does. My devotion led me to this scripture this morning and it warmed by heart so and brought me to tears of thankfulness. I read it out loud. These 4 verses give us the strength that we need to face whatever comes our way.

Do you not know? Have you not heard? The Lord is the everlasting God.

Sitting alone at my desk in the quiet of the morning knowing that my life is in shambles, I know my Lord loves me and is here to bring strength in my time of weakness. I struggle to get through the days yet I soar like an eagle. If you do not know the Lord as your personal savior you may not understand this. Now is the time to seek him and allow him to bring us to our knees. He longs to carry us every step of the way. He longs to overcome our weakness with his strength. He longs to love us in a way that no one or anything else can. We can run and not grow weary. We can walk and not be faint. This reminds me of a time that a group of us hiked up Chimney Rock Mountain in North Carolina. We thought we would surely die of exhaustion but we made it. As we took off our shoes and socks and waded in the cool waterfall we were exuberant in the fact that we reached the top. The struggle up the rocky path was quickly forgotten. As I looked out over the ledge I could feel closer to God's presence. We don't have to long to be close to him. He is with us when we seek him. He helps us reach the mountaintop of our desires. Seek his presence today. Allow him to strengthen you in a special way today. Tell him the desires of your heart and your fears. He gives strength to the weary and power to the weak.

Dear Lord thank you for your promise to provide the strength we need just when we need it. Thank you for the gracious promises I find in your Holy Word. Help me today. Help me as I struggle with life. Help me to trust you and stay focused on your love for me. I need you and I seek your presence. Amen.

332

Excuses
Luke 14:15-24

I am 55 years old and I do not exercise or I didn't until today. Guilt finally got the best of me and I joined a small women's gym. I thoroughly enjoyed it today and hope to keep my commitment. I am not in this to once again weigh 105 as I did years ago. I simply want to accomplish a commitment to exercise on a regular basis with no excuses. I know it is what I must do to care for my body as I should and I have run out of excuses. We are always full of excuses when it comes to doing something we really don't want to do for whatever reason. We often miss out because of our lame excuses. We often miss out on opportunity to glorify God because of our excuses.

Jesus uses this parable to warn the Jews that their rejection to God's invitation would result in God's rejection of them and his invitation to the Gentiles. When we pass up opportunity to serve God he will offer it to someone else. When we allow other interests to take priority we miss out. When I lay up watching *Gunsmoke* episodes rather than exercising my lame excuses show in weight gain and being grossly out of shape. When I make excuses to God when he invites me to do something for him I miss out on the blessings that come from doing service in his name and growing his kingdom. Many will sorely regret making excuses and refusing God's invitation to allow him to be Lord of their life and the opportunity to spend eternity in his presence.

What excuses are you making today? Let's take time to stop and think and pray about that.

Dear God show me today where I need to stop making excuses. You are an awesome God and I want to serve you well. Sometimes I serve my excuses better than I serve you. Forgive me. Help me to be honest with myself and honest with you. What excuses do I need to stop making today? Give me a heart of commitment. Amen.

333

Refreshment
Acts 3:19

Don't you love refreshments? It was our favorite time in Vacation Bible School – cookies and Kool Aid. Wedding and baby showers – delicious punch and finger food. I always loved those homemade cheese straws. Sunday mornings when the Sunday School teacher surprised the class with warm glazed doughnuts. Refreshment. And what about the freshness after a good hard summer rain? When the sun comes back out everything is a beautiful shiny green that looks bright and clean. A swim on a hot day in a crisp cool pool or lake. When you step out and wrap up in a towel you feel squeaky and refreshed. Getting a hug from your child after a bubble bath. Their hair is still wet and they smell like sunshine.

Acts 3:19 tells us to repent, then turn to God so our sins will be wiped out and a time of refreshing can come from him. Repentance is turning from sin. The Lord gives us refreshment when we repent of our sin. When I am convicted of a sin and I know I need to repent I often forget about the refreshment that comes afterwards. The peace that only our Lord can bring. Repentance brings refreshing change. We feel clean again. In 2 Chronicles 7:14 God tells us to humble ourselves and turn away from wicked ways and pray and he will forgive us and heal us. The refreshment of a clean heart. It just doesn't get better than this. We need to ask God daily to remind us of our sin and ask him to convict us. It is so sweet to trust in Jesus in all that we do.

Lord, keep me mindful that you are a God of forgiveness and refreshment. Thank you for the wonderful refreshments we enjoy and help me to remember that repentance can be just as sweet and squeaky clean. Help me to repent and turn to you so that my sins may be wiped out and I can enjoy the refreshment that comes from only you, as you forgive. Amen.

334

He Restores Me

Psalm 23:1-4

This has been a difficult week. One of those weeks that makes it easy to become depressed and feel hopeless. However this verse has kept my faith strong. The Lord is my shepherd. I rest in him. He brings me peace like a calm river. Even though times are difficult I go to him and he restores my faith and my confidence. God is in control and I am glad.

There is a doctor's office that I have been to a couple times and in the waiting room the TV continuously shows peaceful scenes of lakes, streams, snow covered mountains, etc., with soft music playing. When I see this I think of God. Even when the waters are rushing past violently there comes a place in the river that is calm. When I rest in God peace comes. The storm may not be over but he brings confidence and moments of calm that reveal to me that he is present. I came across Romans 4:20 this week. Abraham did not waver through unbelief regarding the promise of God but was strengthened in his faith and gave glory to God. We too can be positive about a negative situation. We, like Abraham know for sure that God will do what he promises. He promises to complete the good works that he starts. We can expect good things.

No passage of scripture is more basic or calming than Psalm 23. It never fails to bring encouragement and confidence and calm into my day. Read it again and anytime you feel discouraged. We have nothing to fear for God is with us. He is our faithful shepherd that restores us daily.

Dear God thank you for your faithfulness. I pray I never waver and doubt you. Give me a desire and commitment to spend time with you daily so that you can strengthen me. You are my shepherd and I need you. You are in control and I am glad. Amen.

335

Praise the Lord

Psalm 103

What a wonderful passage. It lists many things that God does and who he is. I can quickly make the following list. You might see others I missed. Circle them in your Bible.

He forgives
He heals
He redeems
He loves
He is compassionate
He satisfies
He is just
He is gracious
He is slow to anger
He does not hold grudges
He is better than fair
He knew us before we were formed
He is everlasting
He blesses for generations
He is King

After reading this passage do you need encouragement to praise him? I certainly hope not. He is sufficient. Why do we get discouraged in difficult times when we have such a mighty God who loves us? Let's commit to read his Holy Word every day so that we are daily reminded of these promises. When we are weak he is strong. His love never fails. He waits for us to come to him every day. He has blessings to give if only we allow him to bless us. Let's drop to our knee and raise our hands. Praise the Lord, O my soul. Forget not all his benefits. Praise His Holy name.

Dear God help me to appreciate how you bless me. You are the great and mighty God and I bless your name. You are everlasting. It's hard to imagine all you are but I praise you and I long to please you. Thank you for your love for me. Forgive me of my sins and use me to further your kingdom. Forgive me when I neglect to seek you and praise you. Amen.

336

Taking Christ Out Of Christmas
Isaiah 9:6-7

It really bothers me when I see someone write Christmas and place an X in place of Christ resulting in Xmas. Merry Xmas? Oh dear, No. Some say it is easier to write and the X really is the cross. Let me suggest differently. Let's use every opportunity to make Christ a part of Christmas. The prophet Isaiah foretold the coming of the Messiah ages before the birth of Jesus. He proclaimed him as Wonderful Counselor, Mighty God, Everlasting Father, Prince of Peace. While we should celebrate his birth everyday it is at Christmas time that we focus on this marvelous truth. Many traditionally have a birthday celebration for Jesus on Christmas Day in order to ensure a focus on Jesus' coming. This week someone brought a special Christmas cake for us to enjoy at work. Looking though the cabinet we could only find birthday plates and napkins. We all joyously agreed that they were very appropriate.

Let's start a new tradition of keeping Christ in Christmas and sharing the promise and truth of Jesus Christ with those around us. This may be the very time that someone will come to know him as the Lord and Savior of their life and each year they will have not only his birthday to celebrate but their new birth as a child of God. There would be no Christmas without Christ so let's not X him out.

Dear God, we get caught up in the hustle and bustle of the holidays and often forget what it is about. We celebrate the marvelous birth of Your Son. We thank you for the gift of salvation through his death and resurrection. I pray that those around me will witness the promise that you bring to my life and see Jesus in me. Happy Birthday my Lord and Savior! Amen.

337

God Longs To Bless Us
Isaiah 30:18-21

God longs to be gracious to us and bless us. He is gracious when we cry out to him. He longs to hear us cry out to him. He allows problems and troubles to plague us but whichever way we turn he is there to guide us. How do we wait for him? Do we wait anxiously or patient, in fear or in prayer, frustrated or with praise and thanksgiving?

When we face problems many different emotions flow through us. It is difficult to anticipate the lesson we will learn as we come through it. It is difficult to look up and recognize that God is pleased to have an opportunity to guide us and walk through it with us. It is easier to be anxious, fearful and frustrated. God loves us and longs to help us just as we long to help our children through problems they encounter. When we wait and anticipate his blessing rather than focus on those negative thoughts he will strengthen us and we will more clearly see him at work. It helps me to write down and list problems that weigh on my mind. When the anxiousness starts I have to acknowledge it and present my concerns and fears to God for help. It never fails that the anxiousness dies and hope and confidence returns. Let's be encouraged to remember verse 18. The Lord longs to be gracious to me. He rises to show me compassion.

Dear God you are gracious to long for me. You are to be praised for longing to bless me. I long for a heart that is pleasing to you. I come to you with praise and thanksgiving and thank you for your blessings. Forgive me when I fail you. Amen.

338

The Spirit Of Christmas
Luke 2:1-20

The story of Jesus' birth found in Luke 2 is marvelous. I hope that it is a familiar passage that you and your children know by heart. I learned it as a child and can still recite it. We need to take time to enjoy the Spirit of Christmas. Some of us pride ourselves in how busy we are but please slow down and take time to enjoy the truth of this season. Christmas is not all about shopping and the hustle and bustle of the holidays. We must remember that we are celebrating the birth of a child born of a virgin, sent to this earth by our Heavenly Father, who grew as a man to make the ultimate sacrifice of giving his life on a cross for mine and your sins. He rose from death to give us eternal life. I hear lots of negative thoughts from people who are too busy and pre-occupied and they miss the truth of the season. I hear some say they dread seeing Christmas come. I work with someone who seems to deliberately try to keep work going at a fast pace during the holidays so that no one can be distracted by Christmas happenings. I just want to shake her and say, Please, enjoy the Spirit of Christmas, for nothing else is more important.

Stop today and take time to read this passage with your family. Make a commitment to read it together several times throughout the Christmas season and throughout the year. I had a Christmas card with the picture of a smiling, excited snowman that read, Jesus is born! That's hallelujah happy news! Take time to enjoy the Spirit of Christmas.

Dear God, please find favor in me and grant me peace. Thank you for your gift of Jesus Christ. That's hallelujah happy news! Help me to find time to celebrate and not allow the festivities of the holidays to cover the truth of these times. Help me to celebrate the joy of this season throughout the year. I pray that others will see the real reason for the season in my actions. Amen.

339

What Can I Give Him?

Psalm 51:16-17

What does God want from us? We give gifts of time and financial offering to him but what he really wants from us is our heart. The sacrifice he desires is our humble and contrite (repentant) heart. Psalm 51 also says, Create in me a pure heart...and grant me a willing spirit to sustain me (verses 10-12). There have been times that I've asked God to change my heart about something but first I have to give him my heart so that he can bring the needed change. I must release it to him. The Brooklyn Tabernacle Choir sings a song that I enjoy during the Christmas holidays but it has such a message for us for anytime.

"I'll Give Him My Heart"

What can I give him, poor as I am? If I were a shepherd I'd bring him a Lamb. If I were a wise man I'd sure do my part. So what can I give him? I'll give him my heart. I'll give him my heart, give him my heart. What can I give him but all of my heart. What can you give him? What can you bring? What can you offer that's fit for a King? Bow before Jesus. That's where you can start. What can you give him? Just give him your heart.

God wants us to love him and seek him in the good times and the bad times. He wants us to bow before him as our Lord and Savior. He is the King. When the shepherds and the wise men visited Jesus there was no need for gifts. God wanted the recognition and honor of acknowledging him as the King and the Savior of the world. It's great when we are blessed and can give large offerings but the sacrifice he desires is our heart. Something that we can give that costs nothing. Bow before Jesus, that's where you can start. What can you give him? Just give him your heart.

Dear God, create in me a pure heart and a willing spirit to sustain me. I bow before you and give you my heart. You are my Lord and Savior and I praise you. Thank you for your blessings. Thank you for your forgiveness. I give you my heart. I give you all of my heart. Amen.

340

A Fear Not Moment
Matthew 1:18-25

Joseph was a warm loving mature man. I see it when I read this passage. The happenings could have brought real trouble for Joseph and Mary. Yes, God had a plan but remember also that he gives us a choice. Joseph could have made different choices. Apparently he considered other choices. I'm sure he had a heart shattering moment when Mary told him she was pregnant. You know what I mean. The way we feel when we hear news and it feels like our heart skips a beat and we have to stop to catch our breath. This passage implies that after the angel spoke to him, he knew what he had to do and he did it. He understood that God was fulfilling his plan. The child's name would mean, God with us. How appropriate. Was Joseph afraid? Of course he was. Was fear in his heart? I don't think so. I think the appearance of the angel assured him that this was God's plan and all he had to do was follow instructions and there would be nothing to fear.

Do you need a fear not moment? Do you need to follow God's instructions in his Holy Word and do what you know you need to do without fear in your heart? Isaiah 35:4 says to be strong and do not fear, for God will come to save you. My Bible captions this chapter in Isaiah as, The Joy of the Redeemed. Joseph may not have had the Bible as we do but he knew God had a plan and he knew he could be confident in it. I can only imagine the joy he felt when he took his first look at the baby Jesus. The Joy of the Redeemed.

Life is full of fearful things. Let's be encouraged that our God never slumbers or sleeps. He is aware of every moment of our day and everything that comes our way. There is no room for fear in our heart when we ask him into our heart and trust him in everything. Fear not. Replace the fear with confidence and joy.

Dear God, thank you for these wonderful stories of people who chose to follow you. I pray that I can have that same confidence and peace as I choose to follow you. I will be strong and I will not fear for I know you will save me. Thank you for this promise. Forgive me when I fail you. Fill my heart with the joy of the redeemed. Amen.

341

Wise Men Still Seek Him

Matthew 2:1-12

Many manger scenes include the three Kings or Wise Men as visitors to the manger of the baby Jesus. The Bible is clear that the Magi were lead by the star to the house and visited the child and his mother. The word magi is the plural of magus which is a sorcerer, magician, scholar or astronomer. So we know there was more than one and they were intelligent or wise men. But they do not appear to be kings and did not visit the manger at the time of Jesus' birth. It is awesome to know that the baby Jesus had matured to a child and the star was still there. According to this passage of scripture these men were very determined and cognizant of King Herod's jealousy and desire to destroy the precious babe. They believed that he was the Messiah for they brought extravagant gifts of gold, incense and myrrh, as they would a king. They bowed and worshiped him. This is a lovely story. I can imagine young Jesus in Mary's arms or sitting on her lap as these men worshiped him on bended knee. I'm sure Mary's heart was full. Jesus is lavished again with very expensive perfume by a woman shortly before his trial, death and resurrection (Mark 14:1-9). We represent these gifts and the gift of salvation that Jesus bought with his life by sharing gifts with our family and friends as well as the unfortunate and in need during the Christmas season.

Wise men still seek him and worship him. We still lavish him with gifts of praise, thanksgiving and obedience. Sometimes we take a journey through situations in our lives determined to seek him and draw to him. As you read through this passage I am sure you will identify many significant points which we can apply to our own lives.

Dear God thank you for the spirit of Christmas and the different stories of this wonderful happening. Help me to seek you in all I do. I praise you for the promises in your Holy Word and find confidence in your plans for me. Forgive me when I fail you. Help me to keep a strong and committed desire to seek you everyday. Amen.

342

Lottie Moon
Acts 20:35

Lottie Moon was born as Charlotte Digges Moon on December 12, 1840 in Albemarle County, Virgina. She rebelled against Christianity until she was in college. In December 1858 she dedicated her life to Christ and was baptized at First Baptist Church of Charlottesville. She was one of the first women in the South to receive a master's degree. Edmonia Moon, Lottie's sister, was appointed to Tengchow, China in 1872 as a missionary and the following year Lottie joined her. Lottie served 39 years as a missionary mostly in China's Shantung province. She taught in a girls' school and often shared the good news of Jesus Christ with women and girls. She challenged Southern Baptists to go to China or give so that others could go. Southern Baptist women collected $3,315 to send workers needed in China. Lottie died aboard a ship in the Japanese harbor of Kōbe on December 24, 1912 at 72 years of age. In 1918 the Woman's Southern Baptist Missionary Union (WMU) named an annual Christmas offering for foreign missions after the woman who had urged them to start it. When I was a child most Baptist churches held weekly classes for girls sponsored by the WMU. It was called Girl's Auxiliary or GAs. We studied about many missionaries including Ms. Moon. For me it is a part of Christmas. The Lottie Moon Christmas Offering is very appropriate as we give a portion of what we have so that others in foreign lands can learn the story of Jesus and find eternal life through him.

Christmas is a time of giving. Sometimes we feel overwhelmed by all the charities during the holiday season. Particularly in difficult economic times mission finances suffer. In this verse, Paul is talking to his church members about the hard work of maintaining for ourselves and providing for the weak. He reminded them of Jesus' words, It is better to give than to receive. When our heart is right we are blessed more when we give than by what we receive. We all enjoy getting presents at Christmas especially something that we've been hoping for all year. Let's remember the true spirit of giving and providing resources for others to hear the Word of Christ. We may have to give up something so there is enough to give. Let's remember Lottie Moon's determination and the words of our Lord when we make our list for giving this season.

Dear God thank you for the abundant blessings I have received this year. Thank you for your faithfulness to supply what we need and more. I am blessed because of your love for me. Give me a heart of giving. I pray the desire of my heart will be for blessings from giving all that I can. Make me a cheerful giver. In your precious name I lift up this prayer. Amen.

343

Growing In Wisdom and Stature
Luke 2:41-52

This passage takes place when Jesus is twelve years old. It reminds me that Jesus was very human as well as the Son of God. While he was aware of his Heavenly Father's plan for him, he was also aware of his responsibility of obedience to his earthly parents. He was growing physically and in knowledge and in favor with God and man. Based on where his parents found him, he was apparently very anxious to grow and learn. According to Jewish law, when Jewish children reach the age of majority (generally thirteen years) they become responsible for their actions. Prior to this the child's parents hold the responsibility for the child's adherence to Jewish law and tradition. After this age children bear their own responsibility for Jewish law and tradition and are allowed to participate in all areas of Jewish community life.

1 Samuel 2:26 refers to Samuel growing in the same way, in stature and in favor with God and man. Hebrews 5:11-14 cautions us about never maturing or slipping back to infancy in our maturity as a Christian. We should be growing in wisdom and stature and in favor with God and man. This is our responsibility as a child of God. We will grow physically with little effort. We grow as we age of course. Growing in wisdom takes effort of our own. I'd like to suggest a few ways to help in maturing as a believer and growing in wisdom.

- Spending time daily with the Lord, reading his Word and talking to him. Remember to set that alarm a few minutes early and spend time with God before you start your day. Start a prayer journal. I promise you once you commit to this you will get out of bed anxious to meet with our Lord every day.

- Regular worship in a house of God. Yes you can worship God anywhere however it is also important to our spiritual growth to recognize the Sabbath and spend time in tangible worship. Make that regular connection of honoring and worshiping God. This connects with the above suggestion. Our worship is of more value when we have spent time during the week preparing for it.

- Fellowship with believers. It is not true that all of our friends must be Christians. There are some non-believers that we should not tolerate however there are others that we can have a positive relationship with and have the opportunity to witness to them if only by our example. I have non Christian friends that know where I am on Sunday mornings. It makes me feel good when they recognize it. Fellowship with believers is beneficial and necessary. Join a Sunday School class or small group or Wednesday night prayer group for regular fellowship.

- Protecting what enters our mind. Garbage in stays in. Be deliberate about what your eyes see and your ears hear. I believe that Satan uses the opportunity to suggest sinful thoughts when we are not careful about the TV and movies we see, music we listen to and books we read. Strive to keep your mind and thoughts pure.

Dear God help me to be mindful of continuing to mature in my relationship with you. I do not want my knowledge of you to remain in infancy. Help me to grow and learn just like Jesus did. Guide me to the right places and people who will inspire my relationship with you. Guide me in being cautious of what my eyes see and my ears hear. Thank you for your love for me. Amen.

344

The Little Drummer Boy
Luke 2:8-20

One of the most popular Christmas songs is "The Little Drummer Boy". I remember singing it every year in our school Christmas programs.

There is much we can learn from this fictional little drummer boy. One of the most disappointing things for some people during this season is the fact that money is tight and they can't give gifts as they'd like. This little shepherd boy had nothing to give to the magnificent child he heard about from the angels. I am a poor boy too, he sang. He knew this child was special but when he saw the birth place he could identify with the poverty. I have no gift to bring that's fit to give the King, he sang. However he did have a special talent that he could offer as a gift. Special gifts do not have to be great in monetary value. A gift from the heart or giving of time or talent can be the best gift of all. I believe that Jesus did smile at this special visitor though he had nothing to bring.

What can we give other than an expensive gift? What kind of gifts can we give that will please Jesus? Do we neglect to give because we can't give what we think is valuable enough? Let's not have a pity party instead. Jesus only wants our heart. He wants a humble heart of thanksgiving and praise. He wants an obedient heart. This little drummer boy did give the best gift. And it did not cost a lot of money. There was no pretty wrapping paper and a big bow. According to this scripture the shepherds were excited about this first Christmas night and fancy gifts were not involved. They left the manger giving the gift of good news to everyone they saw. I'd like to suggest that we can give the same kind of gifts when our money is short. We can have someone over for a meal (cornbread and vegetable soup on a cold night!!). We can offer a free night of babysitting. We can rake someone's yard. We can bake someone cookies and candy. We can invite someone to the Christmas Eve service and then have them over for desert. We can give of our self. We can give the gift that pleases Jesus. If a purchased gift is not an option, think about the people on your list and think about what they need or want that can't be purchased in a store. Write them a special note and tell them how much you love them and why you are giving what you decided to give. I believe it will be their best gift ever and the best that you ever gave. Merry Christmas!!

Dear God thank you for this wonderful time of the year. Help me to focus on the reason for this season and not on material things that I cannot afford. Help me come up with ideas on how I can share my love for others in a special way this year. I pray that others will see Jesus in me as I share the Christmas spirit. Amen.

345

Finding a Quiet Place
Luke 5:16

Christmas time is not the only busy time of the year. Everyday is busy for most of us. We rarely find a time of peace and quiet for ourselves. Some of us feel guilty if we try to do that especially away from our kids. I believe it is important to find quiet time for ourselves. It is as important as work and rest. Just a few minutes alone and quiet can make a world of difference.

Luke 5:16 says Jesus often withdrew to lonely places and prayed. Mark 3:7 says Jesus attempted to withdraw from the crowd with his disciples but in this case the crowd followed them. Later in Mark 6:46 Jesus went to the mountainside to pray. These are a few examples of Jesus taking time to get away from his busy life. He had much work to do to further his Father's Kingdom but still recognized that he needed quiet time and time to pray. We need that too. There is something that we can do less of to make a few minutes for ourselves. We need a time of quiet and a time for prayer. Allow time for the Lord to have you lie down in green pastures and beside quiet waters – time for refreshment and rest - to restore your soul (Psalm 23:2-3). We have to commit to make the time; it isn't going to just happen. Sometimes the crowd may follow you but try again. Jesus did and he often succeeded in finding a quiet place.

Dear God help me to find a time for quiet and a time for prayer. Help me to recognize that I need this time. Help me to find it and help me to spend it wisely. I know that you want to spend time with me too. Thank you for your love for me and how you graciously bless me everyday. Amen.

346

Our Reflection
Philippians 2:5-11

I've been watching *Gunsmoke* again. One of my favorite actors is Ken Curtis as Festus Hagan. Part of his job as Deputy Sheriff of Dodge City is to walk the streets of the city at night checking the doors of the businesses to be sure they are locked. He came up on a couple of scoundrels who were trying to rob the freight office by cutting through the wall. He had a few of his choice words for them, such as, I'll get after you like thunder after lightnin' faster than you can say rat run over the roof with a piece of raw liver in his mouth. He did have a way with words. He played the rough, tough deputy and often lazy bachelor but had a heart as big as my house. I believe as a person he was the same way. He is one of those people whose rough talking voice sounded nothing like their beautiful singing voice. The sound of Ken Curtis singing in no way reflected the grungy and grumpy Festus Hagan. I once read words that he wrote reflecting on his life. He wrote, If there are to be prayers said for me, let them be said in the hearts of my friends and those whose lives I may have touched during my lifetime – by all means let there be no sadness or grief – I want my family and friends to remember only the happy times we had together, my attributes (if any) and try to overlook all of my faults (that should keep you busy until the time we all meet up again!!). Ken Curtis seemed to be a great guy in fiction and in real life. He reflected an honest caring attitude toward others, took his job seriously and was never afraid to be himself. I'm not sure if I'm talking here of Ken Curtis or Festus Hagan but I think you get my point.

Out attitude should be humble, obedient and reflect our relationship with the Lord Jesus Christ. God made each of us individually. We should never put on heirs or try to be someone we are not. I have recently started exercising. It makes me feel good about myself. I haven't made a lot of progress yet but the feeling of doing the right thing is worth all the sweat. We need to feel good about our self. Our attitude about our self reflects in our attitude toward others. Is there something about your attitude that you need to change today? Ask God to reveal it and give you the strength to make any needed adjustments.

Dear Jesus Christ, I want my attitude to be the same as you and reflect my relationship with you. Show me the changes I need to make in my attitude toward others. Show me how I need to change my attitude about myself. I know you have plans for me and I pray these plans will be accomplished in me. Thank you for your blessings and your gracious love. Amen.

347

Organizing the Tupperware
1 Corinthians 11:23-29

Does anyone out there have an organized Tupperware cabinet that stays organized? It seems like no matter how hard I try to keep my plastic ware organized, when I open the cabinet door it all comes tumbling out. I have bowls without lids and lids without bowls and it is all in disarray. This morning at church we experienced the Lord's Supper. This passage requires that I examine myself before eating the bread or drinking the drink proclaiming the Lord's death and resurrection. It requires me to examine my heart for sin that lingers unrepented or coveting a sour relationship without resolving it and offering forgiveness. I need to match up the right and wrong and organize my relationship with God and with others so that I glorify him as I take of the bread and drink. Otherwise I partake of the Lord's Supper in an unworthy manner. No matter how hard I try to keep my relationship right with God, I need to regularly reorganize so my heart is not in disarray. It takes daily time with God and constant study of his Holy Word to keep my heart in order. I need to commit to this regardless of when I take the Lord's Supper. Mark 1:35 says very early in the morning while it was still dark, Jesus got up, left the house and went off to a solitary place where he prayed. If Jesus Christ the Son of God, who was without sin and perfect in every way needed to take time to pray to his Heavenly Father, how much more do we need it? Jesus knew the importance of keeping his relationship with God the Father in order and active. He was committed to daily time with God. I hope that this book of devotions will assist you in developing your relationship and strengthening it with daily time with God. Maybe it will even help us keep our Tupperware organized.

Dear God I pray that I would never disappoint you by partaking of your supper without first examining my heart. Help me to take such occasions seriously. Help me in committing to daily time with you. Help me to commit to keeping my heart in order. Thank you for your forgiving love and compassion. My hope and my trust is in you. Amen.

348

The Desire Of My Heart

Galatians 5:22

Do you notice that reading a verse often affects us in a different way each time we read it? This verse spoke to me today. I was reminded to pray for my character that it will reflect the fruits of the spirit. Recently I have hesitated to ask God to change my heart because I am afraid of what it will bring. I am dealing with a very difficult relationship in my life. I have separated myself from this person's self destructive ways that directly impacted me and our relationship. I do not want to go back into that relationship because it was very painful and I was only enabling this person to continue and not change the behavior. Many times in the past couple months I have cried out to God not to make me return. I know God does not want relationships to end and I was afraid if I prayed for God to change my heart, he would ask me to return. I felt burdened with guilt because I was afraid I was not living up to God's plan. Now this verse makes me realize that I must do two things. I must trust God completely every day, every step of the way in each word that comes from my mouth and in each and every decision that I make. And I must pray that the desire of my heart is love, joy, peace, patience, kindness, goodness, faithfulness, gentleness and self-control. I must be willing to give my heart to him completely and trust him with everything in me, asking him to give me the desire for his plan. There is no need to struggle with what may be revealed from my asking. When I pray that my heart has the qualities of the fruit of the spirit given in this verse, I can let go of the burdens of the 'what ifs' and allow God to be in control of this difficult situation. I hope this helps you. Let's strive to remember that when our heart is right, we can do a better job of allowing God to take care of the rest. Satan lies to us telling us that we aren't handling problems as we should and our relationship with God isn't what it should be. Don't listen to him. Trust and pray for the right heart qualities. Let God take care of the rest. We can't trust him and try to handle it on our own. This gives me a good feeling and peace in my heart. I hope it helps you as well.

Dear God thank you for being in control. Thank you for showing me the peace and confidence that comes when I trust you completely. Help me to let go of the burdens and lies that Satan puts in my mind. He is a liar and you are victorious in all things. My job is to strive to have the right heart and you will take care of the rest. Help me to recognize the peace that you bring. I struggle with the right words, so I'll say that I trust you completely and I love you as best I know how. Amen.

349

Our Teaching Example
Titus 2:6-8

This passage encourages us to live a teaching example. It tells us to set an example by doing what is good. I recently heard this passage connected to Proverbs 22:6 that tells us to train a child in the way he should go and when he is old he will not turn from it. As adults, the best way we can teach is by our example. I believe this is our responsibility for our own children as well as the children around us in our daily lives. Childhood directly impacts the qualities and character of an adult individual. I don't think we take that seriously enough. Something we say or do in a moment's time can affect the adulthood of a child in our presence. I find that heavy...and scary. I also find this another reason for the importance of our daily walk and talk being focused on our Lord and the instructions given in God's Holy Word. How can we take this responsibility serious without insuring that our relationship with God is daily nourished and developed?

We may need to change our whole way of thinking. Some of us want so badly to be a friend of our youth that we try to live like them and be their friend by living our life younger than we should. Yes, we want to be their friend but our priority must be living a teaching example as their mentor and guide. We must be constantly aware that they will do as we do and say what we say, good and bad. Many parents have been embarrassed when our child repeats something or tells something that happened in the privacy of our home. While I'm preaching to the choir here folks, we must live our daily lives knowing this will happen and be careful of what we say and do in what we think is private. And of course, our God sees and hears it all as well. As this passage reminds us, we are always under a watchful eye. Sometimes it is the eye of someone trying to catch us in sin or inappropriate example or it may be a young person looking for an example to live by. This is a huge responsibility and can only be accomplished in a strong focused relationship with Jesus Christ. Be encouraged to strive to live by this teaching and use it as a prayer as we live daily.

Dear God help me to encourage the young people around me to be self-controlled. In everything, I want my example to be good. I want my example to be of integrity and serious about my relationship with you. I pray my speech will always be appropriate. I pray my example will always be clean and not offensive to you or anyone around me. Help me to remember that my focus on you will reflect in my daily actions and speech. Help me to take this responsibility and my relationship with you seriously. Thank you for the blessings I will receive as I strive to live for you and according to your teachings. Amen.

350

Christmas Spirit Restored
1 Peter 5:10-11

A dear friend lost her son in 1994 in an automobile accident. She tells me that each holiday that followed became an unwelcome season of despair. Grief and sadness were overwhelming and severe. As Christmas approached in 1996 a poem about Jesus' birth started to form in her head. She kept writing and editing and soon the first Christmas poem was finished. She put it into their family Christmas letter and folks responded to the thoughts and words expressed. She praised the Lord! As each season now approaches, instead of dreading it she finds herself anticipating the possibility of another poem. Each year the Lord puts in her heart a new poem to be written and shared with others. She testifies that as the years have passed the joy of the Lord has become her true strength. When we are weak he is strong. Our hearts can be healed and we will no longer suffer severe grief and loss. Now as Christmas nears, Mrs. Lee Tinneny, you and me can look forward to what the Lord will bring. Isn't God so very good? With her permission, I share below her 2009 poem.

WHEN JESUS CAME

Gabriel was sent from God up Above,
bringing to Mary a message of love.
Chosen by God because she'd found favor; Mary's
conception would bear the world's Savior.

How could this be for a virgin to deliver? A Babe
such as this; she'd have to consider.
The Word of the Lord she'd heard very clearly.
God's Gift was accepted by this maiden so dearly.
How to prepare for God's Son to arrive? She
humbled herself and did not strive.
She'd joyfully honor the Lord's mighty plan. A
blessing to cover her whole life's span.
As she and Joseph waited, the word was sent out,
that all must be counted; there was no doubt.
To Bethlehem city they would go. Their lineage
recorded for the Romans to know.
The days were completed for the Babe to arrive.
The Son of God sent, would amazingly thrive.
The birth, though lowly, of this child in a manger.
His life brought to all; He'd ne'er be a Stranger.
The shepherds; the angels; the wise men all knew,
that Jesus, the Christ came for all to view.
He came here by choice, high Heaven leaving; Grown
into manhood no earth-honor receiving.
Why would He come here, one might inquire?
Love for mankind was His purest desire.
Obeying the Father, Christ left His High Seat. The
work of salvation...done; total; complete!
Again, He now lives at His Father's Right Hand.
Return He will surely and make His last stand.
"Are you ready to go if it were this day?" "Yes,"
is your answer, I most earnestly pray.

Dear God above, thank you for your healing power. Thank you that
you send your grace and mercy just when we need it and often in an
unexpected way. I pray that Lee's poems will touch many hearts and restore
the spirit of Christmas for others and their relationship with you. Amen.

351

Forever
Psalm 103:15

This passage reminds us that our days are as grass. The soul of man does not end in physical death. Verse 14 says that God remembers that we are dust. The life of man on earth is referenced twice more in the Bible as the withering grass in 1 Peter 1:24 and Isaiah 40:6. Our earthly lives will wither as the grass does and will blow away into the wind, forgotten. We are made different from other creatures. Our soul lives on forever. Either we choose salvation in Jesus Christ and will live with him forever or refuse salvation in Jesus Christ and live forever separated from him. There is a forever for each of us one way or another. We must live our lives preparing for our eternity. I encourage you today to make the choice of where you will spend forever. When we take our last breath forever begins. We cannot choose after death. We must choose now. God is a gentleman. He does not force himself on us. He allows us to make the choice. He longs for us to seek him and know him and accept his free gift of eternal life but he does not force it on us.

If you know Jesus Christ as your Lord and Savior, welcome to forever with our Lord. If you are not sure where you will spend forever, stop right here and ask Jesus Christ now for forgiveness of your sin and accept his offer for salvation and eternal life with him. Your life and earthly body will blow away as withered grass and dust but your soul can find life in Jesus Christ forever. Seek it today and find it. It is free. It is forever.

Dear Lord forgive me of my sin. I am a sinner and you are my Savior. Thank you for the free gift of salvation. I accept it today and ask you to live in my heart. Become the Lord and Savior of my life. I believe Jesus Christ died for me and paid the price for my sin to purchase a place for me to live forever with you. Guide me in a daily walk with you. Place people in my path that can nurture my relationship with you and help me to grow in following the instructions of your Holy Word. Thank you Lord Jesus. Thank you for giving me an eternal forever in your presence. Amen.

352

A New Heart
Ezekiel 18:30-32

The first surgery on the heart itself was performed by a Norwegian surgeon on September 4, 1895 and the patient died. For several years heart surgery was practiced and became successful but was considered extremely major and patients were kept in the hospital for weeks. Today it is almost common. People are given a new lease on life through open heart surgery or a heart transplant and live perfectly normal lives afterwards. God has blessed us with the knowledgeable and persistent surgeons who developed and perfected these procedures.

This 18th chapter of Ezekiel is God continuing to speak of divine judgment. God warns that he will judge according to our actions. Repent, he says, and turn away from sin. God takes no pleasure in death with unbelief by anyone. He promises us a new heart and a new spirit for our repentance and belief - a brand new heart. Not surgically performed but from our Lord and Savior. I have mentioned before, our ministry to the psychiatric ward in prison. Last night my friend giving the devotion spoke on this passage. She encouraged the prisoners to pray a prayer of salvation and receive their new heart and new spirit. Their circumstances would not change, they would still be behind bars the next morning but they would have a new heart and a new spirit. We sometimes allow life to raise bars and walls around us and hinder our relationship with Jesus Christ. We allow obstacles and lies of Satan to put us in a state where we need a renewed heart and spirit. This promise of a new heart in Ezekiel is repeated in 36:26. God promises to transform our mind and heart. His spirit is within us to enable us to do his will. He provides what we need to accomplish what he asks of us. Kneel before him today.

Dear God, search my heart for sin and show me what I need to repent of and change. You promise me a new heart and spirit and I thank you. You bless me more than I deserve. The desire of my heart is to seek your will and accomplish your will for my life. I pray others will see you in me today. I kneel before you and praise your name. Amen.

Pray Over It

Philippians 4:6-9

I take prayer seriously. I am not perfect at it but I try. Sometimes I find it easier to pray over the easy things than the big things. I pray over the cookies that I bake for the prison ministry. I pray that the men will remember with each bite the words of God that we present and sing. I pray over my luggage that it won't get lost by the airline. I pray over my car when I have to leave it in the parking lot overnight, that no harm will come to it. I pray over cards that I write and ask God to change the words if I didn't get them right. I pray for parking spaces. I pray when ambulances or fire trucks pass me. I pray before making a decision or responding to requests (this is the hard part for me; the waiting before acting). After a difficult week, I decided to have a stress management week end. I made no plans for Saturday. I slept in, ate a late breakfast, read a good book and went to the gym. On the way home I couldn't decide whether to call a friend for dinner or spend time at home alone. So I prayed and asked God to direct me or have someone call. Late in the afternoon a friend called. Before I realized it I was inviting her over for dinner. I made my famous meatloaf, threw a couple potatoes in the oven and she brought dessert. As we talked over dinner we discussed our week, encouraged each other and had a great time of fellowship. Call it what you want. I call it answered prayer.

This passage of scripture says not to worry about anything but in everything by prayer and petition with thanksgiving present our requests to God. There is nothing specific about what we take to God, it says everything. There is nothing to misunderstand about everything. Everything means everything. We take everything to God with thanksgiving knowing as we present them to him, he will respond. Sometimes I feel overwhelmed and I have to quickly find a quiet spot to pray. Nearly everyday I go to my prayer journal to lay my thoughts and fears at the feet of my God. I could not survive without my link to God. Yes I worry and yes I have fears and sometimes I have to fight against them for awhile but comfort always comes when I seek peace from God. Worries always seem not quite so big or even diminish when I take them to God. And then something else comes along and I go before him again with my new requests. Folks this is the only way to make it without giving up and giving in to our fears, big and small. Whatever you have learned or received or heard from our Lord, directly from him or through someone else, put it into practice and the God of peace will be with you each time you seek him. Pray over it, whatever concerns you. Start now.

Dear God thank you for allowing me to come to you and give you my requests. You are my friend and my God and I adore you. Where would I be without you? I do not want to know. Thank you for how you bless me. Forgive me when I fail you. I do not want to be anxious about anything. I need you every hour of everyday day. Amen.

354

The Pruning
John 15:1-8

Pruning is a horticultural practice that involves the selective removal of parts of a plant such as branches, buds, or roots. Pruning is necessary to remove dead growth, shaping to control or direct growth and improving or maintaining overall health of the plant or tree to enhance the quality of flowers or fruits. The practice requires targeted removal of diseased, damaged, non-productive, or unwanted growth. This so applies to my life in Jesus Christ.

Jesus Christ is the vine and God the Father is the gardener. My relationship with Jesus Christ makes me branches from the vine. As long as I stay attached to the vine growing healthy flowers and fruits from my relationship with him, I will thrive. When I allow sin to hinder my growth and my strength from him my branches will dry up, wither and become unproductive. Then I need pruning. The bad is cut away and separated from me so that I can thrive and become productive again. Sometimes I need just a routine pruning to reshape and redirect my life. I glorify God the Father when I produce beautiful flowers and fruit. I like the idea of God tending my life, pruning and snipping way at the bad decisions I have made or unhealthy relationships I have gown to get me back on track. Psalm 1:1-3 says blessed is the man who delights in the law of the Lord. He is like a tree planted by water with leaves that do not wither and yields fruit. Proverbs 11:30 says the fruit of the righteous is a tree of life and he who wins souls is wise. God the Father is an expert pruner. Sometimes we might resist the pruning, wanting to take off in our own direction with our own plans. I'd like to suggest that we will enjoy our relationship with him more if we strive to remain in him, following him, allowing him to snip at our lives rather than get to the point that he has to hack and get out his heavy duty pruner. It is our choice. He gives us the freedom to choose his way or our own. Any plant or tree grows better with regular attention. Our lives grow better with regular attentiveness to our Lord and Savior rather than irregular time with him. Little snips here and there are better for me. What about you? Let's be encouraged to commit to regular time with our Lord so we can thrive as he maintains our growth and direction in life.

Dear Lord thank you for pruning my life. Sometimes it hurts but you are always there to provide comfort and peace in the good times and the difficult. Show me today where I need to yield to your pruning. Show me what I need to drop or let go of. Help me to stay attached to Jesus Christ who is the vine. I don't always understand but help me to trust you completely. I love you Lord and I want to honor and glorify you with the flowers and fruit of my life. Amen.

355

Discover the Joy
John 15:9-17

In this passage we read about a promise of joy for those who believe in Jesus. The source of that joy is our relationship with him. We tend to strive for happiness more than joy. We seldom realize that happiness can come and go. Happiness comes when our circumstances allow it. We can be happy but not have the joy that this passage speaks of. Joy runs deep within me and remains regardless of my circumstances. My joy is the foundation for my happiness. Psalm 146:5 reminds me that my help and my hope come from the Lord. This brings me joy. We have to work at being joyful and make the choice to choose joy. We can find things that make us happy but it is the joy that truly helps me cope and get through each day. Sometimes I have to fight for my joy. I have to fight through the depressing situations that try to torment me and bring me down allowing hopelessness to seep in. My relationship with Jesus Christ helps me ignore the lies of Satan that tempt me with depression and try to take my joy. Joy comes from God the Father and he wants the joy to complete me and make me whole. Joy comes from knowing what is to come. I noticed a note written by my Mom in her Bible – We are meant to enjoy eternal life now. Awesome! She also marked John 16:22, underlining ...no one will take away your joy. True joy comes from Jesus Christ and nothing can take it away. Just like our salvation and promise of eternal life. No circumstance can destroy that promise of hope. Hold on to it. It is our lifeline. Discover the joy.

Dear Lord Jesus, send forth your light and your truth. Let them guide me. Let them bring me to your holy mountain to the place where you dwell. Then I will go to your altar, O my God, my joy and my delight. (Psalm 43:3-4) Amen.

356

God Is Working
Habakkuk 1:2-5

Habakkuk complained to God about injustice, violence and destruction. He felt like the world was falling apart and full of corruption. We all feel that way most mornings when we watch the news. Sometimes we feel it personally as we face strife and difficulties in our lives. God responded. He told Habakkuk to just watch and be amazed at his work. God was working even in the corruption. He is working today we just don't see it sometimes. I often wonder why the Lord waits to return. I wonder how much longer he will wait before he returns when I hear horrible stories in the news. I wonder what he thinks of it. I am sure it grieves him yet he loves us so much he is willing to wait so that no one will perish. And he is working through the bad things. We need to look for the good and know that it is God. We see the peace that God brings to Habakkuk in 2:20. He says, the Lord is in his holy temple, let all the earth be silent before him. The false idols of the people were silent and were worthless yet God was worthy of honor and adoration. Habakkuk's final words in 3:16-19 are beautiful. He trusts in God regardless of his circumstances. He declares that even though he experienced difficulties, suffering and loss, he would still rejoice in his Savior. He speaks of the joy that comes from knowing God the Father. This passage, in fact the entire book of Habakkuk, bursts with hope and promise. My God and Savior has not forsaken me. He knows of the difficulties in my life and he cares and he is working. This encourages me to stop and look for the goodness that surrounds me. Let's not listen to the negative and the lies. God is on his throne and he is the King. He will not be defeated. Our hope and trust is in him. He will prevail and I will praise him for that.

Dear God when I am worried you bring direction. When I am afraid you bring comfort. When I get angry you bring peace. When I seek you, you find me. Praise your name! In spite of everything I still trust and honor you as my God and King. Close my ears and heart to the lies. You are the truth and the way. Thank you for your love for me. Amen.

357

God's Loving Care
Matthew 10:28-33

I am not a supporter of tattoos and wonder why anyone would want to permanently scar their skin in such a way but I heard an interesting story about the common sparrow tattoo. Such a tattoo generally symbolizes God's concern for the most insignificant living things. In this passage Jesus speaks of God's loving care for the sparrow. He tells us that the life of each sparrow is significant to God. If he cares for the sparrow in such a way, how much more would he care for us who he made in his own image and allowed his son to die for our transgressions. In the same way God loves and watches over the sparrow, he knows each person is unique and to be treasured and consequently surely watches over each of us. The passage goes on to say that God even knows the number of hairs on our head. This is unimaginable for us to even think of and I believe that is Jesus' very point. Generally, sparrows tend to be small birds with short tails. They scavenge for food like gulls or pigeons and happily eat virtually anything. They require very little maintenance compared to us. Yet God cares for each of his children and the little sparrows. Jesus refers in the same way to God's caring for the birds in the air in Matthew 6:26. This is the God we trust. Never should we think of ourselves as insignificant. Never should we think of ourselves as alone or unloved. We are special and unique in God's eyes and he is an awesome God that we trust. He is the truth. At the time of judgment he will recognize and acknowledge those who call him Savior. He will deny those who have not. If you haven't already, acknowledge him today. Acknowledge his love for you. Wrap yourself in his loving care.

Dear God I love to hear how you care for me as you care for the simple sparrow. Your eye is on the sparrow so I know you watch over me. Help me to trust you more. Help me to trust your Word that is full of promises for me. You know me by name. I am never alone for you are always with me. I pray the desires of my heart will be your will for me. I want to love you more. Amen.

358

Following Instructions
Deuteronomy 4:1-2

Chapters 4, 5 and 6 of Deuteronomy are very clear that we are to be obedient to God's instructions. Deuteronomy 4:1-2, 9, 29-31, 35, 39-40; 5:6-21, 29, 32-33; 6:1-25. There is no room for saying scripture is not clear after reading through these passages. Sometimes poor or unclear instruction prevents obedience. Sometimes poor listening or deliberate lack of understanding prevents obedience. We often have to be very specific when we give instructions to our children, such as Take a bath, use soap and wash your hair, use shampoo. Or do not call me at work unless the fire truck is in the yard. Or do not make any stop on the way home except at the Stop sign or traffic light and even then our instructions are often not followed. We sometimes have to be very specific with adults as well, such as, the speed limit is 60 no matter how other cars are traveling or the dress code says no flip flops and a flip flop is a flip flop. We often resist instruction because we do not like the barriers they can create, barriers that keep us from doing what we want to do. God's instructions are clear. He repeats them over and over. Each one is as important as the other. We live in a country that allows us to read God's Holy Word openly. Most homes have more than one Bible per person yet they sit and gather dust or stay in the back seat of the car for next Sunday. As I read through the passages in Deuteronomy my heart was pierced as God pointed out to me things that need to change. I hope the same for you. God's instructions are to give him honor and glory through our obedience and for our benefit. Good things come from following God's instruction. Decisions we make, our overall attitude and our relationship with others are blessed when we are careful not to forget the Lord (6:12). He never promised no troubles but he did promise to stay with us regardless. He instructs us to keep his commands so that life will go well for me and my children after me and we will live long in the land that he gives us for all time (4:40). God offers blessing for obedience. Let's not use excuses any longer. Let's commit to study God's instruction daily, seek him when there are any questions and commit to applying his instruction in everything we do. Keep a prayer journal and track the changes that will come as a result. Be amazed!

Dear God thank you for giving clear instruction and offering blessing for obedience. The desire of my heart is to honor you by obeying your commands. Forgive me when I am selfish and think I know what is better for me. I am not you and forgive me when I think I am. Forgive me when I use excuses or claim that I don't understand. Search my heart and show me what I need to change. I will strive to follow your instruction. Help me for I am weak. Amen.

359

Nip It In the Bud
Psalm 128

Our favorite Deputy, Barney Fife from the old Andy Griffith Show is known for this saying, Nip it in the bud. I remember Barney saying, 'Nip it in the bud! Nip it! Read any book on child discipline and you'll find it in favor of bud nippin. That's the only way to take care of it.' He used it often and not always necessarily regarding raising kids. He was always for nipping it; stop something before it got worse was his philosophy. Barney wasn't portrayed as a very smart person but he was sure accurate on this account.

What do I need to nip? Sin can start with only a thought or a glimpse and will grow if not nipped. We are urged in 2 Corinthians 10:5 to take captive every thought to make it obedient to Christ Jesus. Take it captive so that it can go no further. Nip it. The Holy Spirit may urge us to extinguish something inappropriate in our life or convict us for neglecting to do something we should. This Psalm says blessed are all who fear the Lord, who walk in his ways. We are prompted every day to walk in the way of the Lord. We are promised in 1 Corinthians 10:13 that we are all temped in the same way; we will never be tempted more than we can bear and God will provide a way out so that we can stand up against any temptation. God allows a way for us to 'Nip it in the bud' without excuse. Ole Barney was pretty wise wasn't he? This is good advice. And if there is sin before the nipping there is forgiveness. Our hope and confidence is in Christ Jesus who has already paid the price for our sin and provides the way for us to kneel at his feet for mercy and forgiveness.

Dear Lord, with you there is forgiveness, therefore you are feared (Psalm 130:4). Thank you for your Holy Spirit who prompts me with conviction. Thank you for your grace and mercy. Speak to me today and guide me. This saying of nipping is funny yet very serious. Help me to take my sin seriously. Forgive me for my wrongs and for the good I neglect. Open my eyes and my heart to your will for me. In your precious name I pray, Amen.

360

Waiting For the Messiah
Luke 2:25-38

Simeon was promised by the Holy Spirit that he would not die until he saw the Messiah. The Spirit led him to the temple on the day Joseph and Mary brought the young child for circumcision and their purification required by religious laws. The baby was probably about eight days old. Simeon took the child in his arms and praised God. He was then ready for death. While the young parents marveled at this they also learned that Jesus' coming would pierce their soul. Anna, a prophetess who lived in the temple also knew the baby to be the promised Messiah, thanked God for him and shared the news of the redemption of Jerusalem.

We too await the Messiah. We await his return. We await his final victory over Satan and the end of suffering and pain. We await passing from this earth to our secured home in eternity with him. Are we watchful everyday as Simeon and Anna were? Do we look for him in all we do? A new year will soon start. Today is a good day to begin our watch for our Messiah. Begin to live everyday as if he could appear at anytime. Begin to be serious about our witness and testimony so that others will come to know him as Lord and Savior. Begin to seek him in all we do. Begin to make time everyday to study his Holy Word and spend time talking to him and listening to him. Begin to live in watchful anticipation of his return with a spirit of praise and worship.

Dear God thank you for your Son and the gift of salvation and eternal life. Forgive me of my sin. Help me to have a heart of watchfulness. Help me to live each day watching for your return. I need to be prepared and see that others around me are prepared too. Thank you for your love and your faithfulness. Amen.

361

Teaching Our Children
Deuteronomy 11:18-28

I heard an announcer on the radio talking about her young son, I believe about 6 years old. She had been having trouble with him obeying her and his father. After trying different forms of punishment they decided to try community service. They took him to the park and made him pick up trash. The first couple times he thought it was fun but that changed quickly. These trips to the park influenced his behavior and his obedience. These parents were determined to discipline their child and influence his behavior even at such a young age.

This passage instructs us to teach God's Word to our children. It is to be routine topic of conversation in our home. Everything we say and do should be influenced by God's Word. Obedience to this instruction brings blessings to us and generations to follow. Disobedience will bring a curse. Our daily habits and routines will greatly affect the adolescent, teenage and adult minds and behavior of our children whether positive or negative. When our relationship with Jesus Christ influences the daily habits and routines in our family, the adolescent, teenage and adult minds and behavior of our children are influenced. Once our children grow up and leave our home they are faced with their own decisions on how to live their life but when we follow this teaching in Deuteronomy in as dedicated manner as we possibly can we will have done our best. The greatest gift we can give our children is showing them a heart that loves and desires Jesus Christ. We cannot force them to love God but we are making it more probable when the environment in which they grow is an example of God's instructions and of his love.

Dear God thank you for our children. Help me to take seriously my task of teaching our children and youth. I know that we learn best by example. I pray that everyday my behavior reflects the ways of Jesus Christ. Give me a heart of love and forgiveness and a desire to please you in all that I do. Amen.

Water Witcher

Numbers 20:1-12

I've been watching *Gunsmoke* again. The episode today was about a water witcher. The land was dry from lack of rain and the farmers were losing their crops and livestock from the drought. A water witcher came to town. The farmers took the last of the little money they had and invested in him to bring rain, putting their last hope in him. When he couldn't find water they instantly hissed and booed claiming they knew all along he could not find water. He insisted that they must have faith in him and believe in his ability. Once he changed their way of thinking, he found water. Hmmm.

In the art of water witching, an individual clutches an A, Y or L-shaped twig or rod, called a witching rod. When passing over underground water, the stick would suddenly pull, twist or jerk. There were also medicine men among the Indians who through various rituals and incantations were known to cause rain. I understand that today there are individuals known to bring rain by using various scientific techniques, such as the seeding of clouds with silver iodide crystals from an airplane. Hmmm.

In Numbers 20, the people had no water and as usual went to Moses and complained. Moses and Aaron fell on their face in prayer before the Lord. God promised water and provided it. He told them to speak to the rock and water would pour. Rather than speaking to the rock, Moses struck the rock but God made his promise good anyway and provided water. Moses had to face the consequences of his anger, mistrust and disobedience. In verse 12, God said that Moses did not trust enough to honor him as holy. This struck me. When we do not trust God we are dishonoring him. God is a true water witcher and rain maker. He assures us that we can put all of our trust in him and he will provide our needs. He provides according to his plan which is always perfect and in his own perfect time. We must resist placing our faith in other people or other things for God is our sole provider.

Dear God help me to trust you more. I love you and I want to honor you by being obedient to trust you in all things. Sometimes I misplace my trust and I ask you for forgiveness. Help me to be patient and wait for you. Help me to resist following my own desires and plans because I know this dishonors you. Amen.

363

Take The Finger Out Of Your Ears
Matthew 13:11-23

We all laugh when someone puts their fingers in their ears, La, La, La, La…I can't hear you. It's funny unless we are the one trying to be heard. Sometimes when someone is speaking to us, we hear them talking but do not hear what they are saying because we are already rehearsing our response. In these instances, is it ever God speaking? There is a difference in listening and hearing. God speaks specifically in an audible voice but are our fingers in our ears? Are we rehearsing our response rather than listening? I have learned that God speaks to me through his Holy Word, in my circumstances, through other Christians and through the Holy Spirit. He tells us in Jeremiah 33:3, Call to me and I will answer you and tell you great and unsearchable things you do not know. Are we listening **for** his response? Are we listening **to** his response? Do we cut him off and speak before he can respond? When we listen, we choose life (Deuteronomy 30:20). Let's spend time today listening to what God has to say. Let's spend a little less time asking and more time in praise and worship. Take the finger out of your ears. If we listen more we will trust more. When we listen carefully we invite and welcome a response.

Dear God help me to listen. Help me to listen for your voice. The more time I spend listening the more I will recognize you speaking to me. You are with me and will never forsake me. Help me eliminate the noise in my head so I can hear you. Help me to replace my desires for me with your will for me. Your ways are perfect. Forgive me when I fail to listen. Amen.

364

Missing the Grace
Hebrews 12:15

I read this scripture in my devotion time yesterday. See to it that no one misses the grace of God. Am I allowing someone to miss the grace? God says to me, yes. There is a particular person I know that I do not like. This person does not respect my position at work, deliberately ignores me when I walk into the room and is often outspoken and rude to others. I feel very uncomfortable around this person. My response to this person is cold and judgmental. After reading this verse, God has put on my heart to pray for this person and find ways to show his grace. This person is missing the grace of God when I do not show it. My feelings toward this person grows bitterness, and yes, sin; my sin, not theirs.

Dear God forgive me for harboring anger and resentment. It is hard when someone treats me differently and hurts my feelings. I react coldly and judgmentally. Forgive me. Help me to see this person through your eyes. I sin and you forgive me. You love this person just like you love me and can forgive this person just like you forgive me. I pray this person will find salvation in you and forgiveness. I pray that you will pour out grace and mercy on this person. Forgive me for thinking that you love me more. Thank you for the peace you can bring when this situation causes frustration and resentment. You are love and I want others to see your love through me. I pray that one day I will have a loving relationship with this person because of your love that can bond us. I love you Lord and I praise your name. Thank you for the peace this brings to me. Amen.

365

A Time For Everything
Ecclesiastes 3:1-14

This is a well known passage. Songs have been written around it yet I can't say that I read it very often. Today it really touched me. Our lives go through many different seasons. Life is full of changes that often leave us feeling like we are on a roller coaster ride but we must remember that God is in control. His sovereignty predetermines all of our seasons. Some seasons are joyful times, some are routine while others can be sad and depressing. I can remember times that I thought life was wonderful and nothing could change. Yet there have also been times that my bedtime prayer was that God would take me while asleep and not require me to wake up to face the problems I had. God orders all things according to his plan and his purpose for us. The past months have been very difficult for me yet I am here to tell you that God loves me and has been with me every step of the way. Through my relationship with him and good Christian counsel I am addressing issues day by day, sometimes even hour by hour.

Verse 14 warms my heart. I know that everything God does will endure forever; nothing can be added to it and nothing taken from it. God does this so that I will revere him. I praise him for this promise and find my hope and strength in him.

What season are you in today? No matter what you have to deal with today, know that God is at your side. He knows and he cares. He can take away the storm or he will calm it with a peace that warms your heart. He will show you what he wants you to learn from it. Draw near to him. Read his Word and fill your mind and heart with his promises. Talk to him telling him of your fear and anxiousness. God will show you how to face tomorrow. Seek good Christian counsel if you need to. Never hesitate to ask for help. There is hope in finding satisfaction and confidence in today. God has made everything beautiful in its time. Ecclesiastes 7:14 says when times are good, be happy; but when times are bad, consider that God made them both.

Dear God thank you for your promise of hope and peace. You have brought me through many storms. I know you have plans for me to prosper. I know that you are in control of my life. Give me courage and strength to put complete trust in you and fear nothing nor be anxious about anything. Thank you for your love for me. Show me what you have for me to learn today. Amen.

The End... Be encouraged to continue time with God everyday.
Coming Soon! Good Morning, Lord – Book 2